"No Christian counselor should be without this cutting-edge book. It will help you accelerate the changes process and save your clients time, money, and pain."

> **Dr. Les Parrott III,** codirector of the Center for Relationship Development at Seattle Pacific University; author of *High-Maintenance Relationships*

"A readable, practical, and proven approach to Christian counseling that may change forever the way that counseling is provided."

> **Dr. Joseph A. Kloba,** director of the Graduate Counseling Psychology Program and professor of psychology at Palm Beach Atlantic College

"An excellent presentation of the principles of brief therapy—clear, concise examples illuminate each point. A must for the library of anyone serious about Christian counseling."

> **Dr. James Osterhaus,** clinical psychologist at the Counseling Center of Fairfax and visiting professor of marriage and family counseling at Denver Seminary; author of *Questions Couples Ask behind Closed Doors*

"This book clearly describes a helpful approach and gives readers specific ways to implement this approach in their counseling ministry. It's refreshing to find a book that is basic, thorough, and biblical in its premise. The authors give counselors hope in how they view the potential for client change."

> **H. Norman Wright,** Christian Marriage Enrichment; author of *Marriage Counseling*

Promoting Change
through Brief Therapy
in Christian Counseling

AACC
COUNSELING
LIBRARY

Promoting Change

THROUGH

Brief Therapy

IN CHRISTIAN
COUNSELING

GARY J. OLIVER, PH.D.
MONTE HASZ, PSY.D.
MATTHEW RICHBURG, M.A.

Tyndale House Publishers, Inc.
WHEATON, ILLINOIS

The American Association of Christian Counselors is an organization of professional, pastoral, and lay counselors committed to the promotion of excellence and unity in Christian counseling. The AACC provides conferences, software, video and audio resources, two professional journals, a resource review, as well as other publications and resources. Membership is open to anyone who writes for information: AACC, P.O. Box 739, Forest, VA 24551.

Visit Tyndale's exciting Web site at www.tyndale.com

Copyright © 1997 by Gary J. Oliver, Monte Hasz, and Matthew Richburg. All rights reserved.

Author photo copyrights: Gary J. Oliver © 1995 by Brennan Photography; Monte Hasz © 1997 by J. B. Photography; Matthew Richburg © 1994 by Diamond Photo. All rights reserved.

Unless otherwise indicated, all Scripture quotations are taken from the *Holy Bible,* New Living Translation, copyright © 1996. Used by permission of Tyndale House Publishers, Inc., Wheaton, Illinois 60189. All rights reserved.

Scripture quotations marked NIV are taken from the *Holy Bible,* New International Version®. NIV®. Copyright © 1973, 1978, 1984 by International Bible Society. Used by permission of Zondervan Publishing House. All rights reserved.

Scripture quotations marked (TLB) are taken from *The Living Bible* copyright © 1971. Used by permission of Tyndale House Publishers, Inc., Wheaton, Illinois 60189. All rights reserved.

Scripture quotations marked KJV are taken from the *Holy Bible,* King James Version.

Scripture quotations marked NASB are taken from the *New American Standard Bible,* © 1960, 1962, 1963, 1968, 1971, 1972, 1973, 1975, 1977 by The Lockman Foundation. Used by permission.

Scripture quotations marked *The Message* are taken from *The Message, The New Testament in Contemporary English,* copyright © 1993. Used by permission of NavPress, P. O. Box 35001, Colorado Springs, CO 80935. All rights reserved.

Designed by Beth Sparkman

Edited by Lynn Vanderzalm

Library of Congress Cataloging-in-Publication Data

Oliver, Gary J.
  Promoting change through brief therapy in Christian counseling / Gary J. Oliver, Monte Hasz, Matthew Richburg.
    p. cm. — (AACC counseling library)
  Includes bibliographical references.
  ISBN 0-8423-5059-4 (alk. paper)
  1. Pastoral counseling. 2. Brief psychotherapy. I. Hasz, Monte. II. Richburg, Matthew, date.
III. Title. IV. Series.
BV4012.2.O56 1997
253′.5—dc21   97-25133

Printed in the United States of America

03 02 01 00 99 98 97
8   7   6   5   4   3   2   1

With thanks to our Lord Jesus Christ
for his goodness, mercy, and grace
and for giving us his inerrant and infallible
Word, which tells the world of the only
solution to mankind's deepest need,

We dedicate this book to our families,

Carrie Oliver
Nathan J. Oliver
Matthew D. Oliver
Andrew M. Oliver

Susan Hasz
Laura Hasz
Bryan Hasz
Billy Hasz

Sara Richburg
Dr. Robert and Frances Richburg

CONTENTS

FOREWORD

As I walked out on the slender knife-edge of Clouds Rest in Yosemite National Park, I was overcome by the wide openness of the bright sky and the depth of the chasms on either side of our path. The drop was a couple of thousand feet on either side of the rocky path. When I looked down that narrow pathway to the end of the knife-edge, about a hundred yards away, my heart was pounding, and I had the overwhelming urge to walk the straight and narrow.

In *Promoting Change through Brief Therapy in Christian Counseling,* Gary Oliver, Monte Hasz, and Matthew Richburg walk the fine line between chasms of excess and deficit. On one side is the chasm that oversimplifies counseling and reduces all change to a formula, which can lead to ugly and dangerous surprises for both counselors and clients. On the other side is the chasm that beguiles clients and many therapists onto the rocks of unnecessary interminable psychotherapy. Oliver, Hasz, and Richburg lead readers down the safe middle of the knife-edge. In this book they suggest practical, solution-based counseling guided by enough examples to direct the readers' steps but with an appropriate reliance on the sovereign work of Jesus Christ in the lives of the client and counselor.

Oliver, Hasz, and Richburg suggest that, just as people need two legs to walk a straight path, the counselor needs two "legs" to counsel effectively. Counseling is centered on Christ and on helping clients develop solutions that the authors hope are consistent with God's will for the lives of most clients. Hence, their approach is Christian and solution based.

Their approach is Christian. My favorite chapter of the book is the last—"Putting It All Together." It attributes change—and indeed life—to Jesus, and it admonishes helpers to rely on the true source of life. I would almost recommend rereading that chapter at the beginning of each of the four parts of the book.

Their approach is also *solution based,* using aspects of problem-focused therapy, which served as a foundation for solution-focused therapy, from which the authors draw heavily. Oliver, Hasz, and Richburg do not accept a solution-focused therapy uncritically. Instead, they offer a Christian critique of both problem-focused and solution-focused therapies and recommend a Christian-modified, *solution-based* therapy.

With the strong solution-focused influences on their approach, Oliver, Hasz, and Richburg walk near the edge of a behavior-focused, technique-centered approach. However, they stay on track through their frequent recommendations for counselors to acknowledge and deal with clients' emotions, Christian faith, and spirituality. They stress the importance of empathic connection by the counselor and the necessity of maintaining rapport with clients. Emotion receives an important place in their approach to counseling.

Another potentially dangerous bend in the trail is the way they treat the issue of agency. On one hand, they give clients a lot of credit for acting significantly in their own lives and treatment. They also provide clear guidelines for how counselors can think of counseling from a Christian, solution-based approach and for how they can practice that approach (including many case examples and sample conversations between counselors and clients). On the other hand, human agency is clearly not the only emphasis in the authors' worldview. God is given rightful credit for sovereign action in the lives of both clients and counselors.

Oliver, Hasz, and Richburg provide a contour map of the territory of brief, solution-based counseling. As you read, you'll know where the dips are, how to walk through the valleys, and how to climb the hills in companionship with clients and the Lord. You'll finish the book looking for exceptions to problems in clients you are working with, searching for the positive instead of getting caught up dwelling on the problems, trying to discern miracles of change lurking in thickets of gloom, and asking *what* questions and *how* questions to help clients discover pathways through problems and discouragement.

With many types of therapies available, it is difficult for authors to walk a balanced trail while still advocating a clear, effective, and biblically consistent approach. In *Promoting Change through Brief Therapy in Christian Counseling,* Gary Oliver, Monte Hasz, and Matthew Richburg have hiked through the forest and emerged into the sunlight atop Clouds Rest. Come walk the path with them.

Everett L. Worthington Jr., Ph.D.
Virginia Commonwealth University

ACKNOWLEDGMENTS

Thanks to the people at American Association of Christian Counselors and Tyndale House Publishers for inviting us to contribute this volume and to Lynn Vanderzalm of Tyndale for her patience, encouragement, and commitment to excellence in the editing process and for pretending to laugh at some of our jokes.

Our sincere thanks to the following clinical staff at Southwest Counseling Associates, who for several years met together with us on a monthly basis to open God's Word and share our clinical experiences, and ask the hard questions in the process of creating a more time-effective way to help people change:

Doug Feil	Bill Myers
Jim Frantz	Cathy Petersen
Carol Golz	Lanell Schilling

and to the following SCA support staff, who, by their gracious spirit and consistent commitment to excellence, have contributed more to this book and the ministry than they realize:

Cora Block	Rita Campbell
Richard Bristol	Sharon Smith

Thanks to Elizabeth Suarez, who helped with the footnotes and proofreading; to Ev Worthington for making the time to read the manuscript and provide a thoughtful foreword; to the staff at the Brief Family Therapy Institute in Milwaukee and the Mental Research Institute in Palo Alto for what they share with us; to Dr. Jim Beck and the administration at Denver Seminary for allowing us to teach this material to the graduate and postgraduate students; and to the students for their good questions and enthusiastic involvement in the learning process; and to Dr. Clyde McDowell and the leadership at Mission Hills Church in Littleton, Colorado, for their vision in facilitating the independent, church-related ministry of Southwest Counseling Associates.

1 / THE LONG ROAD
to
BRIEF THERAPY

Only true Christian ministry can put grace in the heart so that lives are changed and problems are really solved. The best thing we can do for people is not to solve their problems for them but so relate them to God's grace that they will be enabled to solve their problems and not repeat them.

It has been said that "the heart of every problem is the problem in the heart"; but the statement is only partly true. Sometimes it isn't what we have done that creates the difficulty but what others have done. . . . People may not cause their own problems, but if they relate to their problems the wrong way, they will make the problems worse. What life does to us depends on what life finds in us, and that is where the grace of God comes in.

WARREN W. WIERSBE, *On Being a Servant of God*

You may have picked up this book from a bookstore shelf and are thumbing through the pages trying to decide whether it's worth buying. Or perhaps you've already purchased the book and are desperately hoping that it has something worthwhile to say. Either way, you have some interest in brief therapy.

Do you remember the first time you heard about brief therapy? What was your immediate response? Was it positive or negative? Were you eager to learn more about it, or did you look down your therapeutic nose at it with disbelief and disdain? To me, brief therapy was an oxymoron. I (Gary) remember my first response: "What? Treat everything in fewer than twenty sessions? You've got to be kidding!"

Like it or not, brief therapy is revolutionizing the way people think about and do counseling. Brief therapy means many different things to different people. Over the years I've collected some counselors' questions and comments that may reflect your response to brief therapy.

- Is brief therapy a form of therapy in its own right or merely a second-best substitute in situations where long-term treatment, for whatever reason, is not an option?
- Is brief therapy merely a stopgap, superficial first-aid measure to pursue until some real, legitimate, long-term therapy is available?
- The only way therapy can be brief is if it doesn't aim to do very much.
- A one-size-fits-all approach won't fit many people very well or for very long.

Much of what is considered traditional therapy tends to focus on problems. Many people don't have the time or financial resources to be able to spend months or years free-associating two or three times a week about their childhood experiences to uncover the root of the problem. Brief therapy, as demanded by managed care and preferred by an increasing number of clients, has become the treatment of necessity for a significant segment of the population. And those numbers are growing. It has also become the treatment of choice for many counselors who don't "have" to use it but are finding brief therapy a time-effective way to help people change.

What do you think of today when you hear about brief therapy? Has your opinion changed? Are you more open to it than you were several years ago? Most counselors are. One of the challenges of discussing brief therapy is that so many different models of it exist. Brief therapy can have a psychodynamic, behavioral, cognitive, or a family-systems base. It can range from one session to over fifty sessions. Some approaches to brief therapy are superficial and offer little more than a Band-Aid approach. Other methods have proven to be effective and can lead to meaningful change.

WHY SHOULD YOU READ THIS BOOK?

This is a book written by Christian counselors for other Christian counselors who want to increase their effectiveness in allowing God to use them to help people change and grow. What you will read is focused on practice and oriented to counselors.

Our purpose is to introduce you to the field of brief therapy and to share with you ways in which the three of us have combined aspects of different models that have increased our effectiveness in helping individuals, couples, and families change. We are not presenting brief therapy as the one and only way to help people change. We are not making an apologetic for brief therapy. Our intention is not to convince, coerce, or convert. Rather, our goal is to inform and encourage. We will be sharing with you our current process of understanding one effective way God can use us to help people.

We are saying that, regardless of the demands of a managed-care environment, brief therapy that emphasizes the present and focuses on solutions more than problems can help a wide variety of people dealing with a wide range of presenting problems. We are saying that, at the very least, we can suggest a method that can get you immediately started on the counseling process, accelerate the change process, and save the client time, money, and pain.

Whether you are a pastoral counselor or a professional counselor, this book has been written for you. Whether you would consider your primary therapeutic orientation to be analytic, object relations, family systems, nouthetic, or cognitive-behavioral, you will find insights and interventions that you will be able to use.

We will repeatedly emphasize our belief that there is no one way to do counseling. There is not one set of techniques or interventions that can be applied in every situation. Truth doesn't change. But the variables of the counselor, the clients, and our clients' problems do change. And those variables affect the ways in which we can help clients apply truth to their unique and specific situation. We constantly need to be flexible in clinical decision making. Counseling must be tailored to the individual.

Beyond introducing you to brief therapy, we want to provide a framework to help you integrate this methodology into the larger issues of sound theology, biblical foundations, and personal spiritual growth. Much of brief therapy will fit well into your life as a Christian counselor; a few parts of it will not. We hope to help you evaluate what to keep and what to discard.

FROM BRIEF THERAPY BY DEFAULT TO BRIEF THERAPY BY DESIGN

I started doing counseling in the fall of 1965. I had just graduated from high school and was a freshman at a Christian college. I had been asked to join the staff of Greater Long Beach Youth for Christ as a club director and was given several high schools to work with. As a club director, much of my time was spent talking with young people and trying to help them. My initial approach was to wait until they took their first breath and then share a Bible verse or two with them. In retrospect I functioned as if counseling were nothing more than cramming truth into the cranium. Since I had memorized hundreds of verses and had a good knowledge of the Bible, I was rarely at a loss for passages to share.

Two years later I was asked to become the second person on the staff of a small Southern Baptist church in Anaheim, California. At the church I counseled not only adolescents but also a surprising number of adults. I had taken the required Introduction to Psychology course in my undergraduate program, but no one had taught me how to counsel. I guess I was just supposed to know how to do it.

It didn't take long for me to learn that I needed to spend more time listening to people talk about their problems. I realized that in my eagerness to "dump" the answer on them, I had pursued excellence in answering questions they weren't asking and helping them solve problems they didn't have.

As I listened and explored the problems with people, it seemed that all they wanted to do was to talk about their problems. But that didn't slow me down. Even if they didn't ask, I gave them answers. Most left seeming to feel better. I thought that was what counseling was. Someone has a problem, you listen, you tell them what to do, they do it. Voila! . . . success!

A few people actually did do what I had suggested. But many didn't. And many came back, again and again, to discuss the same issue with me. Over time I began to sense that what was most helpful to them was my legitimate care and concern for them rather than dumping truth on them. Some people seemed more interested in the fellowship and attention than in making change.

Early in my ministry I became interested in brief counseling. But it was not an interest by design; it was interest by default. Most people wanted to meet only a couple of times to discuss their problems. Some stayed only long enough for me to stop the emotional hemorrhage and give them an encouraging word. I remember reading articles and hearing discussions indicating that the only way meaningful change could take place was through years and years of in-depth therapy. The people I was working with didn't have the time, and I didn't have the training, for in-depth therapy. So I did the best I could. I was doing a lot of counseling; I didn't consider myself a counselor.

The more I worked with adolescents and families, the more I realized my need for more effective ways to help them. As more and more people came to me for answers, I found myself asking more and more questions. Counseling tossed me out of the security of the theoretical and immersed me in the practical. I found myself asking questions like, What does it mean to be made in the image of God? How did sin damage and distort the image of God in us? On a very pragmatic and practical (not just positional) level, what does it mean to be *in Christ?* If Christ died so that we could be more than conquerors, why do most Christians walk around acting as if they've been conquered? How can I know as much of God's Word as I do and still have some of the same struggles that I had years ago? What kinds of changes can non-Christians experience?

By this time I was a seminary student majoring in systematic theology. I was learning Greek and Hebrew. I was getting excellent training in theology. But of the couples I saw, none of them were considering divorce due to their inability to agree on the nature of the hypostatic union. No adolescents were suicidal or wanting to leave home because of their inability to understand the kenotic implications of the Incarnation. No clients were clinically depressed because they were unable to decide on the most biblical position on the Rapture.

I'm not minimizing the importance of these doctrinal issues. But they weren't the kinds of concerns that would bring people into my office. They weren't what was getting people sidetracked in their walk with the Lord. They weren't the kinds of things that stymied their growth in the process of sanctification. They didn't pose the kinds of crises that threatened people's jobs, marriages, families, and lives.

I said to myself, *Gary, you know the manual [Bible] that reveals the ultimate solution [Jesus Christ] to life's ultimate problem [sin], but how do these truths relate to helping these dear people deal with the day-in-day-out stuff of life such as fear, hurt, frustration, anger, depression, anxiety, suicide, obsessive-compulsive disorders, eating disorders, divorce, rebellious teens, child and spouse abuse?*

These people have real problems. They're not just asking why. *They need to know the how and the what. They want answers to their questions: How can I cope? How does truth apply to this specific problem? What does God have to say about my situation? What are some specific things I can do to change?*

As I studied the seminary curriculum, I discovered that the only counseling training I would receive was part of one course in which we would learn how to marry and bury people. Well, people struggle with lots of things besides marriage and death. When I realized that my three years of theological education wouldn't include any meaningful training in counseling, I decided to take every elective counseling course that I could.

One of my first courses introduced me to the concept of family systems. I learned that a person's behavior happens within the context of relationships, that those relationships influence the person's behavior, and that, in turn, the relationships are influenced by that person's behavior. When there is a change in the way family members interact, it becomes more likely that the individual will change. When the individual changes, the rest of the family system will respond. This opened up a whole new way of looking at people and problems.

Some people said that family systems are not merely influential but determinative. I came down on the side of those who said they were influential. Either way, it became clear to me that looking at the individual in light of the person's family system, identifying subsystems, considering coalitions and boundaries, and understanding the significance of who interacts with whom gave me another new way of looking at helping people change. I realized that the problem is not just *in* the person but also *around* the person. I started looking not only at the person but also at the family and other relationships around the person.

I was introduced to people like Virginia Satir, Carl Whittaker, Salvador Minuchin, Jay Haley, Murray Bowen, and Milton Erickson. As far as I could tell, they were not Christians. They had little to offer me on *who people are,* but they had a lot to offer on *how people change.*

I was also introduced to other counseling theories. After some examination, I became especially comfortable with the cognitive-behavioral approach. It made sense that what we think and how we choose to interpret the events of our lives clearly influence what we feel. The interpretation we make of events often determines how those events affect us. We all have cognitive distortions that keep us from seeing clearly. I constantly checked these models against what for me is the infallible benchmark of the Bible. I was surprised that much of what I read was consistent with what I read in Scripture.

After graduating from seminary, I moved on to work toward a master's degree in theology with an emphasis in systematic theology. I was still involved in church ministry. I had been accepted for a doctoral program in religion at a European university with the intent to teach theology at a Christian college or seminary in Europe.

In 1976 I moved to central Nebraska to help a close friend begin a quality training and study center for the many rural churches of the area. My friend asked me to come for a year to help him get it started, and I felt comfortable postponing my plans to go to Europe, at least for one year.

During my first year in Nebraska, God began to turn my heart from getting a doctoral degree and teaching theology to getting more training in counseling. This was a difficult and even agonizing shift for me. Was I responding to a "lesser" calling and settling for second best? Would I be asked to compromise or even abandon the rich conservative evangelical heritage that meant so much to me? Was I exchanging my theological birthright for a psychological mess of stew? I could never do that!

During that time I was rereading Francis Schaeffer's classic book *The God Who Is There*. It was subtitled *Speaking Historic Christianity into the 20th Century*. I remember thinking that's what happens when I counsel. Counseling gave me a unique opportunity to be used of God to speak the truths of historic Christianity into the lives of twentieth-century people struggling with the twentieth-century effects of sin, stresses, and problems. After a lot of prayer, consulting, and soul-searching, I realized that if my ministry focus changed to counseling, I wouldn't have to compromise or abandon anything.

I continued to teach, preach, disciple, and do a lot of counseling. I discovered two Christian psychology professors on the faculty of the

University of Nebraska in Lincoln and began to take a few counseling courses. I never dreamed I would end up getting a third master's degree as well as a Ph.D.

In the late seventies I was introduced to a provocative book about change: *Change: Principles of Problem Formation and Problem Resolution*. Written by Paul Watzlawick, John Weakland, and Richard Fisch of the Brief Therapy Program at the Mental Research Institute (MRI) in Palo Alto, California, this book challenged some of the standard ways of looking at change.

Several years later some authors from MRI published another significant book that laid out their well-developed, step-by-step model of brief therapy. *Tactics of Change* put shoe leather on some of the ideas discussed in the first volume. It emphasized problem *solving* rather than problem *exploration*. While I couldn't agree with all of their philosophical presuppositions and theoretical assumptions, I did find much of what they said thought provoking and helpful.

In 1986 I was introduced to the concept of a distinctively solution-based perspective when I read a book by Steve de Shazer, *Keys to Solution in Brief Therapy*. That was another book I ended up reading several times, even though I strongly disagreed with some of its assumptions. It represented a paradigm shift, a move from focusing on problems to focusing on solutions. It wasn't a totally brand-new approach to counseling. But there was something different about it. It introduced some new concepts and pulled together and helped me gain a new perspective of some things that I had already been doing.

This book proposed a counseling approach that didn't begin with the exploration of pathology. Instead, it actively focused on client strengths, resources, and competencies. It suggested that counselors should move from asking, "What's wrong with this client?" and "Why does he or she keep on doing these stupid things?" to "What does this client want?" and "How will he or she know when things are even a little bit better?"

To be quite candid, my first response was one of skepticism. But the more I read and thought and weighed the ideas in light of my biblical and theological presuppositions, I found that what had begun as skepticism and doubts were soon replaced by a respectful admiration for the effectiveness of this approach. I especially liked the emphasis on having clients take responsibility for what they could do in the here and now. It seemed to minimize the blame game.

One of my biggest frustrations with many schools of counseling was that they seemed to legitimize making someone else responsible for my problems. They promoted a victim mentality and legitimized the Adam-and-Eve syndrome. It's one thing to be the victim of unfortunate and painful circumstances; it's another thing to go through life blaming all of your problems on those events. It's one thing to admit that you made a mistake; it's another thing to have the courage to accept responsibility for it. Consider the following examples:

- The Menendez brothers killed their parents. But it was really the parents' fault.
- An FBI agent, fired for stealing money he then lost on bets, won his job back when a judge ruled him a victim of compulsive gambling.
- A man on trial in Butler, Pennsylvania, claims a sleep disorder made him shoot and kill his wife.
- A Lebanese man who shot and killed two Hasidic Jews in New York says he did so because he was emotionally scarred by his childhood in Beirut.
- Stella Liebech spilled hot coffee in her lap. But it was really McDonald's fault: The coffee was so hot that when she put the cup between her legs, pried off the lid, and spilled the coffee in her lap, it caused severe burns. A jury ordered McDonald's to give her $3,000,000, although a judge cut the award to a mere $600,000. McDonald's appealed, but recently the corporation settled the lawsuit for an undisclosed sum.

For many years America was known as "the land of the free and the home of the brave." Today it has become known as the land of the guilt-free, fault-free, and responsibility-free. It doesn't seem to matter what actually happens; everybody is a victim. Whatever problems a person has are really somebody else's fault.

One of the main characteristics of healthy people is that they have learned how to recognize their mistakes, admit them, accept responsibility for them, and grow through them. Everyone faces the temptation to stay stuck, play it safe, pass the proverbial buck, and become a victim. This victim mentality leads to whining rather than winning.

With candor and clarity Haddon W. Robinson writes that

> Adam and Eve's descendants—especially those in the United States—have refined victimization to a fine art and an article of faith. . . . If you want to get rich, invest in victimization. It is America's fastest growing industry. Millions make a fat paycheck by identifying victims, representing victims, interviewing victims, treating victims, insuring victims, counseling victims, preaching to victims, and, of course, being victims.
>
> The difficulty that Adam and Eve faced was that their Creator was not a talk-show host. If they were to indulge in the forbidden fruit today, Geraldo or Donahue would feature them as victims, the serpent would be their enabler, and some lawyer would be waiting in the wings to assure them they had a strong case to bring against God for damages.[1]

Counseling that encourages the victim role helps people avoid responsibility and leads them in the wrong direction. They believe they are blameless. The devil (or somebody else) made them do it. They are not responsible. They had no choice. All of their choices since that time are someone else's fault. The other person is the one who needs to pay. That person owes you. You are a victim.

The tragic part is that the victimization mentality causes people to look for a scapegoat rather than a Savior. If I'm not responsible for what I do, if someone else is always to blame, then I don't need a Savior. The other person does. Our culture has changed the words to an old spiritual. The original lyrics say, "Not my mother, not my father, but it's me, O Lord, standing in the need of prayer." Now we sing, "It's my mother, it's my father, it's not me, O Lord, standing in the need of prayer."

In 1986 I moved from a counseling ministry with several Christian family-practice physicians in Lincoln, Nebraska, to help begin a church-affiliated Christian counseling center in Littleton, Colorado. At that time I might have described myself as a biblical counselor with a cognitive-behavioral orientation and a family-systems perspective. I was already doing what was beginning to be called brief therapy. Most of my clients were seen for twenty or fewer sessions. However, by this time I was doing brief therapy by design, not by default.

Most of the clients we see at Southwest Counseling Associates (SCA) are Christians who come from a wide range of denominational backgrounds. From what our clients tell us, most of those who come to our clinic come because of a recommendation and our reputation for providing time-effective biblically based counseling. Over the past ten years, God has brought to SCA a group of born-again counselors who bring a rich mixture of theological and theoretical orientations and who are committed to being used of God to speak the truths of historic Christianity into the lives of hurting people. It is from this ministry and relationship base that Monte, Matt, and I have come together to collaborate on this book.

At SCA we have more than a global, evangelically sensitive, metaphysical commitment. In addition to our counseling education, most of us have seminary training and ministry experience. All of us believe in the sufficiency of Christ and that salvation comes from faith in Christ alone. We believe that the Bible is the inspired and infallible Word of God. We believe that he chooses to reveal himself and work through people. We believe that the church is the healing community and that the Holy Spirit is the change agent. We are, in the paraphrased words of David Seamands, simply disposable tools the Holy Spirit chooses to use for a short time in people's lives to facilitate the process of sanctification.

CONCLUSION

In some ways all counselors are brief therapists. It has been documented that the modal number of sessions a client attends is one; from 75 to 80 percent of clients attend fewer than five sessions; and the overall average number of sessions is between four and eight. In a study conducted in 1980, Smith, Glass, and Miller found that the major impact of psychological treatment occurs within the first six to eight sessions. After this, there is a reduction in impact that lasts for the following ten sessions. In addition, "comparative studies of brief and unlimited therapies show essentially no differences in results."[2]

Our experience supports the view that "a psychotherapeutic program that flexibly applies a number of strategies and techniques will probably be more successful than will a very rigid and doctrinaire approach."[3] Over the past ten years we have developed an integrative solution-based approach to brief therapy that builds on a solid biblical base and combines aspects of cognitive-behavioral therapy, the MRI strategic problem-solving model, and solution-focused brief therapy. With a wide variety of people over a broad range of presenting problems, we have found that it provides a unique and practical way not only to understand but also to facilitate meaningful change.

This book is an introduction to what, for many counselors, is a different way of helping people change. It is only an introduction. We hope to introduce you to some new concepts, share some helpful interventions, challenge some of your assumptions, and perhaps put a few wrinkles in the theoretically stay-pressed mind. We will share some fresh and different ways to increase your effectiveness in fulfilling the call God has placed on your life to help people grow into the likeness of his Son. We want to stimulate you to ask questions. We'll help you answer some of them. Others you will have to figure out for yourself.

There are a lot of things that we're not going to talk about. We will not delineate and defend a comprehensive theory of problem-formation, pathology, personality, or therapy. We will not discuss at length the essential characteristics of an effective counselor (e.g., expertness, attractiveness, trustworthiness). We will not define what is or isn't Christian counseling. Other resources have done a good job of addressing those issues.

Solution-based brief therapy isn't the treatment of choice for every client and every situation. It isn't the way or the truth. You don't have to "become" a card-carrying solution-based brief therapist to benefit from what you are about to read.

In some cases the client's trauma or disorder is so pervasive that lasting change is unlikely to occur apart from a long-term therapy relationship that involves an in-depth exploration of a client's ineffective attempts at self-protection and survival. In these cases long-term therapy is the treatment of choice. But our clinical experience and a review of the literature make it clear that these cases are the exception rather than the rule.

We agree with psychologists John Preston, Nicolette Varzos, and Douglas Liebert, authors of *Every Session Counts: Making the Most of Your Brief Therapy,* when they say, "Sometimes, brief psychotherapy is simply not enough.

Some people have gone through tremendously difficult times and have very deep emotional wounds that require longer treatment. Their problems involve not just one major focus, but several. Serious difficulties may affect many aspects of life. Brief therapy can provide a starting point for such folks, and many are able to make some gains. But those who have a lot of healing or growth to do, while able to benefit from brief treatment, may subsequently enter either a support group or longer-term therapy."[4]

Some emotional and psychiatric difficulties clearly require intensive and lengthy psychological treatment. However, a person doesn't need to be in serious emotional pain to benefit from long-term therapy. Some people choose longer-term forms of counseling for resolution of complex psychological issues and personal growth. As we discuss the strengths of brief therapy, we don't want to underrate or discount the need for and value of long-term counseling for some disorders and problems.

Brief therapy can be helpful in most situations and in many cases is the treatment of choice. Perhaps the client has the time and money for only six sessions. Perhaps you are on the staff of a local church and have limited time to provide counseling for your parishioners. Maybe you work in a homeless shelter. Perhaps you are a military chaplain who may have only two or three times to meet with someone. Or you might work in a setting similar to ours.

The insights we share in this book will focus on working with a Christian population; however, we have found that these principles can also be effective in helping non-Christians. About a fourth of my caseload are non-Christians who are well aware of my orientation.

Where Do We Go from Here?
At the core of brief therapy is a view of how people change. Since one of the main goals of counseling is change and growth, the next chapter will consider the essential elements of the change process.

Part 1 will introduce you to some models of brief therapy. Since some of you are new to the idea of brief therapy, chapter 3 will present an abbreviated history of brief therapy and some ways in which the assumptions of long-term therapy differ from those of brief therapy. In chapter 4 we will turn a corner and get even more specific with a look at one of the oldest formal brief-therapy models, the strategic problem-solving approach of the Mental Research Institute (MRI). Then in chapter 5, we will look at how the problem-solving approach differs from the solution-focused model of Steve de Shazer and Insoo Kim Berg.

Part 2 will present a problem-sensitive, solution-based model for helping people change. Chapter 6 will address the theoretical and theological assumptions of this model. In chapter 7 you will get an extensive look at what the critical first interview might look like. Chapter 8 will give you specific ways to develop clear treatment goals and help clients construct solutions. In chapter 9 we will focus on what to do after the first session, with specific ways to help clients maintain progress during and after treatment.

Part 3 will explore what solution-focused brief therapy might look like with some specific populations: adolescents (chapter 10), couples and families (chapter 11), and difficult clients (chapter 12).

Part 4 concludes with a chapter focused on the wide research that has been done in the development of brief therapy (chapter 13). Chapter 14, an essential chapter, puts it all together, stepping back to summarize how solution-based brief therapy is integrated into a sound psychology, a sound theology, a biblical foundation, and a need for personal spiritual growth.

As you go through this book, keep an open mind. When we make a general statement or share an illustration, don't immediately think of all the exceptions and all the ways it might not work. You'll have time for that later. Read it, process it, try it. Test what we say in light of God's Word. Then accept what you can and discard what you must.

2/ CHANGE HAPPENS, *but* GROWTH TAKES WORK

Most people are willing to change, not because they see the light, but because they feel the heat. UNKNOWN

But speaking the truth in love, we are to grow up in all aspects into Him, who is the head, even Christ, from whom the whole body, being fitted and held together by that which every joint supplies, according to the proper working of each individual part, causes the growth of the body for the building up of itself in love.

EPHESIANS 4:15-16, NASB

People go to counselors for many reasons. A pastoral or professional counselor provides safety and confidentiality. When people talk about their problems, they are often able to clarify those problems. When people talk about problems, it helps them feel as if they are doing something about them. Some people have the idea that if they talk about something long enough, something good will happen.

If counselors nod, grunt, groan, laugh, or ask questions while a person talks, the counselors imply that they are paying attention to what the person is saying. It implies that they believe the person's problem is significant enough for them to listen to, which implies that the *person* is significant enough to listen to. If counselors don't disagree with the person, it might even mean that they agree. Just having someone listen can help the person feel better. At least for a while.

As a young and obviously naive youth director, I (Gary) thought that everyone who came into my office to talk about a problem was open to change. If someone asked to see me for counseling, it was obvious that person was eager to hear what I had to say and try it. Right?

Wrong!

It didn't take long for me to discover that people like to talk about their problems. They want their lives to be different. But that doesn't necessarily mean that they are looking for solutions. That doesn't necessarily mean they are willing to change.

Change happens. Change is always taking place. But it's not always constructive change. It can be for the better, or it can be for the worse. Counseling is designed to help people change for the better. Several fundamental questions lie at the heart of what we know as counseling. The ways in which we answer these questions will influence, if not determine, our approach to and effectiveness in counseling.

1. Can people change?
2. Can people help other people change?
3. What is it about change that makes it so difficult?
4. What kinds of barriers keep people from changing?
5. What are the general principles of change?
6. Are there basic patterns or stages of change?
7. Is the change process different for different people?

It's obvious that people can change. Noted psychologist and university professor Michael J. Mahoney writes, "Were there any doubt that human beings are capable of substantial psychological change, the events of the twentieth century would offer ample and diversified testimony. In no other period of history have so many aspects of human experience been so dramatically changed."[1] It's equally obvious that people can help people change.

Most people know that unless they change, they'll remain stuck in dead-end jobs, mediocre and unsatisfying relationships, or other depressing and self-defeating situations. Still, many people make up excuses, procrastinate, or do anything they can to avoid change. We've all heard comments like these:

- Why should I be the one to change? I'm not that bad. I know a lot of people who are worse than I am.
- I'll never be able to change; it's just the way I am. My father

and grandfather were the same way. I was born this way, and it's too late to do anything about it now.

- You can't teach an old dog new tricks.

But have you ever had a client come into your office and announce, "I've decided that I want to be mediocre, stay stuck, play it safe, and stagnate. I want to be a spiritual, emotional, and relational midget"? I haven't. For most people, hanging on to old familiar habits, even though those habits are hurting them, isn't a conscious choice. Avoiding change is a reflex action, an unconscious and automatic response.

What little sense of safety and security some people enjoy can be threatened by change. Most people hope that if they wait long enough, the problems will take care of themselves. Who can blame us for wanting to wait for a perfect and preferably painless solution to our problems?

CHANGE IS IMPORTANT TO GOD

You don't have to read very much of the Bible to realize that one of God's primary goals for us as Christians is growth. The Bible has a lot to say about growth, change, and becoming mature. *While God loves us just the way we are, he loves us too much to leave us that way.* Because he loves us, he wants to see us "become like his Son" (Rom. 8:29). Because he loves us, he wants to help us "grow up in all aspects into Him, who is the head, even Christ" (Eph. 4:15, NASB).

The apostle Paul expresses concern over the Corinthian Christians because they haven't grown. He writes, "Dear brothers and sisters, when I was with you I couldn't talk to you as I would to mature Christians. I had to talk as though you belonged to this world or as though you were infants in the Christian life" (1 Cor. 3:1). In Hebrews 5:11-14, the writer expresses concern that the readers haven't changed; they haven't deepened or matured. He begins chapter 6 by exhorting them to "press on to maturity" (Heb. 6:1, NASB). What he is really saying is, "Hey, folks. Wake up! It's time for you to make some changes. It's time for you to grow up."

A careful study of Scripture reveals that a willingness to change, learn, and grow is God's love language. Our choice to change says that we believe in him, that we trust him, that we are willing to become who and what he wants us to be. Being open to change is our way of taking his hand and following where we don't always understand, where we fear, even where we don't want to go, with the knowledge that we can trust him. He will never give us more than we can handle (1 Cor. 10:13). He can cause all things to work together for our good (Rom. 8:28). And he will supply all of our needs according to his riches in glory (Phil. 4:19).

In the spiritual sense, change means being open to surrender, a kind of giving up and letting go. *Surrender* is not a popular term in our society. It flies in the face of our culture's cult of individualism. In the Christian life, change starts with and involves a continuous surrender of our flawed, sinful self. "What this means is that those who become Christians become new persons. They are not the same anymore, for the old life is gone. A new life has begun!" (2 Cor. 5:17).

The process of becoming more like Christ—what theologians refer to as the process of sanctification—involves letting go of the old life so that we can put on the new life. What we lose pales in comparison to what we gain. But Satan doesn't want us to see the *product* of sanctification. He wants us to see only the sometimes painful *process.*

How do we grow up? How do we mature? How do we become who God would have us to be? How do we learn to honor one another, to serve one another, to prefer one another, to esteem others as more important than ourselves? How do we overcome overwhelming depression? How do we learn not to worry about anything or to be angry and yet not sin?

It's a process. It doesn't happen overnight. It takes time. In the first chapter of 1 Peter, Peter gives a powerful word picture to help us understand this process. He describes it as a refining process. In verse 6, Peter compares our lives to gold that is purified by fire. In the first century, the refining process involved several different "firings" in which the heat brought the alloys and impurities to the surface of the molten gold so that the goldsmith could remove them. God's refining process takes time and hard work, but the product is worth it. The end result is gold that is pure.

In conferences around the country I've asked hundreds of people to complete the sentence "Change is. . . ." Here are some of the most frequent responses:

hard	a crossroads
refreshing	unavoidable
positive	essential for maturity
takes work	the opposite of dying
stressful	a tremendous source of fear
uncomfortable	easier to require in others than
exciting	in self
scary	like walking through a
painful	minefield
an attitude	easier for some than others
awkward	an opportunity for self-
threatening	examination

A quick glance at the dictionary will reveal that the word *change* means to make different; to give a different course or direction; to replace one thing with another; to make a shift from one to another; to undergo transformation, transition, or substitution (e.g., winter changing to spring).

However, most people see change as something negative—something that implies inferiority, inadequacy, and failure. Many clients come into counseling having been pressured to change. They've gotten the message that who they are doesn't measure up or that what they're doing isn't acceptable. No wonder so many people run from or resist the idea of change. Who wants to admit feeling inferior and inadequate?

CHANGE IS THE PATHWAY TO GROWTH

Read through the following list of words and ask yourself what your response might be if someone were to encourage you to do one of these. Would your response be positive or negative?

become	bud
expand	shoot up
develop	progress
enlarge	thrive
swell	bear fruit
augment	prosper
supplement	flourish
extend	luxuriate

mature	bloom
advance	blossom

As you read through that list, you probably guessed that each one of those words is a synonym for *grow*. Each one of those words describes a positive change. Most people have a more positive response to the word *grow* than to the word *change*. Yet without change, there is no growth. I remember hearing Warren Wiersbe say that "we can benefit from change. Anyone who has ever really lived knows that there is no life without growth. When we stop growing, we stop living and start existing. But there is no growth without change, there is no challenge without change. Life is a series of changes that create challenges, and if we are going to make it, we have to grow."[2]

Believe it or not, people are a lot like trees. They either grow or die. There's no standing still. A tree dies when its roots become blocked. God has made us in such a way that we become mentally, spiritually, and eventually physically dead when we choose to be victimized and allow the circumstances of our life to keep us from growing. Pastors and therapists spend their lives trying to help people who have chosen to stop growing.

Someone might respond, "Well, I don't want to grow. I want to stay just the way I am." Unfortunately, that isn't an option. Either we are growing, or we are doing the opposite. What's the opposite of growing? Take a look at these words and phrases:

stagnating	atrophying
deteriorating	decaying
degenerating	coming to a standstill
declining	going stale
going to seed	becoming sluggish
going to pot	going dormant
vegetating	dying
hanging back	

What's your first thought after reading that list of words? Mine was *yuck!* I don't know of anyone who would like to be described as stagnating, deteriorating, and atrophying. Yet the reality is that this is what we are choosing when we choose not to grow.

Tim Hansel tells a great story about what it's like to be around people who have chosen to play it safe, to stay stuck, to refuse to grow:

> A close friend of mine was asked back to his forty-year high school reunion. For months he saved to take his wife back to the place and the people he'd left four decades before. The closer the time came for the reunion, the more excited he became, thinking of all the wonderful stories he would hear about the change and the accomplishments these old friends would tell him. One night before he left he even pulled out his old yearbooks and read the silly statements and the good wishes for the future that students write to each other. He wondered what ol' Number 86 from his football team had done. He wondered if any others had encountered this Christ who had changed him so profoundly. He even tried to guess what some of his friends would look like, and what kind of jobs and families some of these special friends had.
>
> The day came to leave and I drove them to the airport. Their energy was almost contagious. "I'll pick you up on Sunday evening, and you can tell me all about it," I said. "Have a great time."
>
> Sunday evening arrived. As I watched them get off the plane, my friend seemed almost despondent. I almost didn't want to ask, but finally I said, "Well, how was the reunion?"
>
> "Tim," the man said, "it was one of the saddest experiences of my life."
>
> "Good grief," I said, more than a little surprised. "What happened?"
>
> "It wasn't what happened but what didn't happen. It has been forty years, forty years—and they haven't changed. They had simply gained weight, changed clothes, gotten jobs . . . but they hadn't really changed. And what I experienced was maybe one of the most tragic things I could ever imagine about life. For reasons I can't fully understand, it seems as though some people choose not to change."
>
> There was a long silence as we walked back to the car. On the drive home, he turned to me and said, "I never, never want that to be said of me, Tim. Life is too precious, too sacred, too important. If you ever see me go stagnant like that, I hope you'll give me a quick,

swift kick where I need it. . . . I hope you'll love me enough to challenge me to keep growing."[3]

Here's the bottom line. When you boil down the Christian life to the basics, the name of the game is change. Those who want to learn, who are willing to look at themselves in the mirror before grabbing the binoculars to criticize others, who resist having a pity party and blaming everybody else, who refuse to stay in a rut, who make time to listen for the still, small voice of the Holy Spirit—those are the ones God is free to use, to bless, to honor. Those are the ones who know what it means to be more than conquerors (Rom. 8:37, NIV).

WHY IS IT SO HARD TO CHANGE?

If change is valuable and necessary, if it is part of God's plan for our lives, if it is essential for our growth, why do so many people avoid it? Whenever I teach about change, I ask people to list what they consider to be the most significant barriers to change.[4] Here are some of the most frequently listed barriers:

we don't know how	security
we've tried before and failed	limited emotional toolbox
fear of the unknown	need for control
lack of role models	fear of self-examination
denial	weakness
it's easier to do it the old way	obligations
disrupts the status quo	fear of failure
it's easy to say no to a new idea	family ties/messages
pride	admitting wrong

People give a lot of different reasons for not being able to change. Have you ever heard anyone say, "I can't change," "It's too hard to change," or "Why try? It won't make any difference"? Time and time again we've found that, of all the many barriers to change, of all the reasons people give, one barrier heads the list. Do you know what it is?

Before I tell you what it is, let me ask you a question. What do you think of when you hear the word *crazy?* Someone who thinks he is George Washington? Someone who has intimate conversations with trees? Someone who has traveled around the world seven times this past month? Someone who has a severely impaired reality orientation? That might be one definition.

How's this definition? *Crazy is to discover what doesn't work and keep on doing it.* Think about it. If you walked into a room and saw me flicking the light switch up and down two or three times, you wouldn't think anything about it. However, if you saw me flicking the same light switch up and down for a half hour, you would know that, at the very least, something was seriously wrong with my thought process and problem-solving skills.

Everybody wants to be different, but few people want to change. Does that sound a bit crazy? It is. But it's the truth. I've worked with thousands of people who have spent twenty and thirty years doing the same dysfunctional dance, refusing to grow, refusing to change, refusing to budge. They have cussed, discussed, and complained about their problems. They've asked the *why* question ad infinitum and ad nauseam. They've talked to their friends. They've talked to their pastors. They've talked to several different counselors. They sincerely want to have a different kind of life, but they are not willing to change. They are stuck in a personal and relational rut. And you know what a rut is, don't you? A rut is a grave with both ends kicked out.

How does this resistance to growth happen? How is it that something that seems so simple can be so difficult? How can someone who has been to Calvary and has a personal relationship with Jesus Christ *not* grow? Why do some people choose to endure pain and mediocre relationships when they could significantly increase their joy?

It's simple. We are creatures of habit. We get used to seeing and doing things a certain way, and after a while it's hard for us to see it any other way. As we get older, we develop our own unique perspective that determines the way things "should" be and the ways people "should" act. That's why it can be hard for us to understand why others don't see things the same way we do. But we usually assume it's their problem and attribute it to their lack of training, opportunity, intelligence, or spirituality. The assumptions we have about the way things and people should be can become so strong that they determine what we do and do not see.

Here's a classic example. When Jesus Christ came in fulfillment of the hundreds of prophecies concerning the Messiah, the experts in the Scriptures didn't recognize him. Not only did they miss him, they *crucified* him. Why? Because he didn't come in the manner they thought he would come. He didn't fit their "model" or paradigm of what the Messiah would look like. They were expecting a mighty and powerful king who would free them from their bondage and annihilate the Romans. They weren't expecting a baby, born out of wedlock, in a manger, to a poor carpenter from Nazareth. They weren't expecting a man who took the form of a servant so that he could die on a cross.

Throughout history people have resisted change. They have chosen to stay stuck in the rut of the safe and familiar. In sixteenth-century Venice, Galileo struggled with people stuck in such a rut. In his day, the assured results of scientific research had "proven" the Copernican theory that the earth and not the sun was the center of the solar system. Galileo looked at the facts and came to a different conclusion. He took the leading scientists of his day to the top of the Tower of San Marco to look through his newly perfected telescope and share his exciting discovery that the earth went around the sun.

Galileo's peers were so antagonized by his shocking assertion that he was threatened with torture if he didn't retract his position. Over time, of course, he was proven right. His ideas won out. But what kept those "experts" from being able to admit what they had seen with their own eyes? The same thing that blinded them can blind us and the people with whom we work.

We all have a set of rules and regulations of how things are and how they should be. These "models" serve as filters that screen the information that comes into our minds. They establish boundaries, show us what is important and what isn't, help us solve problems, and define what is normal or abnormal, healthy and unhealthy. So far, no problem.

However, a problem arises when our models of reality become *the* model, the only way to do things. It's easy to get stuck in the rut of seeing things the way we (or our parents, denomination, or graduate school) have always seen them. Anything different can be threatening and make us feel uncomfortable. Most of us tend to see ourselves the way we want to be, should be, or are expected to be, rather than see ourselves the way we really are.

People's models of how things should be can blind them to areas that need changing. They can keep clients from being open to change. They can keep a counselor from trying something new. Sometimes, even in the face of overwhelming evidence that what we're doing isn't working, it's easier for us to stay in the rut of the safe and familiar rather than venture out into an area that has risk but also has the possibility of leading us to maturity and growth. Our perspective becomes paralyzed by our limited perception. It doesn't matter how bright or talented we are. It doesn't matter how successful we've been. All of us suffer from this tendency.

CONSTRUCTIVE CHANGE INVOLVES SETTING REALISTIC GOALS

Sometimes change is easy, but other times change can be difficult and even painful. Even positive changes like a promotion, a new house, or a bonus can produce stress and anxiety. It involves our doing something that is different, and that takes some adjusting. It moves us out of our comfort zone. Sometimes unlearning an old habit, no matter how small or insignificant, can take a lot of emotional, mental, and even physical work.

Recently one of my older friends told me about a struggle he was having with his golf game. Bill said, "Gary, I've played golf for close to twenty years. I play several times a week. But over the years I've developed some bad habits." Because of his love for the game and his desire to become a better player, he decided to take some lessons from a profes-sional golfer.

Bill reported later, "I couldn't believe how difficult it was to change a few simple aspects of my game. Unlearning unhealthy and automatic ways of swinging my club was a lot more work than I had thought." He had to spend hours and hours working on some new techniques. "At first I felt silly doing some of the exercises the instructor made me do. And after the first few practices my arms ached. But now," he said with a smile, "it doesn't hurt me at all." His smile got even bigger when he added, "And I've lowered my handicap by six strokes."

I don't golf. But I know enough about the game to know that dropping your handicap by six strokes is a significant accomplishment. How did Bill do it? What brought about his growth? What led to his increased sense of confidence and competence? How was he able to improve on habits he had practiced for over twenty years?

His desire to grow, to improve, to increase his skill and competence made him willing to risk some pain, to risk looking awkward, to risk confronting some feelings of inadequacy, to risk the challenge of change. He took the risk, paid the price—and won.

Bill was open to change. But he had learned one of the secrets of effective change. He set realistic goals. One of the potential pitfalls of change is the tendency to attempt too much too soon. That is true in both golf games and counseling. Sincere but misguided attempts to achieve complete change at the beginning of counseling will almost always result in frustration, discouragement, and failure. Setting unrealistic and un-reachable goals can become a self-fulfilling prophecy that is destructive to the change process.

As clients continue to pursue solutions that don't work, the ultimate goals appear further and further out of reach. This perpetuates the clients' misbeliefs that they can't change. "Why try again? It won't make any difference. I'm a failure. I'm a loser. I always have been. I always will be." While it is important to keep the ultimate goal in mind, we need to help our clients focus on the individual steps.

Charles Swindoll has written that "change—real change—takes place slowly. In first gear, not overdrive. Far too many Christians get discouraged and give up. Like ice skating or mastering a musical instrument or learning to water ski, certain techniques have to be discovered and developed in the daily discipline of living. Breaking habit patterns you established during the passing of years cannot occur in a few brief days. Remember that. 'Instant' change is as rare as it is phony."[5]

It's true. Change takes time, and it can be hard, painful, discouraging, and difficult. But think of the alternative. What is the cost of not changing? of choosing to stay stuck?

What has been your view of change? What is your client's view? Has it been positive or negative? Remember that change doesn't always involve losing old things. It often means adding new things. Growth or development can enrich. Where you had only one way to respond, you may grow to have two. Where you had only one way of looking at things, you may grow to have several. Where you had only one tool to work with, you may grow to have an entire toolbox. God can use change to help you become fully equipped for "every good thing God wants us to do" (2 Tim. 3:17).

THE STAGES OF CHANGE

So far we've looked at the nature and importance of change and some of the barriers to change. One of the essential ingredients for successful counseling is understanding the complexity of how people change. What are some things we need to know about change to become more effective in our counseling? Do all people change in the same way or at the same pace? Are there any identifiable stages people go through?

For over fifteen years psychologist and researcher James Prochaska and his colleagues at the University of Rhode Island have studied how people intentionally change. Initially they interviewed ten thousand people who were trying to give up smoking. Since then, their studies on change have involved more than thirty thousand people dealing with various kinds of change.[6] They looked for an underlying structure of change that might be common to both self-administered and therapeutic courses of treatment. It was clear that people can change. They do successfully resolve complex problems and addictions with and without counseling. What they wanted to know was whether there were some basic principles that made successful change more likely.

Prochaska and his team studied hundreds of different counseling theories, looking for any common components of change. After a lot of hard work they were able to identify nine of the most common and powerful processes of change: consciousness raising, social liberation, emotional arousal, self-reevaluation, commitment, countering, environmental control, rewards, and helping relationships.

They also found that these nine processes of change use a wide variety of techniques to help accomplish that change.[7] In fact, they discovered that for each process, there may be hundreds of different techniques. For example, they found that a particular smoking-cessation group relied on more than 130 different techniques to quit permanently. A technique that is effective for one person may not be helpful for another. In fact, research suggests that counseling is more likely to have a positive outcome if a person is given two choices of how to pursue change rather than one. The success rate increases even more when there are three or more choices.[8]

So far so good. But the researchers didn't stop there. As their ambitious project continued, they struck gold. They found that successful change follows a powerful, controllable, and predictable course. This course consists of various well-defined stages. Each stage involves a series of tasks that need to be completed before moving on to the next stage. One stage doesn't automatically lead to the other. It is possible to get stuck at one stage and not experience change.

Most approaches to helping people change have followed the "action paradigm," which assumes change will occur dramatically and discretely. For the past several decades, this action model has been the foundation of behavior-change programs dealing with problems such as smoking, alcohol, and weight. After going through the program, people are expected to be able to take action, make the change, and adopt a different (healthier) lifestyle. If for some reason they fail to take the action or are unable to maintain the change, they are blamed for a lack of willpower, motivation, or commitment.

Prochaska's research revealed why this approach had such a consistently high failure rate. People who are successful at making positive changes follow a controllable and predictable course. At each stage of the change process there are different dimensions of change. They found that, contrary to popular opinion, no one stage is any more or less important than another. The key to success is knowing what stage you are in for the problem you want to overcome and using the appropriate coping skill at the appropriate stage.

Let's take a brief look at these stages in the context of counseling.

Stage 1: Precontemplation

At this stage clients have little desire to change themselves. Quite frankly, they don't see the need to change. Perhaps they were pushed into therapy. In some cases they don't think that they are able to change. They may be more interested in seeing the people around them change.

Stage 2: Contemplation

At this stage clients can acknowledge that they have a problem and are beginning to consider doing something about it. It is a point of ambivalence; they have a good idea of where they want to go, but they're not sure they're ready to do it. They spend time going over and over the pros and

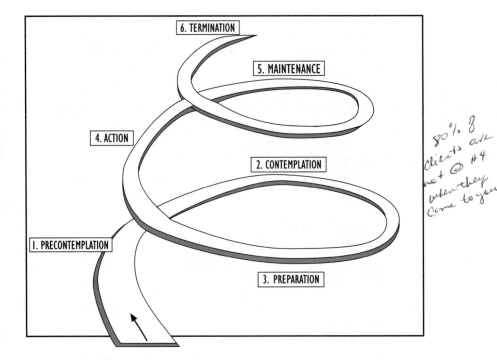

(handwritten note in right margin: 80% of clients are not @ #4 when they come to you)

cons. In fact, it's not unusual for people to spend years telling themselves that someday they are going to change. Some people spend a major part of their life in the contemplation stage. *Thinking about* something gives the illusion of actually *doing* something.

People who eternally substitute thinking for action can be called chronic contemplators. When contemplators begin the transition to the preparation stage, their thinking is clearly marked by two changes. First, they begin to focus on the solution rather than the problem. They then begin to think more about the future than the past. The end of the contemplation stage is a time of anticipation, activity, anxiety, and excitement.[9]

Stage 3: Preparation

By the time clients reach the preparation stage, they are planning to take some action within the month. They have dealt with their ambivalence, made a decision, committed themselves to that decision, and drawn up a plan. They haven't taken any specific steps but are working out the final details.

Stage 4: Action

In stage four, clients have moved beyond contemplation and preparation and are doing something specific. This is the stage that takes the most time and energy. The changes that take place at this stage are the most obvious and thus usually receive the greatest recognition. However, changes can occur in all of the other stages. "Although modifying your behavior is the most visible form of change, it is far from the only one; you can also change your level of awareness, your emotions, your self-image, your thinking, and so on. And many of those changes take place in the stages that precede action." [10]

Stage 5: Maintenance

It's easy to forget about this important stage. It is here that clients consolidate the gains they made during the preceding stages. This is where they struggle to minimize lapses and prevent relapse. Depending on the problem being addressed, this can be a long, ongoing, and, at times, difficult process.

The best way to minimize relapse is not to focus and dwell on the possibility of relapse, what it might look like, what it might feel like. One of the most effective ways to maximize the change is to provide clients with a posttreatment plan for maintaining progress and continued growth. Without this, people are likely to experience a lapse that can easily lead to a relapse.

Stage 6: Termination

This is the stage the clients have been waiting for. The problem has been solved. The goal has been reached. Change has taken place. It's time to move on.

Prochaska and his colleagues found that people who try to accomplish changes they aren't ready for end up setting themselves up for failure. "If you spend too much time working on tasks you have already mastered—such as understanding your problem—you may delay acting upon it indefinitely." [11]

From looking across a representative sample of more than fifteen high-risk behaviors, the study found that "fewer than 20% of a problem population are prepared for action at any given time. And yet, more than 90% of behavior change programs are designed with this 20% in mind." [12]

This also helps to explain why "over 45 percent of clients drop out of psychotherapy prematurely, since treatments too often don't match the stage clients are in."[13]

In the beginning, Prochaska and his associates assumed that there was a linear progression through the stages: Precontemplation → Contemplation → Preparation → Action → Maintenance → Termination. What they found is that linear progression can occur, but it is a rare phenomenon. Most people slip up at some point and return to the contemplation or even the precontemplation stage.

What is significant is how people respond at the point of a setback or failure. When relapse occurs, all isn't lost. A relapse doesn't prove that the client is a failure. More likely, a slip is proof of a person's humanity. Most people spend years struggling with various problems. Often it is a fear of failure that keeps people stuck in the contemplation stage. The reality is that failure and the lessons learned from failure can be an essential and invaluable part of the change process.

Another important insight is that people *rarely* go through the process just once. Most go through it three or four times before the change is sustained for six months. Prochaska and his colleagues studied those who were successful at making change and found that only 5 percent made it through the cycle of change without at least one setback. Based on the results of years of research with thousands of subjects, Prochaska doesn't talk about *relapse* anymore. He calls it *recycling.*

Based on this replicated research, it's obviously critical for us as counselors to tie our intervention and intervention strategies to where people are on the change cycle. As you read through this book, you will be able to understand better how essential these insights are to effective brief therapy. We can't treat every person the same way and be effective. If someone is in the precontemplation stage, we would treat that person differently from the way we would treat someone at the action stage (i.e., for people in contemplation we want to lower the resistance to change). This research dispels the myth that good therapy involves treating everyone the same.

Understanding where clients are in their stage of readiness to change can dramatically promote both efficiency and the behavior change clients desire.[14] People can be at different places of this change process for different areas of their life. People can be in denial or ambivalent about one aspect of their life and be at the action stage for another part of their life. This model has obvious implications for treatment planning.

CONCLUSION

Christian psychologist David Dillon has written that change is part of everyone's life but channeling change into growth is paramount in counseling. Because people have the freedom of choice, we must work with them and not try to force their will. We must get their attention so that they can receive new or correct information for cognitive processing. Finally we need to help them convert what they learn into new behaviors that become self-reinforcing. Once they try and succeed, they are more likely to follow a new course.[15]

People tend to look at change in terms of what will be lost rather than what will be gained. When people see the possibilities for change, when they understand that change means more rather than less, when they see that the long-term benefits outweigh the short-term discomfort, they will be more likely to take the first small step.

Since change is occurring all of the time, the counselor can help the client pursue productive change by providing basic parameters to direct the change that is naturally taking place. Attempts to sabotage constructive change don't stop the change process. Change happens! It simply increases the probability that the inevitable change that is taking place will be in the direction of stagnation or decline.

We humans cannot change many things about ourselves and our world. But by God's grace there are many important things we *can* change, like our thoughts, our feelings, our behaviors, our choices. I have seen people change deep-seated patterns. I have seen men and women break multi-generational bondage to unhealthy and destructive anger patterns. I have seen God breathe hope into the "hopeless" and provide help for the "helpless."

God has a wonderful way of not changing himself but of changing the way he deals with his people. He is immutable, but he is also flexible. He didn't talk to everyone the same way. He didn't perform every miracle the same way. He gave us four Gospels to help us understand the one gospel. Even though we change, God does not change. Yet one of his desires is to orchestrate change in his people. Philippians 1:6 states, "And I am sure that God, who began the good work within you [justification], will continue his work [sanctification] until it is finally finished [glorification] on that day when Christ Jesus comes back again."

PART ONE

Models of Brief Therapy

3 / WHAT IS BRIEF THERAPY?

Brief psychotherapy—treatment concluded in no more than twenty sessions—is often seen as a compromise. During the training of the dynamic psychotherapist, the idea becomes firmly imprinted that longer is better. Experience has taught me, however, that shorter is anything but second-best. In a majority of cases, short-term treatment, effectively applied, enables the patient to reach the same therapeutic goals as long-term psychotherapy, while offering the added advantage of relieving the patient's psychic stress that much sooner. Moreover, I believe that one cannot decide arbitrarily, on the basis of either symptoms or character structure, that a patient will not benefit from brief therapy. Indeed, it is my position that all patients who are not psychotic or suicidal should be thought of as candidates for brief psychotherapy until proven otherwise.

At first blush it may seem odd for a card-carrying psychoanalyst to be writing about short-term treatment. But I am not suggesting that brief psychotherapy is a substitute for either psychoanalysis or open-ended psychotherapy. The point is simply that very few of the people referred to me for treatment need such extensive therapy.

MICHAEL FRANZ BASCH, *Doing Brief Psychotherapy*

When people seek counseling today, they are faced with what can be an overwhelming and confusing array of choices. There are thousands of different counselors, who practice hundreds of different approaches to helping people change. However, it wasn't always this confusing. In the 1950s it was estimated that there were thirty-six different types of counseling. In 1975 a report of the Research Task Force of the National Institute of Mental Health indicated that there were over one hundred and thirty modes of counseling. In 1980 R. Herink identified over two hundred different forms of therapy, and just six years later, in 1986, psychologist Alan Kazdin referenced over four hundred different techniques.[1]

What makes the choice especially difficult for clients is that all techniques claim to be effective. All of them have at least one charismatic proponent with great illustrations of almost miraculous cures. All of them have a list of testimonials singing the praises of that particular approach.

Yet with this proliferation of therapies that emphasize different therapist behaviors and therapeutic procedures, no one approach has risen to the top as the most effective one. If one approach had demonstrated clear superiority over the others, it would be a household word by now, and therapists using any other method would be out of business.

Many changes have taken place in the counseling field in the past thirty-five years. One of the most significant has been the surprising increase in the acceptance of brief and short-term therapies. Until recently the dominance of psychoanalytic thought led most people to assume that good therapy had to take a long time.

> Because the personal difficulties of the patient supposedly developed over a period of many years, it was believed that a reasonably long period of time would be required in order for significant improvement to be obtained. Accompanying this view was the belief that only by helping the patient to secure insight in the unconscious conflicts causing his or her difficulties could he or she be helped. . . . Too quick an attempt at uncovering repressed material might also lead to the shattering of the patient's defenses and to possible disintegration of personality. Furthermore, if one did not get to the source of the neurotic difficulty and concentrated only on treating the symptom, the result would be the eventual appearance of substitute symptoms.[2]

The sociopolitical climate of the eighties, with its push for cost containment, created an environment in which the brief-therapy movement began to flourish. As creative therapists pursued innovative techniques to promote change rather than gradual growth through understanding and insight, the brief-therapy movement began to take off. An increasing number of therapists became more directive and began to use strategic approaches.

The significant increase of published reports on brief therapy indicated that some clients made rather quick progress without acquiring deep insights or working through complex issues. Many studies showed that the average number of sessions in therapy was much fewer than previously assumed. As studies were published on premature termination and length of stay in outpatient therapy, counselors began to take a second look at their previously unchallenged assumptions. The results of this new research suggested that, in many cases, brief therapy is as effective as long-term therapy; sometimes it is even more effective than long-term therapy.[3]

In the nineties, changes in the social and political climate have continued to fuel the mental-health revolution that has accelerated the popularity and growth of brief approaches to therapy. The belief that therapy had to be long-term to be effective has given way to the reality that in many cases significant and lasting change can be achieved in a short period of time. Whether it be by intentional design or by default, brief treatments are becoming the norm of counseling practice.

Probably the greatest impetus toward the growth of brief therapy has been the powerful influence of the rapidly growing managed-care movement. It's obvious that the desire of the insurance industries to cut costs and increase profits has been a driving factor in promoting various forms of brief therapy. In fact, one of the major criticisms of brief therapy has been that its only purpose is to satiate the money-hungry managed-care companies. Based on this assumption, it would be logical to condemn it as a shallow, superficial, Band-Aid approach to change.

While the interest in and growth of brief therapy has been accelerated by the realities of managed care, brief therapy is not the invention of managed care. Brief therapy is not the new kid on the block. Brief therapy has been around for much longer than most people realize. Many counselors are surprised to discover that brief, intermittent psychotherapy throughout the life cycle has been subjected to an unprecedented thirty-five years of outcome research.[4]

In 1966, before the advent of managed care, psychologists E. Lakin Phillips and Daniel Wiener wrote, "We believe therapy as conventionally practiced is usually loaded down with a superstructure of theory . . . which diverts therapists and patients from the problems and solutions at hand. Instead, it burdens them with speculations which may be intended for use in carrying out grand concepts and advancing scientific study— but not primarily in helping individuals as directly and effectively as possible. Parsimony is ignored. It is as if therapists had been trained to look at patient problems through glasses which distort, suppress, elongate, and foreshorten, so that the view of therapy may be delightful, creative, or fantastic, but never entirely realistic."[5]

Unfortunately the fear, frustration, and paranoia produced by managed care has led to an antagonism that has spilled over to brief therapy. Some look at brief therapy as the illegitimate child of legitimate (read *long-term*) therapy. It is an epidemic that threatens to contaminate the entire counseling field. This negative view has been fueled by some extreme and irresponsible brief-therapy proponents who talk as if it is a miracle cure that all counselors should use with all clients regardless of the presenting issues.

In a recent edition of *Family Therapy News*, several counselors wrote a humorous article detailing the diagnosis and treatment of what they call "brief therapy addicts."

> Judge and Killem (1988) report the following personality characteristics in brief therapy addicts: (1) obsessive and inordinate attention to detail and concern for concrete information about the obvious; (2) delusional faith in clients' resources and ability to change; (3) pathological concern for therapy outcome, even with schizophrenics and borderlines; (4) marked feelings of over-responsibility resulting in a manic and frenzied effort to "do something different"; and (5) compulsive desire for efficiency. Name and Blame (1989) have proposed a new diagnostic category for brief therapists, which encompasses the above characteristics and is called Pragmatic Personality Disorder (PPD). The objective of treatment is recovery of the brief therapist, control over the craving for rapid change, abstinence from brief therapy, and realization that he or she can cope with the unchanging problems of clients and lead a more rewarding life without brief therapy.[6]

The fact is that brief therapy is much more than an attempt to meet the demands of insurance companies. It is much more than compacted and compromised long-term therapy. Based on our experience and a growing body of anecdotal and research evidence, it is clear that regardless of the forced financial realities of managed care, brief therapy has a place in the toolbox of effective counselors.

WHAT IS BRIEF THERAPY?

You can call it focused, short-term, strategic, solution-oriented, cost-effective, time-effective, time-limited, time-sensitive, or just plain old brief therapy. Some therapists have other less clinically oriented names for it. They believe not only that it is inferior but that it really isn't even therapy. It is a betrayal of what any responsible, conscientious, and ethical counselor should do.

Other clinicians would say just the opposite. Psychologist John Cooper believes that contrary to the assumptions of some clinicians who associate brief therapy with inferior care or even denial of care, brief therapy may in reality be more consistent with ethical practice than many longer-term approaches. "Specifically, it is consistent with the notions of using least invasive procedures first, informed patient consent (since treatment is collaborative), and respect for patient autonomy (presenting complaints are taken seriously and clients are considered the primary arbiters of treatment success)."[7]

From the beginning, "brief" therapy has been defined in contrast to "long-term" therapy. In 1966, Phillips and Wiener stated that many therapists believe that short-term therapy is only a poor substitute for long-term therapy. "To them, short-term therapy is for the poor, the lower classes, the naive, the 'unmotivated,' and the nonfluent of speech, and is equated with superficial insight and temporary effectiveness. Long-term therapy, on the other hand, is likely to be regarded as 'deep,' 'intensive,' 'long-lasting,' and more 'insightful.'"[8]

So what is brief therapy? A simple definition isn't as easy as you might think. It can't be defined merely in terms of number of sessions, length of sessions, or total time elapsed between the first and the last sessions. Brief therapies can range from one session to over twenty sessions; sometimes they may include as many as fifty sessions. The length of sessions can range from twenty minutes to several hours. The total time elapsed can be a few hours or a period of several years.

One of the reasons for the difficulty in definition lies in the fact that there are well over fifty forms of therapy that would call themselves *brief,* and that number continues to grow.[9] Most models integrate aspects of a variety of theoretical orientations, including psychodynamic, family-systems, cognitive-behavioral, problem-solving, solution-based, and inter-personal therapies.

At its core, brief therapy is a way of *thinking about change* as much as a way of *helping people change.* Psychologists and brief-therapy pioneers Simon Budman and Alan Gurman said it well when they suggested that one of the critical criteria for defining the nature of brief therapy is "a state of mind of the therapist and of the patient."[10] The bottom-line goals are helping clients overcome the difficulties that are keeping them from functioning in healthy ways and, in the process, giving them new ways to handle future problems in a more effective manner.

Psychologist Sol Garfield says that "the general goal of brief psycho-therapy is to help the client overcome the problems or discomforts that lead him or her to seek out someone for psychotherapeutic help. Relief of pain, discomfort, or unhappiness are what the client seeks and hopes to receive from therapy."[11] He goes on to suggest that a secondary goal of brief therapy might be helping the client develop coping skills to handle and prevent future problems more effectively.

According to researchers Mary Koss and James Butcher, "Most brief therapists strive to accomplish one or more of the following goals: removal or amelioration of the patient's most disabling symptoms as rapidly as possible; prompt reestablishment of the patient's previous emotional equilibrium; and development of the patient's under-standing of the current disturbance and increased coping ability in the future." [12]

Psychologists Nick Cummings and Mike Sayama state that the goal of brief therapy "is to release the patient from situations that thwart the natural process of growth."[13] Ideally, therapy is brief and intermittent throughout the life cycle and is needed at times when old defenses no longer suffice and the client is most receptive to change.

BRIEF THERAPY BY DEFAULT OR BY DESIGN

Most counselors do a form of brief therapy. Therapist and professor Hanna Levenson writes that at the beginning of her seminars in time–limited dynamic psychotherapy, after she asks the participants why they have decided to attend her seminar, she inquires how many of them do brief therapy, either in private practice or in an agency or institutional setting. "After a show of hands, I confess it is a trick question: They all do brief therapy whether they intend to or not. . . . The reason is that most patients choose to stay in therapy only a short time."[14]

Unfortunately, much of what is called brief therapy has taken place by default rather than by design. What is brief therapy by default? Many surveys relating to the length of therapy in the United States have revealed that, de facto, most therapy tends to be brief. Theoretical attrition curves predict and empirical evidence confirms that 60 to 75 percent of all outpatients drop out of treatment before the eighth session. These findings hold even for psychodynamic treatments that are intended to be long-term.

A number of research studies with a variety of patients and with a wide range of settings and agendas showed that a large number of patients tended to drop out of therapy early. The studies established that, regardless of the type of outpatient treatment, the great majority of patients are seen for only six to eight sessions.[15] The counselors behind such treatment practiced a brief therapy whether or not they meant to.

Yet, an increasing number of competent therapists are choosing to do brief therapy not because they have to or because managed-care companies are forcing them to, but because they believe it is the treatment of choice for many of the people they see. At the very least, it is the most effective way to begin the counseling process. Brief therapy by design takes place when, at the outset of the counseling process, the counselor chooses to make the most of limited time.

HOW IS BRIEF THERAPY DIFFERENT FROM LONG-TERM THERAPY?

Brief therapy is more than just a set of clever techniques or compacted long-term therapy. One of the most effective ways to differentiate brief therapies from long-term therapies is to examine the underlying assumptions of each approach.

In 1983, Simon Budman and Alan Gurman wrote what has become a seminal article on the practice of brief therapy.[16] They identified and contrasted sixteen core assumptions of brief and long-term therapy. We have modified and edited the original sixteen down to fourteen different assumptions. Seven reflect long-term therapy, and seven reflect brief therapy.

Read through the following list of assumptions and put a check by the statements that most reflect your practice and make you the most comfortable.

☐ 1. Seeks change in basic character.

☐ 2. Prefers pragmatism, parsimony, and least radical intervention and does not believe in notion of "cure."

☐ 3. Believes that significant psychological change is unlikely in everyday life.

☐ 4. Maintains an adult development perspective from which significant psychological change is viewed as inevitable.

☐ 5. Sees presenting problem as reflecting a more pervasive underlying pathology.

☐ 6. Emphasizes patient's strengths and resources; presenting problems are taken seriously, although not necessarily at face value.

☐ 7. Believes the therapist needs to be there as patient makes significant changes.

☐ 8. Accepts that many changes will occur after therapy and will not be observable to the therapist.

☐ 9. Sees therapy as having a timeless quality and is patient and willing to wait for change.

☐ 10. Does not accept the timelessness of some models of therapy.

☐ 11. Views psychotherapy as almost always benign and useful.

☐ 12. Views psychotherapy as sometimes useful and sometimes harmful.

☐ 13. Sees the patient's being in therapy as one of the most important parts of patient's life.

☐ 14. Sees the patient's being in the world as more important than being in therapy.

If the majority of your checks were next to the odd-numbered statements, you are probably most comfortable with long-term therapy. If more of your checks are next to the even-numbered statements, you are more comfortable with brief therapy. Now that you are more aware of what your bias might be, you are ready to move on. After a thorough review of a wide range of the brief-therapy literature, we have identified seven core assumptions that distinguish most brief therapies.

Limited and Specific Goals along with Maintaining Clear, Specific Treatment Focus with Clearly Defined Outcomes

Rarely does a client walk into a counselor's office and announce, "I have one and only one issue to discuss with you." Real people have multiple problems in multiple settings, and it's easy for the focus of treatment to become complicated. Brief therapists believe that the focus needs to be clarified from the very beginning.

In my own counseling, teaching, and supervision, I have found that the most common reason for counselors' getting stuck is related to inadequate and unclear goals. Matthew Selekman, a social worker who specializes in work with adolescents, writes that when a counselor is stuck or frustrated with a particular case, the counselor "may be lost in a sea of information about problems, he or she may not know what the client's treatment goal is, or the treatment goal may be too monolithic. Our job as therapists is to negotiate solvable problems and realistic treatment goals."[17]

Along this line, psychiatrist James Mann writes,

It has long been my conviction that long-term psychotherapy with insufficiently or inaccurately defined treatment goals leads to a steady widening of and diffusion of content. This creates a growing sense of ambiguity in the mind of the therapist as to what he is about, and, while it may affect the patient similarly, it surely increases the patient's dependence on the therapist. The result is that patient and therapist come to need each other, so that bringing the case to a conclusion seems impossible. Since treatment is the responsibility of the therapist, the problem of excessively long treatment lies in the domain of the therapist and not the patient. Further, it has been my position that the constant exposure to large doses of severe psycho-pathology that is a rather natural consequence of training programs in psychiatry tends to diminish the young therapist's peripheral vision, so to speak, so that he is unable to appreciate the assets of the patient before him. He tends to develop very little confidence in his patient's ability, capacity, and motivation to help himself. It is a short step then to being convinced that no patient can long survive without his close and indefinitely prolonged attention.[18]

Brief psychotherapy is focused. The challenge isn't how brief we can make it. The challenge is to identify the need and then clarify what can and can't be accomplished in this episode of treatment with the resources that are available. At a later time, you can move on to another focus.

A Conscious and Conscientious Use of Time

Traditional approaches to psychotherapy are based on the assumption that the presenting problem is not the real problem but merely a symptom of a much deeper psychological or interpersonal problem that must be uncovered, interpreted, and worked through. These approaches assume that real change takes place through an understanding of the problem and a focus on it. In order to be effective, therapy must be intensive, reconstructive, and time-consuming.

Effective brief therapy involves a rapid assessment and integration of assessment within treatment. We have found it helpful to hit the ground running and look at every session as possibly the last session. The past can be acknowledged in the context of moving on in the present, but the emphasis is on intervening in the present. We want clients to take away from the session something that is useful, helpful, and beneficial to them. This involves frequently reviewing progress and discarding ineffective interventions.

Practicality   Expense

An Emphasis on Pragmatism, Parsimony, and Change versus "Cure"

According to Steve de Shazer, "'Brief therapy' simply means therapy that takes as few sessions as possible, not even one more than is necessary, for you to develop a satisfactory solution."[19] At any given time any client has a variety of concerns and problems that might be helpful to discuss in a counseling context. However, the focus of brief therapy is the problem or issue that is keeping the person stuck and hindering him or her from functioning in healthy ways.

My own experience, as well as that of my students and supervisees, has demonstrated that therapy is prolonged not because of the client's need but often because the therapist does not know how and where to intervene. I understand that some people have deeper issues that in principle are dealt with through an exploration of early childhood. But that doesn't mean that is the route all psychotherapy must take. Psychiatrist and psychoanalyst Michael Franz Basch observes that that would make about as much sense as deciding that since insulin is a life-saving treatment for diabetic patients and that since everyone has a pancreas, insulin is the treatment for all bodily ailments.[20]

We find it helpful to emphasize the direction of change rather than the magnitude of change. More is not necessarily better. We ask clients *what*, *where*, and *how*, rather than *how much*.

Creative, Pragmatic, and Flexible Use of Techniques

Some therapists assume that whatever the clients' needs are, they will fit into one correct theoretical mold. The best therapy listens to the needs of the clients and shapes the therapy to meet those needs. In all of my Introduction to Counseling courses at Denver Seminary, I remind the students of the danger of operating from a single orientation or perspective. I believe it was Abraham Maslow who said, "If the only tool you have is a hammer . . . [you tend] to treat everything as if it were a nail."[21]

While the goal of change for two people may be similar, the pathways to that goal may be significantly different. An intervention that is effective for one client may be absolutely useless for another. The best brief therapists have a variety of tools in their therapeutic toolbox.

A Belief That Therapy Is Not Timeless but May Be Intermittent throughout a Person's Life

Brief therapy is rarely officially terminated. Rather it is interrupted, and the client is encouraged to return if, in future life stages or traumas, another episode of therapy would be helpful. We've already seen that brief therapy deals with the presenting problem. While dealing with the presenting problem, there is an opportunity to address subsequent problems. However, there is no belief that the course of this person's life will not lead to a future problem that could benefit from treatment.

One of the criticisms of brief therapy is that many patients come back for more. There is some research indicating that within a year of terminating a course of treatment, some patients return for additional therapy. These include patients whose outcome was labeled either successful and unsuccessful.

The assumption is that a patient who returns for more therapy was either a failure or has relapsed. If they had received "real" help, they would have no need to return. That certainly is one way of interpreting that data. Perhaps the treatment was inadequate. Perhaps they were given a band-aid. Perhaps they didn't receive any meaningful help.

Another, and we believe a much more realistic model, is to look at the doctor-patient relationship in medicine. If you go to see your family practice physician and receive successful treatment for a particular virus, it doesn't mean that you will never have to deal with that virus again for the rest of your life. It does mean that when you return for another visit, both you and the doctor will remember the symptoms and be able to much more quickly identify the treatment that worked.

Many therapists are moving towards a general practice model of treatment much like that of internists or pediatricians where a professional relationship may not be continuous, but may last over an extended time period.[22]

Use of and Emphasis on the Client's Strengths and Resources

Some therapies have a tendency to look for and focus on shortcomings, symptoms, defense mechanisms, syndromes, and dynamics. When looking through these lenses, counselors could rate a successfully functioning person as "sick." However, the brief therapist has an orientation to health or strength rather than to sickness or weakness. Saleeby has written a great summary of this perspective: "At the very least, the strengths perspective obligates workers to understand that, however downtrodden or sick, individuals have survived (and in some cases even thrived). They have taken steps, summoned up resources, and coped. We need to know what they have done, how they have done it, what they have learned from doing it, and what resources (inner and outer) were available in their struggle to surmount their troubles. People are always working on their situations, even if just deciding to be resigned to them; as helpers we must tap into that work, elucidate it, find and build on its possibilities."[23]

A Belief That Small Changes Can Be Significant

Somewhere in my early years of training, I got the idea that complex problems always involved complex solutions. Problems that took a long time to develop took a long time to solve. This led to a tendency to overlook or to minimize small changes. One key assumption of brief therapy is that small changes can be, and often are, significant. In his foreword to *Tactics of Change,* Milton Erickson wrote, "Psychotherapy is sought not primarily for enlightenment about the unchangeable past but because of dissatisfaction with the present and a desire to better the future. In what direction and how much change is needed neither the patient nor the therapist can know. But a change in the current situation is required, and once established, however small, necessitates other minor changes, and a snowballing effect of these minor changes leads to other more significant changes in accord with the patient's potentials."[24]

In recent years therapists have differentiated between two levels of change.[25] *First-order* change involves an adjustment to the structure of the existing system without changing the system itself. *Second-order* change requires a transformation at the operational, not structural, level. It involves an alteration of the system itself, making it operate in a different manner.

Some therapists believe that unless they have helped the individual or couple achieve second-order change, they have not done effective work. Brief therapists believe that it is naive to elevate second-order change over first-order change. First-order change is often the first step toward more substantial change. Many people who come into counseling need and want only first-order change. Do they need more? Perhaps. Do they want more? Maybe or maybe not.

WHO CAN BE HELPED BY BRIEF THERAPY?

One of the main questions many counselors ask is, Who can be helped by brief therapy? I agree with psychiatrist and psychoanalyst Lewis Wolberg, who over thirty years ago stated that "the best strategy, in my opinion, is to assume that every patient, irrespective of diagnosis, will respond to short-term treatment unless he proves himself refractory to it."[26] To a great degree, that has been our experience.

A different way to look at this issue is to ask how much help can be given with the time and resources the client has available. If you are a professional counselor, your client may be approved for only six visits. If you are a pastor, you may be able to meet with your client only three or four times. If you are a military chaplain, you may have only one or two sessions with your client. When you have less time to work with people, can they still be helped, or is it a waste of time? If the person has the resources for only three sessions, can you do anything of value for him or her? What other approaches to counseling would help you maximize those three visits?

Our own experience over the past ten years supports the literature that suggests that some forms of brief therapy can help a wide range of people with a variety of presenting problems. It's not just for the "worried well."

WHERE DO WE GO FROM HERE?

In the first chapter, we explained that this would be a book not primarily about history or theory but about the nature of brief therapy and how you might integrate it into your counseling ministry. With the foundation we've laid in the first three chapters, we're now ready to turn the corner and become more practical.

Given the fact that over fifty different ways of doing brief therapy have been identified, you have lots of options to consider. Among this diversity are several brief-therapy schools that have been especially influential in the development of our own thought and practice. For example, the "focused psychotherapy" of Nick Cummings and the "time-limited therapy" of Simon Budman have provided us with invaluable insights for helping people change.

However, of all the models of brief therapy, the two that we have found most helpful have been the strategic problem-solving model that came out of the research conducted at the Brief Therapy Center, which is part of the Mental Research Institute (MRI) in Palo Alto, California, and the solution-focused model pioneered by Steve de Shazer and Insoo Kim Berg at the Brief Family Therapy Center in Milwaukee, Wisconsin. In chapter 4, Matt will present and critique the MRI model, and then in chapter 5, I (Gary) will present the solution-focused model.

4/ PROBLEM-SOLVING BRIEF-THERAPY MODELS

But oh my God and Lord, how everything is ruined by the vain habits we fall into and the way everyone else follows them! Our faith is so dead that we desire what we see more than what faith tells us about—even though what we see is that people who pursue these things end up with nothing but misfortune. —TERESA OF AVILA

My dog, Charlie, loves his backyard. Not only does he love his yard, but he also loves the yards of all of our neighbors. Six-foot privacy fences mean nothing to my fifteen-pound mutt. He quickly digs under the most formidable fences and finds his way into the neighbor's yard. Within a matter of minutes, he can free himself from the neighbor's yard and move to the next yard. When doors to houses are open, Charlie sees it as an invitation to explore other peoples' kitchens, basements, and even bathrooms.

My wife and I love our dog, but we knew we needed to do something about his escapades when he showed up in our neighbor's house while she was taking a bath. We frantically tried dozens of ways to keep Charlie from digging under the fence. We piled dirt next to the fence. He dug it out in one day. We removed the dirt under the fence and put wood deep into the ground. Surely he couldn't dig under the wood. He did. We put twenty-pound rocks around the perimeter of the fence. He went between them. Nothing could stop this dog. Finally, we called an animal behaviorist, a doggy psychologist of sorts, and he noted the folly of our attempted solutions to our problem with the wandering dog. He explained that the dog must not be allowed even to get near the fence. Once he is at the fence, he will surely find a way to escape. An electric fence placed at the perimeter of the yard, two feet away from the fence, kept Charlie away from the fence and in our yard.

The point of my story is this: Sometimes the solutions we attempt only become part of the problem. When this happens, we must try something new.

While the previous chapters have described the merits of solution-focused brief-therapy models—which focus on the future, exceptions, and solutions—we don't want to ignore the value of problem-solving models of brief therapy. At times the problem-solving tools can be equally effective because they help us understand what has not worked. *Problem-solving models rely on the assumption that attempted solutions have become the problem.* By understanding these attempted solutions, we can help clients generate a new solution and solve their problem.

This chapter will challenge you to think about problems in new and creative ways. Some counselors have adopted the problem-solving model exactly as it is explained. Others have chosen to use pieces of it. We have found this model to be especially helpful as it encourages us to avoid doing more of what hasn't worked and to try something new with our clients. The solution-based and problem-solving models are two different ways of looking at how people change. Each provides important tools. Read carefully as you uncover another tool that may help you in your work with your clients.

A BRIEF HISTORY OF PROBLEM-SOLVING MODELS

With all of the models of brief therapy available, you may wonder why we have chosen to explain the Mental Research Institute (MRI) model of brief therapy. With over thirty years of research and experience, this is one of the oldest models of brief therapy. While the MRI model has many of its own strengths, it also laid the foundation for many of the great clinicians of the last thirty years to do their work. People like Jay Haley, Virginia Satir, Steve de Shazer, Insoo Kim Berg, and other solution-based clinicians share a strong heritage with the research conducted at MRI. Further, the work of the MRI practitioners introduced the realm of systems theory to therapeutic thought, integrating new ways of thinking about problems and solutions into the research and practice of family therapy. Let's explore some of the beginnings of the family-systems movement in order to understand the development of the problem-solving models of brief therapy.[1]

In 1958, Don Jackson, a psychoanalytically trained clinician, founded the Mental Research Institute, which paved the way for much of the brief-therapy movement as well as the family-systems movement. Jackson was heavily influenced by the thinking of Gregory Bateson, an anthropologist who introduced cybernetic systems theory to the realm of interpersonal and family functioning in the 1950s. Bateson challenged many long-standing beliefs, one of the most important being the notion of *linear causality* in psychopathology. The linear causality model sees events from the past—including relationships, learning, disease, deprivation, and others—as the direct cause of present symptoms. For example, through the grid of a linear model, adult depression may be seen as the result of anger directed at the self because of a faulty infant-mother relationship. Bateson and other anthropologists challenged this model by introducing the concept of *circular causality*. Circular causality recognizes the importance of the interactions between members of a system, noting that interactions, in turn, influence the present symptoms. For example, circular causality would suggest that symptoms of depression may be related to a problematic relationship between a husband and wife. Not only does the depression worsen the relationship, but the relationship also deepens the depression. Several factors both cause and maintain problems.

An understanding of circular causality has helped practitioners from many schools understand the *feedback loops* that maintain problems in any system. We have all encountered these feedback loops or "vicious cycles" many times in our clinical work and everyday lives. I saw the dynamic recently in a couple who came for counseling. The husband stubbornly resisted any of his wife's requests for help with the children. She in turn became more angry and more aggressive. In response to her aggressiveness, he became more resistant. She further turned up the heat. You get the picture. It wasn't a pretty one.

Don Jackson believed that positive feedback loops or "vicious cycles" determine the nature and course of problems. While each family unit encounters various difficulties throughout life, the *response* to these difficulties determines whether or not they become a problem. John Weakland, Richard Fisch, Paul Watzlawick, and Arthur Bodin—pioneers in the MRI model and family-systems theory—suggest that when members of a family encounter a difficulty, they tend to apply more of the same solutions. These solutions may provoke more of the same problem, leading to an escalation in the problem to the point that it becomes unmanageable. Watzlawick describes this succinctly by noting that "the solution is the problem." In this model, *problems are unsuccessful attempts to resolve difficulties.*[2]

In a problem-solving model, therapy is focused on the resolution of the presenting problem. Once this occurs, therapy is over. Einstein once said that it is impossible to solve a problem using the same kind of thinking that created the problem. On a practical level, the MRI model tries to interrupt the vicious, problem-maintaining cycle. This model focuses on changing the behavior of individuals in the system in order to help them avoid doing "more of the same." The counselor helps the family or the client try something new in hopes of resolving the problem.[3]

Before we explore other facets of this model of brief therapy, let's exercise your problem-solving skills. Grab a pencil and prepare to think creatively.

Find the four groupings of nine dots. Starting with the first group of dots, your job is to connect the nine dots. Sounds easy, right? Before you start, though, you need to know the rules: You must use only four straight lines to connect all of the dots, and you may not lift the pencil from the paper. You've got four attempts to do this, so don't be afraid to write in your book. The answer is provided at the end of this chapter.

How did you do? Did you get it the first time? the second? the fifteenth? Some people never get it.

Our solutions are often limited to a handful of prescribed notions. We forget that we can go outside the lines, expand our options, and bring about meaningful change.

But how do we do that in counseling our clients? The problem-solving model is another way to stock our toolboxes with additional options.

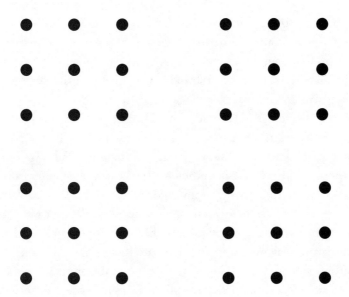

SEVEN STEPS OF
THE PROBLEM-SOLVING MODEL

The MRI model of problem-solving therapy includes seven steps that are applied uniformly to clients' problems. While the sequence of the steps does not change, interventions vary from case to case. You may find this model extremely valuable as it is explained, or you may choose to use only parts of it. After we look at the seven steps, we will evaluate the model from a Christian perspective.

1. Define the problem
2. Establish the goal of therapy
3. Explore the attempted solutions
4. Determine the main theme of the attempted solutions
5. Design an intervention
6. Elicit the client's cooperation
7. Monitor progress and terminate[4]

Step One: Define the Problem

The first step of the MRI model is to define the problem. This entails defining who is the "customer" for treatment. Those who complain may be seen as customers whether or not they appear to be part of the problem. For example, a man who complains about his wife's annoying habits may be seen as the customer for help even if his wife is not the person who comes for counseling.

Once you determine who the customer is, you need to get the customer to describe the problem in concrete terms.[5] Two questions will help you obtain specific and concrete information: "Who is doing what to whom?" and "How is it a problem?" For example, a father's answers to these questions might tell you this information about his trouble with his teenage son. His son (who?) is skipping school two days per week (is doing what?) and is on the verge of expulsion by the dean of students (to whom?) and may not be able to graduate (how is it a problem?).

When you are attempting to define the problem, make sure that you ask about recent examples of specific behaviors because these will shape the intervention you will choose to use. In the case of the father and the teenage son, for instance, you would want to know when the son skips school, what specific days he tends to skip, and what he does with the time he's not in school. It is also important to ask the father why he chose to come for counseling at this time. Answers to these questions will provide further clues about the nature of the problem and the attempted solutions. Finally, if clients come to your office with more than one problem, ask them what problem they would like to fix first. After prioritizing, pick a starting point.

Step Two: Establish the Goal of Therapy

An old proverb says, "If you aim at nothing, you will surely hit it." In the second step of a problem-solving model, you establish a goal for this episode of treatment. Because problem-solving models assume that successful therapy occurs when problem behavior changes and that small changes will lead to larger changes, the goal of this step is to elicit change that the client will observe.[6] You and the client can set this goal by having the client answer this question: "What would be a small, concrete sign that would let you know that the problem hasn't yet been resolved but that you are heading in the right direction?" This small sign guides the subsequent steps, plants the seeds of hope, and maintains an optimistic stance. Make sure the goals you set are behaviorally anchored, measurable, and attainable. Chapter 8 will provide further explanation about setting effective goals.

Let's look at a hypothetical example. Martha comes to your office with a twelve-year-old daughter who will not do her homework. Martha has tried everything she knows to make her daughter do her homework. At first, Martha asked her daughter about her studies. When this didn't help, the mother turned up the volume and nagged, every hour on the hour. Still her daughter did no homework. Martha tried new techniques. She grounded her daughter and took away privileges. All to no avail. Out of desperation, Martha resorted to bribes, then to shame, and then to despair. Finally, she just left her daughter alone. All the while, the daughter completed no homework. As Martha sits in your office, she pleads with you to help her find a way to get her daughter through school. She also tells you that she doubts anything will help. After all, she has tried everything she knows to do.

Using the problem-solving technique, you ask Martha, "What would be a small, concrete sign that would let you know that while the problem hasn't been resolved, you are heading in the right direction?" After much thought and discussion, Martha decides that if she were to see her daughter studying for five minutes per night, two nights of the week, she would feel they were making progress. Martha has just established the initial goal of therapy.

Step Three: Explore the Attempted Solutions

The MRI model holds that problems are unsuccessful attempts to solve other problems.[7] This simple statement sets the stage for the rest of the model. If we accept this, then this model's goal is to understand and change the attempted solutions that have fueled the vicious cycle. The counselor's job is to discover and understand the attempted solutions the client has already tried. To elicit this information, ask the client this question: "What have you done in your best efforts to resolve the problem?"[8] You may find it helpful to write down all solutions the client has attempted, even if those attempted solutions do not seem relevant at the time. By knowing all of the solutions our clients have attempted, we can avoid doing more of the same.

If you remember my struggle with Charlie, our dog, you will remember that my wife and I attempted several solutions. First, we placed dirt around the fence. Second, we placed wood underground, extending the fence below the existing structure. Third, we used rocks to block the fence. We also chided the dog, eventually yelled at him, and finally threatened to send him to reform school. None of these worked. With Charlie, the attempted solutions actually became part of the problem because they provided only a greater challenge for him.

Step Four: Determine the Main Theme of the Attempted Solutions

Each set of attempted solutions carries with it a common theme. While these themes are never stated explicitly, they determine and prescribe the nature of the solutions the client has used. As you understand this theme, you will help your client break out of past attempts at solutions by thinking creatively and ultimately developing new solutions that will solve the problem.

Let's return to Martha, the client who was experiencing difficulty with her twelve-year-old daughter. Using the problem-solving model of therapy, you ask Martha to describe all of the ways she has tried to solve this problem. Together, you generate a list of attempted solutions that looks something like this:

- Acting interested in her daughter's homework
- Asking lots of stimulating and insightful questions about her daughter's school and homework
- Suggesting ways and times to complete work
- Regularly reminding about grades, deadlines, and punishment
- Grounding
- Taking away phone time with friends
- Bribes of candy, food, and trips to the mall
- Yelling
- Shame
- Hiring a tutor
- Ignoring her daughter

Each of these attempted solutions is consistent with a theme. After eliciting all solutions, the theme of the attempted solutions can be understood by organizing them within the context of one of two statements. Solutions to most problems frequently suggest that someone, usually the focus of the presenting problem, either *must do* something or *must not do* something. By organizing the attempted solutions within the framework of either "You must do_____" or "You must not do_____," the main theme can be discovered. As you examine the list of attempted solutions generated above, you see that the theme of Martha's attempted solutions was "You must do your homework." Pretty easy, huh! When Martha tries to solve the problem based on the premise that her daughter *must do* her homework, her daughter refuses, becoming more entrenched in her position.

Let's look at another example. Wendy, a hardworking wife and mother, became concerned about her husband's tendency to sleep through his alarm. John loved his rest and was on the verge of losing his job because of consistent oversleeping. Out of concern for her husband, Wendy sought counseling. Her therapist used a problem-solving model and asked Wendy to list all of the ways she had tried to prevent her husband from oversleeping. These included waking him up herself, setting multiple alarm clocks around the bedroom, yelling at him, and sending the dog in to greet him. None of the attempted solutions had worked. As Wendy and her therapist examined these attempted solutions, it became apparent that the theme of the solutions was "You must not oversleep." By understanding the theme of the unsuccessful solutions, Wendy and her therapist were able to create new solutions that brought about meaningful change.

The problem-solving models assume that each of us has a certain amount of rebelliousness that keeps us locked in dysfunctional patterns. How similar this sounds to the rebelliousness of our sinful nature: "I don't understand myself at all, for I really want to do what is right, but I don't do it. Instead, I do the very thing I hate" (Rom. 7:15). When we are pressured and told we must or must not do something, our sinful nature resists, making change difficult. By understanding the themes of attempted solutions, we are able to try something new.

Step Five: Design an Intervention

The research from the field of social psychology helps us understand what happens when we do more of the same, hoping either to change others or to change ourselves. Charles Kiesler studied the consequences of public behavioral commitment, both in the laboratory and in real-life situations. Here's what he found: When examining social and political beliefs, Kiesler discovered what he calls a *boomerang effect*. That is, when people are publicly committed to actions that are consistent with their beliefs, counterarguments actually intensify their beliefs. That's right; when strongly held beliefs are argued against, the beliefs become even stronger. This dynamic creates a vicious cycle.[9] For example, when a person with moderate beliefs is confronted with opposition, the person often strengthens his or her beliefs and actions. This has two possible outcomes. First, it makes this person more accepting of even stronger beliefs, beliefs the person may have previously found unacceptable. This in turn makes the person even more likely to elicit opposing views that may, in turn, strengthen the existing beliefs. The vicious cycle has begun.[10]

Many people try to solve a problem by trying to convince the other person of the need to change. Martha did everything she knew to encourage her daughter to do her homework. The theme of her interventions became "You must do your homework." Our understanding of the boomerang effect and other social psychological research suggests that this type of command, whether stated or implied, often causes the other person to dig in his or her heels and resist change. That's right; the harder we are pushed, the more we resist.

This information provides important clues to use when designing an intervention. The MRI model recognizes that vicious cycles often escalate the problem. In response, strict adherents to the problem-solving model help clients make a *180-degree change*. This means that the person attempts solutions whose main theme is the opposite of the previously attempted solutions. For example, instead of saying, "You must do your homework," Martha would attempt solutions whose theme is, "You must not do your homework." Similarly, when the main theme of an intervention is "You must not do_____," then the intervention focus would be "You must do_____." The 180-degree change accomplishes two important things. First, it helps avoid doing more of the same. Second, it encourages the

client to interrupt the vicious cycle and cause an imbalance. If Martha uses the 180-degree change, she will certainly cause an imbalance, and it may lead her daughter to reevaluate her position and try something new.

Looking again to social psychology, William Swann and his colleagues provide interesting research that further explains this phenomenon. They used *paradoxical interventions* with people who were certain about their beliefs and resistant to changing them. By using a *superattitudinal leading question* with these clients, they were able to help them change their attitudes dramatically. Here's how they did it: Clients with strongly held beliefs were asked to defend similar beliefs but ones that were *even more extreme.*[11] For example, those who believed strongly in socialized medicine were asked to argue an even stronger point of view, such as government control of all business ventures. These people still resisted, but they resisted so that they argued against the more extreme position. In short, they argued against their own beliefs, causing them to take a more moderate stance. This study and others demonstrate that by paradoxically joining people in their beliefs, we may actually cause them to change and move toward a more workable position.

You may already sense that these interventions are not always appropriate. Read on to see our critique at the end of the next section.

Step Six: Elicit the Client's Cooperation

Client cooperation helps ensure that changes will be made and gains will continue. Whether or not we care to admit it, persuasion is an important part of any counseling. In the therapy hour, we persuade our clients about many things. Persuasion can be subtle, like nodding to affirm a client's feelings, or it can be more overt, like suggesting an intervention we believe will help the client function better. And whether we challenge distorted thinking, set limits with an angry child, or suggest that the client forgive a parent, we continuously engage in a process of persuasion, helping people to see the value in these interventions. Instead of pretending that counseling does not include persuasion, the problem-solving models recognize that persuasion is a powerful tool that can lead to greater cooperation and more effective treatment.

The MRI model of brief therapy suggests that by understanding the client's position, we can more effectively persuade in the direction of healthy change. Position is synonymous with beliefs.[12] We all have beliefs, values, and attitudes that are reflected in how we see a problem and how we define it. Whether we are selling used cars, time on the Internet, or a therapeutic intervention, we must understand the beliefs and position of those with whom we work. As counselors, our job is to listen closely to words, watch nonverbal cues, and understand the client's position. By doing this, we can frame interventions in the most appealing way and help persuade the clients to try something new.

A traveling salesman came to town extolling the virtues of organically grown Jamaican jicama. Two men approached the salesman to purchase his goods, but each came for different reasons. Healthy Harry wanted the vitamins, nutrients, minerals, and fiber available in jicama. Pretentious Phil, on the other hand, wanted the status associated with organically grown Jamaican jicama. Because these men have very different reasons for purchasing this product, the salesman must use a different approach for each. The words that the salesman uses to sell his product may make or break his sale. When talking to Healthy Harry, the salesman sings the praises of Jamaican jicama, noting its many healthy benefits, including more energy and longer life. By doing this, he is enlisting the values (position) of the customer. But if he touts the status and prestige associated with eating Jamaican jicama, he will miss his customer's momentum and may even drive him away. He must speak his customer's language if he hopes to make a sale.

When counselors enlist the cooperation of the client, they are, in effect, "selling their intervention."[13] Somehow, the client must see a benefit in trying something new. How can the counselor sell an intervention to Martha? The counselor hears Martha say, "I just don't know what to do with my daughter. I have tried everything I know to help. I'm just so tired that I feel like giving up. But I really want her to succeed. I sure hope something will fix her." From these few sentences, it seems that Martha holds a position of hopelessness. She genuinely cares about her daughter, but she is beginning to wonder whether anything will help her. Even though she feels hopeless, her involvement with her daughter suggests that she sees herself as part of the solution.

The counselor must work to understand the client's position. Let's listen in on how the counselor can join the client in her pessimism while affirming her love and commitment to her daughter.

> *Counselor:* It must be frustrating to have tried so many things to help your daughter and found that none of them have worked. You have done your best to remind her. You've taken away privileges. You've used the power of your anger, and you've gotten help from a tutor. You've even gone out of your way to provide extra money and gifts in the hopes that she will complete her assignments. I think I'm beginning to understand why this must feel so hopeless after you have worked so hard. I am aware of how much you love your daughter and just how much concern you have for her. In fact, I wonder if in all of your love for her, you have done too much.

> *Martha:* What do you mean?

> *Counselor:* It seems that by trying all of these wonderful things to help your daughter, you may have stolen her motivation. That was certainly not your intention, but all of your care and helping acts may have robbed her of her motivation. Because you are still concerned, I wonder if it is time for you to give your daughter her motivation back. I think the best way you can do this is by joining with her and discouraging her from doing her homework. In fact, if you really want to give her motivation back, you may want to prevent her from doing her homework.

> *Martha:* How would I do that?

> *Counselor:* Well, I suppose that you could distract her when she tries to study. You could turn up the music or talk to her. Use your imagination.

By understanding Martha's position, the counselor was able to join her and persuade her to do something different. In doing so, the counselor elicited Martha's cooperation, and she was open to the suggestion that her daughter must not do her homework.

You may be thinking, *I would never encourage a parent to tell her child that she must not do her homework.* Good point. This is one of several places where we as Christians disagree with the standard MRI approach. We have found that most of the time only a small change is needed, and we opt not to use the 180-degree change. Once we understand the theme of the attempted solutions, we can try something that is a little bit different. With a little creativity and a willingness to move slightly outside of the prescribed solutions, change can occur. With Martha, doing something that is different might include having her set a schedule with her daughter, noting the times she would do her homework. After setting the schedule, Martha might be encouraged to back off and allow natural consequences to run their course. Or with a bit more creativity, Martha might decide that she will sing "Jingle Bells" as loudly as she can at the first sign of frustration with her daughter. Not only does this avoid doing more of the same, which hasn't worked, but it may imbalance her daughter enough to motivate her to try something new.

Step Seven: Monitor Progress and Terminate

Once you have designed and implemented the intervention, conduct one or two follow-up sessions. Ask clients what kind of change or progress has occurred. When Martha followed the intervention suggested by her counselor and acted as if her daughter must not do her homework, something unusual happened. Not only was her daughter amazed that her mom wasn't on her back, but she began to rebel against her mother's new stance and actually started to do her homework. Martha responded with skepticism, suggesting that this change may not endure. This spurred on her daughter to continue. Somehow, in this process, the daughter internalized her motivation to do homework as she no longer reacted to her mother. By trying something new, Martha solved the problem.

If change has occurred, remind the client that change is more enduring when it happens slowly. Because of this, it is important to go slowly and make small changes. This again encourages clients to take responsibility for change. After one or two follow-up sessions, terminate therapy.

CRITIQUE

The MRI problem-solving model provides a useful tool when working within a brief model. We see several strengths and a few weaknesses to the model.

Strengths of the Problem-Solving Model

While Watzlawick, Weakland, and Fisch may not have intended it, they have adeptly illustrated in a psychological model some of the effects of our sin nature.[14] The positive feedback loops that result in more vicious cycles remind us of our propensity to remain stuck in our sinful patterns. Jeremiah reminds us, "The human heart is most deceitful and desperately wicked. Who really knows how bad it is?" (Jer. 17:9). Who can understand the deceit of our sinful nature, the deceit that keeps us locked into old patterns that don't work? Somehow, the problem-solving practitioners recognize this. While they present an amoral view of mankind, failing to recognize the ultimate cause of these vicious cycles, we as Christians are able to use this model within the context of ultimate truth. In doing so, some of the insights and techniques described can be helpful tools with our clients.

While the MRI model does not work for every problem, principles from it can be applied to many situations. Perhaps the greatest strength of the MRI model is its ability to help us understand what has *not* worked. By learning about all of the things our clients have tried to do to solve their problems, we are able to recognize themes of attempted solutions. From this, we can help our clients imagine new solutions and create the possibility for change. In addition, we can avoid prescribing and doing more of what is not working.

The ability to break away from patterns of failed solutions both requires and promotes creativity. When our clients are limited to a small range of solutions to solve their problems, creativity is stifled and options are limited. As helpers, we also easily become limited by our clients' attempted solutions and miss opportunities for creative change. The Genesis account of Creation reminds us of the infinite creativity of our God. When used responsibly and in ways that are consistent with Scripture, creative interventions open a new range of possibilities that help our clients change

The MRI model worked well with a client who was a chronic worrier. John worried about everything: his job, his family, his house. You name it, he had anxiety about it. When asked what he had done to solve this problem, he explained all the solutions he had attempted. None had been met with any success. I encouraged John to write out four Bible verses on the topic of worry and look at them three times each day. In addition,

I suggested that he really didn't know how to worry well. He needed to enhance the quality of his worry, making sure that he was truly proficient at it. To accomplish this, John was instructed to set aside one hour per day in which he would worry with as much strength, intensity, and perseverance as he could find. After just a few days of this, John discovered the folly of his anxiety and began to report significantly less worry in his life.

We have also found the MRI model to be especially helpful when working with problems that include two or more people. The MRI model allows the person who comes for counseling—even if that person is not the heart of the problem—to be a valuable part of the change process. By working with the person who comes for counseling, the counselor can influence the larger system, which, in turn, will influence the target of the initial complaint.

As counselors, we often deal with a parent who comes to our offices because of a problem child, but the child will not come to counseling. Or we have one spouse come to us for marital counseling, claiming that his or her partner does not see a problem and is unwilling to come to counseling. Traditional therapy models suggest either that we cannot treat the individual independently of the system or that treatment must be focused only on the identified client. The problem-solving model frees us to see whomever comes to us for treatment. By finding the attempted solutions the client has used to try to change the other member(s) of the relationship, we can help the client make changes that will have positive effects on that relationship.

Weaknesses of the Problem-Solving Model

While the MRI model can be a helpful tool, it is also weak in several important areas. Therefore, we do not advocate mindless acceptance of this model.

Perhaps the most serious criticism of the problem-solving model is its heavy use of paradoxical interventions. These interventions raise the eyebrows of some and elicit scorn from others. Some have criticized paradox as being dishonest and manipulative. After all, we subtly work to persuade our clients to do something that may seem absurd or even harmful.

Others have criticized paradoxical interventions for their apparent lack of morality. Proponents of the MRI model seem to suggest that the "end justifies the means." When used irresponsibly, the 180-degree change may promote immoral behavior. For example, a person who struggles with a persistent sin may have employed a range of solutions organized around the theme "I must not sin." We would be foolish to use paradox, suggesting that this person must sin in order to solve his or her problem.

Finally, others have noted the ethical dilemmas associated with paradox. If we truly believe in doing no harm, we must closely examine the use of certain paradoxical interventions. Encouraging suicidal patients to think of all of the ways they could harm themselves would certainly introduce the possibility of further harm, not to mention a myriad of ethical dilemmas.

What do we do with these apparent problems? After all, we desire to be responsible and ethical Christian counselors. Is there any way that Christian counselors can use paradoxical interventions?

While it may seem hard to imagine, paradox is powerfully used in the Bible. One example is in 1 Kings 3:16-28, where two women come to King Solomon because they are fighting over whose baby had died and whose had lived. Both claimed ownership of the living baby, and each claimed that the dead child belonged to the other woman. Solomon, instead of doing more of the same and engaging in the fight, employed a paradoxical intervention. He replied, "Bring me a sword. . . . Cut the living child in two and give half to each of these women!" (1 Kings 3:24-25). By trying something different and avoiding doing more of the same, Solomon was able to discern which of the women was the mother of the living baby.

Paradox can be used effectively, but using it requires great caution and training. We suggest that you use paradox sparingly and only under competent supervision. We have discovered that designing something new to respond to the theme of the attempted solutions does not always necessitate a paradoxical intervention. With some creativity, we have been able to develop new solutions that are not paradoxical.

A second major criticism of the problem-solving model is that it feels like a cookie-cutter approach to counseling. After all, if good counseling relied solely on following seven steps with each client, anyone could do it. To many counselors, this appears stifling, impersonal, and even inappropriate.

We present the MRI model as a resource God can use to help people change. At times we follow the model closely with a client, but more often we integrate some of the principles of this model into our treatment. For example, when we become stuck with a client and are unable to generate solutions (as we will discuss more fully in the next chapter), we are flexible and shift gears. Or, when we encounter clients who must talk about their problems and are unwilling to look at exceptions, then we may find it helpful to use parts of the problem-solving model. As you read this book, you will find cases and examples in which principles from the MRI model are integrated with solution-based principles. These will help shed light on the flexibility and compatibility of these two models of brief therapy.

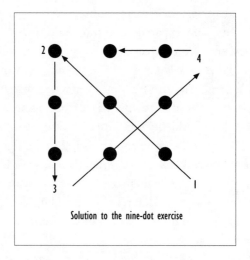

Solution to the nine-dot exercise

5/ FROM PROBLEM-FOCUSED
to
SOLUTION-FOCUSED

I do not view brief therapy as a "wonder therapy" that is amazingly applicable and effective in every situation, but I appreciate what brief therapy has to offer as both a technique and a way of viewing persons and their problems. Most significant to me personally is the emphasis on the hope and encouragement brief therapy can offer to many clients, even within the context of a single session, and the disciplined focus on well-defined goals clients create in cooperation with the therapist.
CHRISTINA RAIMO
Becoming Solution-Focused in Brief Therapy: A Personal Response

Imagine that you work in a gas station. A woman drives in and tells you that she has a problem. She is lost and is already late for an appointment. She asks you for directions.

You have a couple of options for helping the woman.

You could respond by telling her, "I can help you if you answer a few questions. Sometimes getting lost can be a multigenerational problem. When you were growing up, did your mom and dad have problems getting lost? Was it more of a problem for your same-sex or opposite-sex parent? Do you know why they got lost? Did they ever blame you for getting lost? What is your first memory of getting lost? How old were you? Were you being toilet trained at the time? Do you have any unresolved issues about that experience? How do you feel when you get lost? Do you feel retraumatized when it happens? When was the last time you really got in touch with the humiliation and shame you feel about getting lost? Does the way I'm asking these questions remind you more of your mother or your father? Why are you leaving?"

Obviously it's absurd to help a person get to an appointment for which she is already late by asking her thirteen questions. However, that's very similar to what counselors do when we approach problems in the time-honored way: question, explore, expand, discuss (and sometimes cuss) the problem. We mistakenly believe that the more we engage in problem talk, the more insight we will gain into the cause of the problem and the more effectively the problem will be solved. Sometimes that approach can be helpful.

But let's get back to the lost woman. A second option for helping her get to her appointment is to help her identify where she is and where she wants to go, get out a map, and help her decide which route she might want to take to get there. After all, some routes are more direct and more scenic than others. We can't assume that the woman wants to take the most direct route. It may be true that she has developed some bad navigation habits in her past. At a later time, she might want to explore what those habits are, where they came from, and why she keeps using them. But right now she is lost, is late for an appointment, and wants to get back on a correct course.

A growing body of evidence suggests that of the more than fifty approaches to brief therapy, those that emphasize finding solutions more than focusing on problems are the most popular. This solution-based method of approaching problems can also be called solution-focused or solution-oriented or solution-centered or solution-directed therapy. In this chapter and throughout the rest of the book, we will use the term *solution-based* to refer to this overall approach to helping people change, and we will use the term *solution-focused* when we are discussing the Milwaukee model of Steve de Shazer and Insoo Kim Berg.

Without discounting the value of insight or the fact that some issues take longer to heal than others do, a solution-based approach is sensitive to the problems people present. However, it doesn't focus or dwell on problems. It focuses on helping people generate solutions. Therapists start in the present and then focus on the future, where problems can be solved. They believe that if both the client and counselor can reorient themselves in the direction of strengths, exceptions to the problem, clarified goals, and strategies for achieving them, then therapy can be quite brief in most cases.

We have found that when counselors learn to look through the lens of solution-based therapy, problems can become filled with options and new possibilities for change. Clients feel encouraged, hopeful, and freshly motivated. Solution-based therapy moves beyond mere insight, blame, and analysis to help people discover *that* problems can be solved, *how* they can be solved, and that they can *start* the change process *before* the first session. We have found that solution-based brief therapy can be effective with individuals, marriages, families, and a wide range of problems.

PHILOSOPHY

At first glance, solution-based brief therapy (SBBT) may appear as nothing more than a collection of questions and techniques. However, it is much more than that. In fact, a solution-based approach is as much a way of looking at change as it is a group of techniques for change. It represents a major paradigmatic shift in looking at how people can change. Brief therapist and author Bill O'Hanlon refers to SBBT as the Third Wave of psychotherapy. The First Wave began with Freud, who laid the foundation for much of what was to follow. The First Wave focused on the past and pathology and was dominated by psychodynamic theories and biological psychiatry.

O'Hanlon identifies the Second Wave as the more problem-focused therapies (behavioral therapy, cognitive therapy, and family therapy) that emerged in the 1950s. These therapies didn't entirely replace the First Wave, but they did attempt to correct the overfocus on pathology and the past. They moved from a focus on the past to more of a here-and-now look at patterns of communication, family and social relationships, stimulus and response, and the role of self-talk.

It was in the early 1980s that a few creative therapists began adopting what O'Hanlon believes was a precursor to the Third Wave—competence-based therapies. "We believed that the focus on problems often obscures the resources and solutions residing within clients. Like the Third Wave that was to follow, we no longer saw the therapists as the source of the solution—the solutions rested in people and their social networks."[1]

Most counseling models acknowledge a variety of influences in their development, and the solution-based approaches are no exception. One of the most significant influences was the therapeutic ideas of Milton H. Erickson. He emphasized the value of narrative—the stories people tell about themselves—in the change process. He believed that whatever clients brought to therapy—their language, beliefs, resources, and sense of humor—could be used by the therapist in constructing therapeutic tasks. In fact, much of what solution-based therapists do is an application of Erickson's *utilization principle*. As Steve de Shazer writes, "This is the key to brief therapy: utilizing what clients bring with them to help them meet their needs in such a way that they can make satisfactory lives for themselves." [2]

The philosophy underlying solution-based therapy is best illustrated by a story Milton Erickson told to Bill O'Hanlon about his encounter with a severely depressed and suicidal woman whose nephew, a physician colleague, had asked Erickson to look her up during a lecture visit to Milwaukee. This woman had been confined to a wheelchair and left her house only to go to church. Whenever she attended church, she avoided people.

When Erickson arrived for the visit that the woman's nephew had arranged, Erickson asked her for a tour around her gloomy house. Everywhere he went, the shades were drawn. Every room was dark until they ended the tour at the woman's pride and joy: her plant nursery.

After the woman had proudly shown Erickson her newly transplanted African violet plants, he told her that her nephew had been worried about her depression, but Erickson could now see what the real problem was. He sternly told her that she wasn't being a very good Christian and doing her Christian duty. She stiffly replied that she considered herself a very good Christian and resented his opinion.

No, he responded, here she was with a sizable inheritance, with time on her hands, with a God-given gift with plants, and she was letting it all go to waste. He recommended that she obtain the church bulletin and visit each person in the congregation on the event of some sad or happy occasion (such as births, deaths, illness, graduations, or engagements) and bring along a gift of an African violet plant that she had grown from her own cuttings.

At this point in telling O'Hanlon the story, Erickson opened a scrapbook and showed O'Hanlon an article taken from a Milwaukee newspaper some years after his visit with this woman. The headline read, "African Violet Queen of Milwaukee Dies, Mourned by Thousands."

When O'Hanlon asked Erickson why he hadn't focused on what was causing the woman's depression, Erickson replied, "I looked around her house, and the only sign of life I saw were those African violets. I thought it would be easier to grow the African violet part of her life than to weed out the depression."[3]

O'Hanlon concludes with the observation, "That, in a nutshell, is solution-oriented therapy—grow the solution/life-enhancing part of people's lives rather than focus on the pathology/problem parts, and amazing changes can happen pretty rapidly."[4]

Some theories start by looking at what is wrong and how to fix it. The solution-based approach is aware of what is wrong but chooses to focus on what is right and how to use it. The counselor focuses more on the strengths and resources that patients bring to therapy than on their weaknesses or limitations. The orientation toward solutions is an attempt to create an atmosphere in which people's strengths can move out of the shadows and into the foreground.

Solution-based therapists emphasize collaborating with people rather than directing or coercing them. Therapists help clients discover their own solutions rather than try to impose solutions. It is a great application of the old discipleship slogan, "Give me a fish, and I'll eat for a day. Teach me to fish, and I'll eat for a lifetime." Solution-based therapy teaches people how to fish. The therapist exhibits expertise but isn't authoritarian.

Therapists and clients work together to identify resources and create solutions for what is problematic in the present and what needs to happen so that the situation can improve. Therapists help clients see numerous resources they might not have considered as part of the solution. As therapists help clients to become clearer about the solutions they want to construct, the solution becomes more of a possibility and even a probability.

HISTORY

In many ways the birthplace for the solution-based movement was the Brief Family Therapy Center (BFTC) in Milwaukee, Wisconsin. It grew out of the soil of the brief- and strategic-therapy movements and is based on over twenty years of evolving work. The solution-based movement has been described and discussed in over a hundred articles and numerous books and has been expanded, adapted, and revised by many other therapists.[5]

The roots of solution-based therapy go back to the 1970s, when a group of therapists who were interested in the Mental Research Institute (MRI) model became frustrated with the limitations of the community agency in which they worked and moved out on their own. This group included Steve de Shazer and his colleague and wife, Insoo Kim Berg. As they began to work with the MRI model, they found some aspects that fit and others that didn't.

De Shazer had worked with MRI and had been influenced by John Weakland and his colleagues. In a book honoring the thirty years of MRI, de Shazer and Berg wrote a chapter describing some of the ways in which the MRI model contributed to the development of what they would call solution-focused brief therapy. At first they started with the three premises—or the central philosophy—of the MRI model:

1. If it ain't broke, don't fix it.
2. If it doesn't work, don't do it again. Do something different.
3. Once you know what works, do more of it.

However, they soon realized that this model was too simplistic. They opted, instead, for a variation of their original philosophy.

> Obviously, a tradition based on such simple premises is frequently going to be seen as deeply flawed. Surely the resolution of chronic human problems cannot be so simple. . . . It came as a shock, as brief therapists, to discover there is a serious flaw in the MRI version of the Central Philosophy.
>
> At BFTC, we serendipitously found out that, when asked in the right way and/or at the right time, most clients will report that there are times when the complaint/problem does not happen, even though they had every reason to expect it to happen! This means that Premise 3 should take precedence over Premise 2, and thus we have been forced to revise the Central Philosophy.
>
> 1. If it ain't broke, don't fix it.
> 2. Once you know what works, do more of it.
> 3. If it doesn't work, don't do it again: Do something different.[6]

Over time, de Shazer and Berg found themselves spending less time in the problem-exploration phase. Eventually they experimented with skipping the full description of the problem and exploration of the attempted solutions. They began to place more emphasis on helping the client identify when the problem was absent and learning how to think about what was different during those times. The therapists spent more and more time encouraging the client to search for those "exceptions."

They discovered that helping a person deliberately replicate an exception—doing more of what has already worked rather than doing more of what didn't work—is a way of doing something different. They found that if exceptions were identified, the therapist could help the client expand these pockets of problem absence. A solution can be developed by building on and doing more of what is already working. "The basic premise of this model is that exceptions to problems offer keys and clues to solving problems and that it is more profitable to pay attention to the activities that center on successful solutions than to the problems. These exceptions become the pathway to future solutions. When and if there are no past successes to build on, the client can be helped to forge a different future by imagining 'a miracle' and identifying small but realistically achievable steps toward that event."[7]

Since that simple beginning, de Shazer, Berg, and their colleagues have expanded and refined their approach. In the process they have not only provided the counseling community with some new tools but also given us a fresh way to use some old tools. These solution-focused tools "are not a bag of tricks; the questions articulated by solution-focused therapists are expressions of an attitude, a posture and a philosophy."[8]

HOW THE SOLUTION-FOCUSED APPROACH WORKS

The remainder of this chapter will introduce you to some of the distinctive features of the solution-focused approach. It will explore some distinctives of the pre-session, the first session, and subsequent sessions, and it will describe the function of many of the question techniques: scaling questions, exception-finding questions, and the miracle question.

You will quickly discover that in addition to emphasizing a solution focus rather than a problem focus, this model uses a variety of questions.

The answers to these questions provide important direction for the counselor and build a sense of confidence and self-efficacy in the client. It might be most helpful to introduce some of these techniques in the context of a hypothetical couple.

Harry and Joyce have been married for seven years. Harry is a rising executive with an electronics firm, and Joyce is a full-time mother with two preschoolers. They are both active in a local evangelical church. Joyce is the one who calls the counselor for the appointment. She and Harry had some counseling several years earlier, but Harry felt it had been a waste of time because the counselor hadn't made many suggestions and had never given them anything specific to do.

Pre-Session Distinctives

One of the unique aspects of solution-focused therapy is that it can begin before the first session, with the phone call to make the appointment. Even before the first session, the counselor challenges clients to consider what their goals are and what change will look like to them. This is an essential first step in that it gets clients to think about solutions. Most people come into therapy prepared to discuss the problem, but few come prepared to talk about the solutions.

De Shazer and Berg developed another pre-session technique. They noticed that some clients came into the first session saying that between the phone call and their first visit, they had already seen some positive change. So in the telephone pre-session, the counselors began to encourage their clients to look for any small signs of positive change.

We have found that we have to ask clients to look for change. Most clients don't think small changes are important, and if they do notice them, they don't believe they are significant enough to talk about. They tend to compare them with the massive problems they are facing, and these small positive changes pale in comparison. Or they compare where they are with where they think they want to be and become overwhelmed with hopelessness.

Understanding that pre-session change can occur and paying attention to it can lead clients to a quicker identification of solutions since they have already proven that they can change, and they have identified areas in which change is taking place. In fact, this client-generated solution is the most powerful kind.

This is part of what the initial phone call can sound like:

Joyce: My husband and I need some help with our marriage.

Counselor: How are you hoping I might be able to help you?

Joyce: Well, we don't communicate very well, and we argue more than I like. I've wanted to get some counseling for a long time, and Harry finally said he'd be willing to come.

Counselor: So Harry wants to come for counseling too?

Joyce: Well, he doesn't really want to, but he is willing to.

After a bit more discussion about the counselor's approach to counseling, fees, office hours, and the like, Joyce asks if she can make an appointment. The counselor closes the conversation like this:

Counselor: Joyce, there are two important things you and Harry can do before our first session. Doing these two things will help you get much more benefit from our time together. Here's the first one. If, after our first session, we agree to work together, what would have to happen for you to know that the counseling had made a positive difference in your marriage relationship? Another way of looking at this is to ask yourself, "When will we know that we no longer need to come in for counseling?" Do you think you and Harry can do that?

Joyce: Sure. What's the second thing?

Counselor: Well, the second task is easier than the first. In the past several years, I've had many couples tell me that they experienced some small improvements between the time they made the phone call and their first session. Between now and your first appointment, I'd like you and Harry to notice any positive or pleasant things that happen in your relationship. You may want to write them down and bring the list with you, even if it is a list of only one thing.

First-Session Distinctives

The first session is a critical part of successful solution-based counseling. In fact, it is so important that we have devoted chapter 7 to it. In addition to the usual first-session tasks (establishing rapport, etc.), one of the counselor's first tasks is to determine the termination criteria. This process began with the initial phone call, and now it continues. The answer to the question "When will you know that you no longer need to come in for counseling?" usually contributes to the successful treatment plan. The counselor can also ask some different kinds of questions.

When Harry and Joyce come in for the first session, they are pleasant and appropriate, but they sit on opposite ends of the couch. It is obvious that they are having a bad day.

> *Counselor:* When we talked on the phone, I asked you to think about what would need to happen for you to know that our work together was helpful. Harry, what did you come up with?

> *Harry:* Well, one of the main things is that we wouldn't argue so much. Sometimes I come home from work, and as soon as I walk in the door, I feel attacked. It feels as if she can't wait to pounce on me.

> *Joyce:* (with a disgusted look and a sarcastic tone of voice) If you'd come home when you say you will, maybe you wouldn't feel so attacked. I'm sick and tired of working hard to have dinner ready, get the kids to the table, and then have you waltz in at least an hour late. And you don't even call to say you'll be late.

> *Counselor:* Joyce, so one of the ways you would know whether Harry was really committed to working on improving your marriage is if he came home when he said he would?

> *Joyce:* Yes, that would be a great start.

> *Counselor:* Harry, how realistic is that?

> *Harry:* I guess I could do that. I mean, I'm on time for appointments at work. But I don't know if I can be on time every night.

> *Counselor:* How many nights do you think it would be realistic for you to be on time?

> *Harry:* (after a pause) Three?

Counselor: Joyce, what would it be like if Harry was on time for dinner three nights a week?

Joyce: That would be great. But I don't think he will do it.

Counselor: Maybe he will, and maybe he won't. We'll find out next session. But, who knows? He may just decide to surprise you. It will be interesting to see what Harry chooses to do.

Harry: (with a smile on his face and with a competitive tone in his voice) Not only will I be on time, but if I am going to be late, I will call you and let you know. How's that?

Joyce: (with a smile on her face) Fat chance! But it would be nice!

After clarifying the small change that Harry would be willing to make, the counselor moves on to help Joyce identify one meaningful thing that she could do for Harry. They discuss exactly what it will be and how it will be meaningful to Harry.

SCALING QUESTIONS

Another unique feature of solution-based therapy is the use of *scaling questions,* which can effectively be used in the first session. Berg and de Shazer write that "scaling questions were first developed to help the therapist and client talk about nonspecific topics like depression and communication," where it is difficult to identify concrete behavioral changes and goals.[9]

With this technique, the counselor asks clients to create a scale, with 1 representing when the problem was at its worst and 10 representing when things are going so well they no longer need to come in for counseling. The counselor then asks clients, "Where are you now?" That can be followed up with a question such as, "What would have to happen for you to be even a half a point higher on your scale?"

So what's the inherent value in using scaling questions? We've found that it gives a spatial component to change. It's a way to use language to create a kind of visual image, and it provides a mutual language for clients and counselors. It also provides a kind of map for the next step. If clients agree that there is a 10, that means that things could be better than they are now. If they say they are currently at a 5, you can respond with the encouraging, "You are already halfway there. What would it take to get it a half-step higher?" Or you can respond with, "What's the closest you have been to a ten? When was it? What was it about that time that made it close to a ten?"

Scaling questions help counselors and clients assess two dynamics: satisfaction and commitment. Let's look more closely at each of these benefits.

Scaling questions are useful in assessing satisfaction. In this first session with Joyce and Harry, we've seen that they know their spouse is in a different place but they aren't sure how their partner's perspective compares with their own. This is a great time to use the scaling question to assess satisfaction:

> **Counselor:** I'd like you to imagine a scale between one and ten. A one means that you are discouraged, dissatisfied, and hopeless about your marriage. A ten means that most of the time you are pleased with your marriage. You enjoy high levels of satisfaction, good conflict resolution, and deep levels of love and affection. How would you rate your marriage?
>
> **Joyce:** (responding immediately) I'd give it about a three. I know that compared to some other couples our marriage isn't horrible. I mean, Harry doesn't beat me or anything. But when I compare it to what it could be, to what I think God would want it to be, I'm discouraged. Harry doesn't talk. He is negative and critical, and he always wants to go to Canada with his friend Don and fish for Northern Pike. At times I think that if things don't change, it's not worth going on.
>
> **Harry:** (with a surprised voice) I didn't have any idea you thought it was that bad! I was going to say a seven.
>
> **Joyce:** A seven? Where have you been?

By using this simple technique, Harry had a glimpse of how Joyce saw their marriage, and Joyce gained some new insight into Harry's perspective. It was obvious that their definitions of what constituted a healthy marriage were quite different. So now they have a clearer understanding of where the other stands. What next?

Scaling questions are also useful in assessing commitment. The questions allow the counselor as well as the clients to understand just how committed each is to making change.

> *Counselor:* Do you think you can do one more scale? Once again, I'd like you to imagine a scale between one and ten. This time a one means that you have virtually no commitment to making your marriage work. Quite frankly, if it falls apart today, that will be fine with you. A ten means that you would be willing to invest whatever it takes, to do almost anything to make your marriage the best it can be. How would you rate your level of commitment?

> *Harry:* (responding immediately) I'm at a ten. I know I've been slow in realizing how bad things are, but I am committed to making our marriage all that God designed marriage to be.

> *Joyce:* (looking at Harry, with a sarcastic tone in her voice) That's a pleasant surprise. (After a long sigh, Joyce continues.) Well, in spite of how discouraged and frustrated I am, I would say that I'm probably at about a six. I do love Harry, and I want our marriage to work, but something has got to change.

As the session continues, it becomes clear that while Joyce and Harry love each other, they have become emotionally estranged. Three years earlier, Harry had been given a big promotion that involved extended travel. Joyce had given up a successful sales career to be an at-home mom to their two children, who are only nineteen months apart in age. Joyce and Harry are committed Christians who attend an evangelical church regularly, but they don't pray together. They haven't had a "date" in over six months. Toward the end of the session, they reveal that they haven't been sexually intimate for close to a year.

EXCEPTION-FINDING QUESTIONS

Another intervention that the Milwaukee group refined is the *exception-finding question*. We've talked about the fact that central to a solution-based approach is the hypothesis that no problem happens all of the time or with the same frequency, intensity, and duration—there are always exceptions to the problem. Exceptions are those times when the problem doesn't occur or doesn't happen the same way.

The MRI problem-solving model emphasized a focus on identifying the patterns of interaction around the complaint in order to interrupt the problem sequence, but Steve de Shazer and Insoo Kim Berg moved to a focus on identifying what has been working in order to identify and amplify these solution sequences. This is where the term *solution-focused brief therapy* originated.

Most clients (and some counselors) see exceptions to the problem as unimportant, insignificant, and certainly not worth spending much time discussing. However, the solution-focused approach says that sometimes the most therapeutic thing a counselor can do is to move beyond clients' picture of the problem and direct their attention to the opposite of that image—to past times when they didn't have the problem. By exploring these times and what was different about them, clients find clues to what they can do to expand those exceptions.

By helping clients capitalize on their existing strengths and resources, counselors help change take place. The basic principle appears simple: Increase what works, and decrease what doesn't work. What are the "exceptions" to the problem? What are clients doing differently at those times when they aren't anxious or depressed? What has worked before? What strengths can clients apply? What would be a useful solution? How can they construct it?

Berg describes two kinds of exceptions: deliberate and random.[10] Deliberate exceptions are those that clients are able to describe in a step-by-step fashion. For example, clients struggling with depression might say that they made themselves get up, fix some coffee, have breakfast, have devotions, get in the car, and go to work. Since they are able to describe what they did and since it was helpful, a part of their task will be to "do more of it."

When a random exception occurs, either clients aren't able to describe the success (i.e., "I just felt better") or they attribute it to someone or something as else if they had no control over it. For example, depressed people might say, "I felt a lot better on Thursday," but they have absolutely no idea what they did to influence that change. Perhaps they received a raise (that doesn't happen every day) or completed a major project at work. In either case, the exception does demonstrate that they are capable of doing and feeling better. There is hope!

Michele Weiner-Davis, Steve de Shazer, and Wallace Gingerich report the following case that illustrates the value of identifying and using exceptions:

> A deeply concerned mother brought her 12-year-old son to the Brief Family Therapy Center. For 30 minutes she described, in great detail, the nature of her son's deteriorating school performance and its multifaceted implications. She postulated that her divorce of several years ago had had a lasting effect on him and that perhaps he was experiencing a deeply rooted depression. Just as the therapist was about to consult with the team behind the mirror, the mother nonchalantly mentioned that for the 3 days prior to coming for therapy, her son "had been trying in school." The therapist stopped for a moment, expressed great surprise, and asked the boy why he decided to "turn over a new leaf." At first, the boy appeared perplexed by this idea but quickly affirmed that, indeed, he had turned over a new leaf because he was "tired of always getting into trouble." The remainder of the session was devoted to helping the boy determine what he needed to do to stick to his resolution. Therapy goals were accomplished within three sessions.[11]

Obviously the mother didn't think that this "exception" was significant. And many counselors would have been so focused on the problem that they wouldn't have noticed it either. However, this counselor was solution-focused and was trained to look for exceptions. Now at this point, you might be saying to yourself, "Come on, guys. How often is a counselor going to catch an exception and close a case in three sessions?" You're right, that rarely happens. But that's not the point of the illustration. The point here isn't that the problem was resolved in three sessions. The point is that looking for and using an exception led to a successful outcome much faster than it would have otherwise.

Exceptions can become building blocks to help clients construct their own solutions. The time when the client is not experiencing the problem becomes very important both for deconstructing the problem and for constructing a solution. Some of the questions de Shazer and Berg use to elicit exceptions include

- Tell me about the most recent time the problem didn't occur.
- Can you tell me more about that?
- How did you do it?
- What was it like for you?
- Who else noticed something different?
- What is your spouse like when he or she is doing that?
- What would need to happen first?
- What is different about the times when _____ is getting along? Or when the bed is dry? Or when _____ goes to school? etc.
- How do you get that to happen?[12]

One of the many powerful things a counselor can do is work with clients to identify problem-solving behaviors that have been effective in the past. It seems that the tendency of human nature is to continue doing the same thing even when it isn't working. Instead of trying something new, we often take whatever didn't work and do it longer, harder, louder, faster. However, as we encourage clients to focus on exceptions and the healthy things that are already taking place in their lives, they are more likely to be able to develop the vision of a more hopeful and satisfactory future.

THE MIRACLE QUESTION

Probably the most talked-about technique of solution-focused therapy is the *miracle question,* which encourages clients to imagine a future in which their problem is solved. "Suppose that, while you were sleeping tonight, a miracle happened and the problem that brought you here was solved. How will you and those around you know a miracle happened? What will be different? What will you be doing differently? What will the people around you notice you are doing differently?" The miracle question helps clients imagine a future in which meaningful change has taken place. It also helps the counselor determine how realistic their goals are and what change will look like.

Counselor: I want to ask you both an unusual question. Suppose that while you are sleeping tonight, a miracle happens and the problems that brought you here are solved. You have changed, and your spouse has changed. Of course, you don't know a miracle has happened because you were asleep. When you wake up in the morning, what might be the first small thing that would tell you that a change had taken place?

Joyce: That's easy. Harry would touch me before we got out of bed. And then maybe he would smile.

Counselor: So you're saying that when Harry touched you and smiled, that would let you know something had happened? If Harry did that, what might you do differently?

Joyce: Well, I'd probably look him in the eyes and say good morning back.

Counselor: Harry, if this happened, how would it be helpful?

Harry: That would be the most positive start to a day we've had in months!

The key to success in the miracle question is to help clients expand all of the possibilities, to give a specific, realistic, detailed, and achievable picture of what change might look like at home, work, play, or church. Encourage them to describe inner feelings as well as outward signs.

FORMULA FIRST-SESSION TASK

Brief therapists believe that change is a constant in life. Nothing happens twice in exactly the same way. Each apparent repetition is at least in some subtle way different. The goal of brief therapists is change that makes a difference to clients so that their lives at the end of therapy will be different from their lives before therapy.

In the early 1980s de Shazer, Berg, and the others in the Milwaukee group began experimenting with a different orientation toward finding solutions by giving all clients the same assignments. They had started to notice that some assignments seemed to be universally effective regardless of the problem. They called these *formula tasks.*

One of these tasks, given in the first session, was to ask clients to observe what dynamics in their lives or relationships they would want to see continue.[13] They found that this assignment helped reorient clients from focusing on the bad things in their lives to thinking about and expecting the good; it was a kind of learned optimism. They also found that this shift in perspective seemed to build on itself, to create a more positive outlook that led to better interactions, which in turn reinforced and expanded that positive outlook.

With the success of these formula tasks, the team decided that perhaps the process of change could be initiated without much knowledge of the problem or the personalities of those suffering from it. They began to focus on ways to initiate and maintain this problem-solving faculty, which they believed was inhibited by a focus on problems and deficits. This thinking led to the development of the miracle question and the exception question.[14]

The formula first-session task is simple. At the end of the session, counselors tell clients, "Between now and the next time we meet, I would like you to notice what is happening in your life that you would like to continue to happen."[15] In our clinical work, we have found that approximately 80 percent of the time, clients have reported in the second session that at least one significant exception occurred after having been given the formula first-session task.

SETTING SPECIFIC GOALS

Most people who come for counseling know what they don't want, but they rarely know what they do want. Our experience is similar to that of de Shazer's in that most of the time, clients' complaints say more about what they don't want than about what they do want. Frequently they may have little idea about what a reasonable replacement might look like.[16]

Goal setting is a critical aspect of solution-focused therapy. While talking about what change may look like has some value, the more important step is implementing the changes. Setting goals for change moves clients beyond the contemplation stage, which change expert James Prochaska talks about, to the action stage. This is an important move, and even if the goals are small (and the best goals *are* small), it lets clients know that if change is going to take place, they need to do something different.

Prochaska writes: "People who eternally substitute thinking for action can be called chronic contemplators. When contemplators begin the transition to the preparation stage, their thinking is clearly marked by two changes. First, they begin to focus on the solution rather than the problem. They then begin to think more about the future than the past. The end of the contemplation stage is a time of anticipation, activity, anxiety, and excitement." [17]

How do we set effective goals? Effective goals are observable, attainable, specific, measurable, and positively focused. They are focused in the present and are indicated by the presence of something rather than the absence of something. They emphasize what people will be doing or thinking rather than what they will not be doing or thinking. Well-formed goals describe the first small steps clients need to take rather than the end of the journey. Scaling questions can also be used to help clients set realistic goals.

> *Counselor:* Harry, at the beginning of our session you said you would rate your marriage at about a seven, and Joyce gave it a rating of three.
>
> *Harry:* Well, that was at the beginning of our session. After what we've talked about, I think I'd probably give it a five.
>
> *Counselor:* Joyce, what would need to happen between now and our next session for you to be able to say that your marriage was at a three point five instead of a three?
>
> *Joyce:* Harry could do two small things that would make a big difference. It would help if he would call once a day to see how we were and if he would come home on time.
>
> *Counselor:* How would that be helpful?
>
> *Joyce:* It would let me know that he is thinking of me, that I count, that I am important to him.
>
> *Counselor:* Harry, how realistic are those requests? Is it too much? Would it be better to do just one of them?

>*Harry:* No, those are easy. I can do both of them.
>
>*Counselor:* How many times have you done that in the past month?
>
>*Harry:* (after a pause) Once or twice.
>
>*Counselor:* Harry, what would need to happen between now and our next session for you to be able to say your marriage was at a five point five instead of a five?

Harry proceeds to give two specific things that Joyce can do. The first session ends by summarizing the strengths of each person and the relationship and by assigning the couple to follow through on what they have agreed to do. Due to Harry's travel schedule, they will not be able to come back for two weeks.

In the context of secular counseling, this might be all that the counselor would do. In the context of Christian counseling, however, we might encourage the couple to share a brief time of prayer together on a daily basis and to read chapters 4 and 5 of *How to Change Your Spouse without Ruining Your Marriage* to help them better understand male and female differences.[18]

Subsequent Session Distinctives

The second session with Joyce and Harry begins with the question "What's been a little bit better since the first session?" The therapeutic task is to discover, amplify, and reinforce any positive changes that have taken place. Many people will focus on what hasn't happened rather than on what has happened. Harry answers the question.

>*Harry:* Well, the past week has been all right except for last Sunday.
>
>*Counselor:* So six out of the last seven days were good?
>
>*Harry:* Well, I hadn't thought about it that way, but, yes, that's right. I mean, they weren't great, but they were all right.
>
>*Counselor:* What was better about them?
>
>*Harry:* We had a great date night on Saturday. We went to an early movie and then had dinner afterward. It was a lot of fun. But it went downhill on Sunday night.

After this opening, it is clear that Harry wants to focus on the one bad day rather than the six good days they have enjoyed. A solution-focused approach doesn't ignore problems or concerns. At the same time, positive change is more likely to take place when we spend more time looking at what has worked, on what has gone well, on the positive changes that have taken place.

At this point in the session, the counselor is faced with a choice. Go for the bait and spend the rest of the session dwelling on the "bad" Sunday material, or continue to expand, explore, and develop the ways in which Harry and Joyce were able to enjoy the other six comparatively good days.

> *Counselor:* Joyce, what did you enjoy about your week?
>
> *Joyce:* Well, for one thing, Harry came home on time *three* nights in a row.
>
> *Counselor:* It sounds as if that's a new record.
>
> *Joyce:* I can't remember the last time that happened.
>
> *Counselor:* How was that helpful to you?
>
> *Joyce:* (as Joyce responds, she looks at Harry and takes his hand) It let me know that he cared enough about me and the kids and the hard work I had done in fixing a nice meal to come home on time . . . and that he is really committed to improving our marriage.

Toward the end of the session Harry mentions that when they came home from their date, they enjoyed their first sexual intimacy in almost a year. One might think they would have talked about that right away when the counselor asked what had gone well. But they didn't. It took most of the session for that positive event to come out. Why? Most people in conflicted relationships are conditioned to dwell on the negative, the deficits, the weaknesses, and the pain of the relationship.

CRITIQUE

After reading this chapter, you might be thinking that this solution stuff isn't so bad after all. In fact, it's better than you thought. It is an effective approach to helping people change. But along with its advocates are its critics. And rightly so. In the remainder of the book, we will continue to point out the strengths and weaknesses of this approach to brief therapy. As we close this chapter, it might be helpful to look at what a few of the critics have to say.

Not everyone is excited about brief therapy, let alone about an approach that emphasizes a focus on solutions rather than problems. A small number of critics have expressed a variety of concerns about the solution-focused approach. They have challenged its simplicity and brevity, and they have questioned the credibility of its outcome claims.[19] For example, in their review of solution-focused therapy, psychology professor Jay Efran and therapist Mark Schenker observe that "whereas Freudian analysts have been accused of interpreting virtually any remark, positive or negative, by a patient as a defense against something worse, solution-oriented therapists can be accused of whitewashing anything negative. In using this sort of strategy, there is the danger of blurring the fine line between encouraging a positive outlook and invalidating a client's perceptions."[20]

Cheryl Storm writes, "I have found that being relentlessly solution-focused is a mismatch for some clients. These individuals insist on talking about the problem in detail and, if ignored, fire the therapist. I thought I was misapplying the approach but now believe I . . . over-emphasized change."[21]

Counselors Don Efron and Kip Veenendall write, "Our experiences do not permit us to completely accept the enthusiastic positiveness of the solution-focused model. . . . When we attempt to use these models and stances exclusively, we build up a sense of wrongness and futility, as if we were somehow pulling the wool over the eyes of clients and ourselves."[22]

Critics ask these questions:

- Is solution-focused counseling anything more than a collection of preordained techniques that encourage people to ignore reality?
- Are counselors really doing meaningful counseling when they only praise, search for exceptions, and define goals?
- Isn't it possible that these insistently optimistic dialogues can

have the effect of silencing people's doubts and minimizing their pain?

- Can clients really trust the feedback of counselors who constantly strive to find things to praise and never challenge or question them?
- Can clients be honest regarding the outcome of their therapy with counselors who seem to want so much for them to feel better about things?

Those are fair questions. At the same time, it is also fair to ask these questions:

- Isn't it more empowering to help people envision their goals and focus on their strengths than to dwell on their problems and deficits?
- Isn't it important for counselors to have clear, concrete guidelines so therapy doesn't become vague and directionless?
- If clients have limited time and limited resources, isn't it more compassionate and professional to provide legitimate (even if limited) hope and encouragement and give them specific tools to get them started in the right direction?
- If people's experience is tied to the way they think and talk about it, then isn't it better to use language that leads people out of pain than language that allows them to ruminate on it?

We've heard some solution-focused advocates portray the model as a way to start therapy on a positive note, with the option to switch to other methods if the problem perseveres. We've heard other advocates talk as if almost any problem can be treated successfully with a few solution-focused sessions.

In our review of the literature, the majority of concerns and criticisms focus on the "relentless," "exclusive," and "uncritical" use of a pure solution-focused approach. Any model—including the solution-focused model—can become overly simplified. The problem isn't so much the solution-focused theory or techniques as it is the rigid ways that some therapists apply them.

In our experience, some of the criticisms of solution-focused therapy are well founded, which is one of several reasons why we don't advocate a "pure" solution-focused model but rather prefer the term *solution-based*. That is one reason why, as you read through the rest of this book, you will find us encouraging an integrative brief-therapy approach that emphasizes a greater focus on solutions rather than one on problems.

For example, a "pure" solution-focused model says that solutions can be pursued with very little or no attention to the nature of the problem. Sometimes this can be effective in helping clients achieve their goals. However, in our experience, sometimes an understanding of "what hasn't worked" is essential to developing effective solutions. In fact, at times an exclusive focus on amplifying possible solutions without clearly defining the problem can actually become a problem.[23]

Even hard-core advocates of the solution-focused model emphasize the need for some flexibility in its application. For example, therapist Eve Lipchik, who was a codeveloper of the solution-focused model, includes discussions of clients' feelings in therapy (what some would consider a major breech of solution-focused orthodoxy) because "I sense within all my clients . . . the desire to be loved and affirmed by a significant other or others."[24]

Michele Weiner-Davis admits that she sometimes lets her clients focus on their problems rather than always pushing them for exceptions. "My clients cry and express pain, anger, disappointment and fears just as they might in any other therapist's office. And I respond with compassion. . . . My therapy story [what she presents in workshops] is not the total picture of how I do therapy."[25]

The challenge is staying solution-*focused* rather than solution-*forced*. It is being solution-*oriented* rather that solution-*obsessed*. That is why the brief-therapy approach that we have found to be most helpful builds on a solid biblical anthropology and uses some of the insights of both the MRI (find out what doesn't work and do something different) and the solution-focused (find out what does work and do more of it) models in facilitating the change process.

The spring 1994 issue of the *Journal of Systemic Therapies,* "Solution Focus: Therapy, Model, or Myth," was a special issue devoted to looking at the limitations and strengths of the solution-focused model. In a subsequent issue, one reader responded to some of the questions raised:

> If solution-focused therapy is more similar to other models than different, why practice it? And, if there is currently no outcome data to demonstrate its superiority over other models, why cave in to pressure from administrators and managed care companies and become "solution forced"? . . .
>
> The answer for me personally is that SFT (solution-focused therapy) provides me with a framework for correcting errors in my practice of therapy: Am I hearing what the client wants? Whose goal are we working on: mine or the client's? Am I getting ahead of my client? Am I noticing small changes? Am I presuming I know what's best for my client or am I acknowledging that they are the best expert on their own lives? If these are things I once knew but forgot, then SFT makes it easier to remember. It also reminds me to be hopeful, not, as some have claimed, relentlessly (and disrespectfully) cheerful.
>
> The answer to the question "Why use it?" for responsible, ethical therapists must not be because someone else (managed care, administrators, etc.) made me. I sometimes wonder if SFT would be getting such a negative response if it weren't seen by some as an instrument of the devil (Oops! I mean managed care). If one chooses to practice SFT, it requires thought, study, practice, supervision and consultation just like learning any other approach to psychotherapy.[26]

While researchers need to do additional work in examining the strengths and limitations of solution-focused therapy, the existing literature demonstrates, and our experience supports, that having solutions as the primary focus of treatment is an effective approach that can be used in a variety of church, parachurch, and clinical settings. It can be especially helpful in situations where the pastor or clinician has a limited amount of time. Proponents say the average number of sessions ranges from three to ten. From our point of view, the most important factor isn't how many sessions it takes; it is the degree to which clients experience meaningful and lasting change. In our clinical experience, more and longer isn't necessarily better.

Throughout the remainder of the book, we will be discussing a solution-*based* rather than a solution-*focused* approach. Solution-based brief therapy is both a way of looking at change and a way of doing therapy. It isn't the treatment of choice for every situation, but in the hands of a well-trained counselor, it can be a powerful and effective tool for helping people change.

However, counselors learning this approach must beware of becoming solution-forced rather than solution-focused. Even in situations in which a "pure" solution-focused approach may not be the treatment of choice, solution-based insights can be an invaluable way to facilitate increased effectiveness in therapy and to help clients experience what God designed life to be.

PART TWO

A Problem-Sensitive,
Solution-Based Brief Model

6/ ASSUMPTIONS *of* SOLUTION-BASED THERAPY

Most of the arguments to which I am party fall somewhat short of being impressive, owing to the fact that neither I nor my opponent knows what we are talking about.

ROBERT BENCHLEY, *Benchley—Or Else!*

Jill, a twenty-three-year-old woman, enters your office and tells you of the depression she has been feeling for the last six months. As she describes her inability to sleep, her lack of appetite followed by binge eating, and her long evenings filled with tearfulness, you must decide what type of treatment you will choose. Jill goes on to tell about long-standing conflict with her mother and her parents' painful divorce when she was eight years old. As she describes these relationships, she notes that she does not see a connection between them and her current depression and that she would prefer not to spend a lot of time discussing them. Jill further describes her current relationships, and she tells you about a recent breakup with a boyfriend of two years. You inquire about her current functioning, and she mentions that she has felt better for the last five days. Because she doubts it will last, she quickly dismisses the changes.

After spending more time with Jill, you learn that she accepted Christ at the age of seven and was active in the church through high school. She tells you that she stopped attending church after she graduated but that she would like to pursue her faith again. Because Jill works weekends, she wonders if she will be able to join a local congregation. She also worries about her lack of money and wonders how she will afford the years of therapy her previous counselor told her she will need.

A counselor might approach Jill's problems in a variety of ways. Dr. Al Ego, a psychodynamically trained clinician, recognizes Jill's early developmental arrests and subsequent conflicts. Because he sees Jill's depression as an expression of deeply rooted internal conflicts that have arisen from the lack of a stable and consistent internal object, Al focuses treatment on long-term personality restructuring. He determines that he must work to strengthen Jill's ego, to help her internalize good objects, and to confront and work through her projective identifications. He believes that insight and interpretation will allow Jill to understand her long-standing conflicts and eventually change her behavior. Of course, none of this can occur without a strong therapeutic bond that will allow Jill to internalize healthy internal objects. Productive therapy will rest on Jill's ability to develop transference with her counselor. Because transference takes time to develop, it may take Jill up to two years to overcome her depression and successfully terminate treatment. Until deep internal personality restructuring occurs, no lasting gains in the level of her depression can be expected.

This comparison is used to provide a clear contrast between the assumptions of brief and long-term therapy. It is not intended to deny or discredit the value and viability of good, long-term therapy in certain situations. It is also not intended to discredit the value of a psychodynamic perspective.

Dr. Bea Brief has a different approach to Jill's situation. While Dr. Brief is aware of the long-standing relational patterns between Jill and her mother and the pain she has experienced because of her parents' divorce, she focuses her attention on Jill's current symptoms. She is less concerned about the cause of Jill's problems and more concerned about what is maintaining her present symptoms. Dr. Brief is struck by the many resources that Jill brings, including her persistence, desire to seek help, and hope for a renewed commitment to Christ. The counselor is especially attentive to the last five days of Jill's life, realizing that while her depression is not over, she may be on her way to feeling better. Treatment begins by asking Jill to explain what has been different during the last five days.

While Al Ego helps Jill achieve growth through an in-depth understanding of her past, Bea Brief focuses treatment on Jill's current symptoms and the behaviors that are maintaining those symptoms. From this, it is apparent that each counselor holds different views about the nature and etiology of problems as well as the maintenance of these problems in the client's life. Perhaps more important, these views shape the course of treatment and the interventions. While one perspective may not be better than the other and while each may help Jill to feel better and experience less depression, it is likely that Al Ego will need considerably more of Jill's time and financial resources to help her accomplish her goals. In addition, while Jill's goals are the alleviation of her depression and a renewed commitment to Christ, Al's theoretical orientation suggests that he cannot do treatment without insight, working through the analysis of resistance, and the establishment of transference. This means that change in the here and now is not likely at this time, and more important, Al must impose his beliefs on the nature of change in order for Jill to feel better.

Al Ego and Bea Brief each have significant training, and both are accomplished counselors. Each also has a unique set of assumptions and beliefs about people and about the nature of change. As we saw in chapter 3, those who work within a brief model hold a set of assumptions that may, at times, be very different from those who work within a long-term model of therapy.

In order to work efficiently within the brief-therapy model, we must have a thorough understanding of the assumptions behind the model. First, an understanding of assumptions provides a theoretical undergirding from which to understand our work. Second, an understanding of assumptions helps guide our clinical work in practical ways. These assumptions become more than theory as they are applied to individual clients. When we become stuck with a client or need new direction, assumptions lay the foundation for subsequent interventions.

This chapter will provide a working understanding of the assumptions of solution-based brief therapy. We will start with the assumptions provided in the current literature on brief therapy and work toward the working assumptions that are consistent with a biblical worldview. These assumptions are evolving and are subject to change. In fact, they may have changed since we wrote this book. While we have contrasted a psychodynamic counselor with a solution-based counselor in this chapter, it is important to remember that these assumptions are not necessarily related to one school of thought. Rather, they are designed to help us understand the processes of change and are applicable to many theories. Whether your counseling framework is humanistic, systemic, cognitive-behavioral, Gestalt, or psychodynamic, you can use these assumptions to understand how individuals change within brief therapy.

ASSUMPTIONS OF SOLUTION-*FOCUSED* THERAPY

Chapter 3 discussed how long- and short-term therapies differ. Many theories of long-term therapy suggest that lasting change can occur only after deep personality restructuring. For many of us, these theories and underlying assumptions are deeply ingrained.

In stark contrast to many of these assumptions is a group of assumptions that are unique to the solution-focused models. These represent a radical departure from other theoretical orientations, even from those of others doing brief therapy of varying theoretical orientations.

Let's look first at some of the assumptions of the solution-focused movement. John Walter and Jane Peller, who have built on the work of Steve de Shazer and Insoo Kim Berg, give us twelve assumptions that provide an important starting place in order to understand solution-focused theory. These are germane to the Milwaukee model of solution-focused therapy and have not been integrated with a Christian worldview. They include the following:

1. *Advantage of a Positive Focus*—Assumption: Focuses on the positive, the solution, and the future, facilitates change in the desired direction. Therefore, focus on the solution-oriented talk rather than on problem-oriented talk.
2. *Exceptions Suggest Solutions*—Assumption: Exceptions to every problem can be created by the therapist and client, which can be used to build solutions.
3. *Nothing Is Always the Same*—Assumption: Change is occurring all the time.
4. *Small Change Is Generative*—Assumption: Small change leads to larger changing.

5. *Cooperation Is Inevitable*—Assumption: Clients are always cooperating. They are showing us how they think change takes place. As we understand their thinking and act accordingly, cooperation is inevitable.

6. *People Are Resourceful*—Assumption: People have all they need to solve their problems.

7. *Meaning and Experience Are Interactionally Constructed*—Assumption: Meaning and experience are interactionally constructed. Meaning is the world or medium in which we live. We inform meaning onto our experience, and it is our experience at the same time. Meaning is not imposed from without or determined from outside of ourselves. We inform through interaction.

8. *Recursiveness*—Assumption: Actions and descriptions are circular.

9. *Meaning Is in the Response*—Assumption: The meaning of the message is in the response you receive.

10. *The Client Is the Expert*—Assumption: Therapy is a goal or solution-focused endeavor with the client as the expert.

11. *Unity*—Assumption: Any change in how clients describe a goal (solution) and/or what they do affects future interactions with all others involved.

12. *Treatment Group Membership*—Assumption: The members of a treatment group are those who share the feeling that there is a goal and state their desire to do something about making it happen.[1]

ASSUMPTIONS OF SOLUTION-*BASED* THERAPY

The assumptions of solution-based therapy differ from the assumptions of solution-focused therapy. While each of the solution-focused assumptions listed above may be important, some are more relevant than others and will be explained in depth below. Those that are explained have become a working part of our understanding of solution-based counseling and are consistent with a Christian worldview. On the other hand, several of the above assumptions are clearly inconsistent with our Christian beliefs. For example, it is idolatrous to believe that people have all the resources they need to solve their problems. Romans 3:23 reminds us that "all have sinned; all fall short of God's glorious standard." Similarly, we also know that "the wages of sin is death" (Rom. 6:23). We are sinful, fallen people who deserve death. Even so, we have hope because we know that "when we were utterly helpless, Christ came at just the right time and died for us sinners" (Rom. 5:6). How exciting!

We agree that God has given each of us resources that can be used in many ways; however, without a personal relationship with Jesus Christ, we lack many things. Similarly, while we must respect our clients' wishes and use the resources and strengths they bring, it is dangerous to assume that the client is the only expert on his or her problem. When carried to its logical end, the assumption that the client is the expert asserts that there is no ultimate reality, no normative standards from which to compare; all that matters is the individual and unique reality of the client. Again, this is incompatible with clear scriptural teachings, which give us absolute, objective truth and guidelines for normative behavior.

The following, then, are working assumptions of a distinctly Christian solution-based brief-therapy model. Solution-based therapy as we describe it is an integrative approach building on the knowledge and contributions of solution-focused, MRI problem-solving, and cognitive-behavioral theories. Some of these assumptions have been described and explained by other authors.[2] We are continuously evaluating and reevaluating our assumptions in light of God's Word. We would encourage you to do the same.

1. People Have the Ability to Change and Grow

Foundational to any perspective on brief therapy is an inherent belief that people are capable of making changes throughout their lives. Development does not end after adolescence. Rather, humans continue to grow and change from birth until death. Accordingly, therapeutic goals are formulated based on this belief, recognizing that when people come to counseling and desire treatment for a problem, they may return to address other problems at later times in their development. Not only does this perspective allow the counselor to focus on the client's present problem, but it eliminates the need to restructure personality or change embedded schemata at one point in time.

From a Christian worldview, a belief that people have the ability to grow and change closely parallels our understanding of the sanctification process. The Scripture promises that "God, who began the good work within you, will continue his work until it is finally finished on that day when Christ Jesus comes back again" (Phil. 1:6). Counseling may be seen as a part of the sanctification process. As the effects of our sin and the sin of others become problematic in our lives, Christian counseling may be used as a tool to further spiritual growth. Similarly, as the sanctification process continues over the course of a lifetime, so does our psychological, emotional, and spiritual growth.

In practical terms, if we believe that people are capable of growth and change, we take clients at their word and work with the issues for which they come to us for counseling. If we think back to Jill, this assumption suggests that we focus treatment on the depression for which she has sought help. We don't ignore the fact that her early relationships may be important; however, if these are not part of the problem for which she has sought help, treatment should not focus on them. In the process of growing, Jill will continue to change, and she may seek treatment at a later time for these problems.

2. Change Is Always Occurring

At a recent concert, the performer described two rules that she learned while on a trip to the Holy Land.

Rule #1: God is sovereign.

Rule #2: Everything changes except rule #1.

How true this is! We have a Father who "does not change like shifting shadows" (James 1:17, NIV). While we have a God who does not change and a consistent set of promises and laws to live by, few of us can name anything that hasn't changed from how it was ten years ago or even six months ago. The Bible promises that societies will wither and disappear. Leaders of the world are overthrown, fads come and go, new scientific theories develop, and technology changes at a dizzying rate.

When we consider the exponential change that occurs around us each day, it can become overwhelming. As Christians, we are fortunate to be grounded in absolute, unchanging truth; however, I think you get my point—change is inevitable. Change happens all the time.

Heraclitus, the ancient philosopher, is quoted as saying that you cannot step into the same river twice. This assumption holds numerous benefits for our work with clients. When we recognize that change is always occurring and that people are continuously changing, we are much more likely to look for change in our clients' lives. We also realize that people's problems are always changing.

By carefully looking for change, we are able to build on existing change and promote further growth in our clients. When we do this, we are able to help our clients see ways in which they are growing and changing while helping them to develop ways to continue to change. Not only does this facilitate growth, but it also builds self-efficacy and increases faith as our clients recognize the subtle growth that God facilitates. This ultimately helps us to watch for future growth.

3. Small Change Can Lead to Larger Change

Jesus in his teachings reminds us of the nature of change when he says, "Whoever can be trusted with very little can also be trusted with much, and whoever is dishonest with very little will also be dishonest with much" (Luke 16:10, NIV). Whether for good or for bad, small change begets larger change.

It is frequently assumed that a large problem requires an equally large solution. Think about people you have seen for treatment. Maybe it was a man who had been married three times, was diagnosed with a bipolar disorder, and was abusing alcohol. Or maybe it was a teenager who was out of control at school and had recently run away from home for the third time. If you are like me, you sat with these clients and thought about the years it would take to treat them and the many interventions you would have to employ to be of any help. We often assume that the interventions used and the therapy employed must be of an equivalent magnitude to the problem described. While this is sometimes true, most of the changes we make occur in small steps. In fact, Prochaska's model of change presented in chapter 2 reminds us of the controllable and predictable course that change takes as we move from precontemplation to termination. When we believe that large problems deserve large-scale interventions, we limit our work and may even prevent small changes from producing more changes. These small steps build on each other, leading to larger changes.

In order to understand how small change can lead to larger change, it is important to consider how problems develop. If you remember our assumption that people change and develop over the course of life and therefore may return for therapy at different times in life, then it is also easy to see that people's problems develop over the course of time. Very few people have problems that suddenly appear. While it may seem that the problems appear suddenly, if we look more closely, we will see that many successive life events led up to the incident for which a client seeks counseling.

Just as problems develop over time, so do solutions. Accordingly, positive growth and changes build on each other, leading to additional changes. Most important, small changes are the building blocks for larger change. Small is not synonymous with insignificant, and any small change that occurs now will affect all future interactions with everyone involved. Wow! That makes one small change seem a lot more important!

I am reminded of a couple who came for treatment for marital conflict. During the ten years of their marriage, they had endured financial ruin, the births of four children, and a significant level of conflict. Because they had identified in our first interview more than eight things they hoped to change, it was necessary to prioritize our treatment goals. Early in therapy, they noted a pattern in which conflict began after the husband arrived home from work. A small change was made, and the couple began to set aside three minutes for communication after the husband arrived home from work. This small change led to a significant decrease in early evening arguments, and this relative peace paved the way for increased positive communication, more time with their children, and an improvement in their financial management because they were able to talk about money issues.

4. An Effective Therapist Can Identify and Amplify Change

Do you believe that change really occurs all the time? Can you recognize change when it happens? In the time it took you to read the previous page, the earth moved twenty-two hundred miles, ten quarts of blood were pumped through your body, sixteen babies were born in the U.S., and nine Americans died. Change continuously happens, and because it happens so quickly, we often miss it.

On a smaller scale, our clients tell us about change all the time. We hear about a day in which a depressed client was able to get out of bed, eat a small breakfast, and walk to the corner before returning home for the day. It doesn't sound like much, but this may represent important change in this person's life. Another client may tell us of one day out of the week in which he did not fight with his wife. In fact, this was the first day in three months in which no conflict occurred. Yes, this probably isn't what any of us would desire for our own marriages, but it represents change—significant change.

Effective brief therapists not only believe that change is occurring all of the time but also are able to identify change and amplify it. You, as a brief therapist, are open to change, and you look for it whenever possible. You see, both of the clients mentioned above demonstrated that they are capable of change, even if the changes appeared inconsequential. By first recognizing change, we are then able to amplify it, to find out what allowed this to happen. When we do this, we are able to help people find ways to continue to make these changes happen.

5. Focusing on the Positive Has Many Advantages

Many contemporary helping theories focus on things that are unchangeable and impossible. By talking only about problems and the past, solutions and change in the future are rarely generated. On the other hand, by focusing on what is changeable, on what is possible, and on the hope we have in the future, the seeds of change are planted, and the process begins. The most effective counselors focus on what is possible and changeable rather than on what is impossible and unchangeable.

As professional helpers, we hear about problems, disturbances, and conflict on a daily basis. These become the lenses through which we see the world. Accordingly, the glass is easily seen as half empty rather than half full as our clients describe their lives to us. While we must be aware of our sinful nature and the pain in people's lives, we limit our effectiveness as counselors when we focus on pathology, weakness, and hurt.

Paul in his letter to the Philippians reminds us, "Fix your thoughts on what is true and good and right. Think about things that are pure and lovely, and dwell on the fine, good things in others. Think about all you can praise God for and be glad about" (Phil. 4:8, TLB). Each person is made in the image of God and is therefore an image bearer. What an exciting thought that each of us bears God's image, even when we suffer from depression, anxiety, or the symptoms of a borderline personality. Who better, then, to see strengths and maintain a positive focus with our clients than those of us who are committed to Christ? When we do this, we recognize the power of the Holy Spirit, the potential for change, and the hope of solutions. As a result, we talk about what can be changed rather than what cannot be changed.

6. Exceptions Suggest Solutions

Jill, the client presented at the beginning of this chapter, told her counselor that she has been depressed for the last six months. In addition, she described family problems that have occurred for much of her life. For those who were trained in traditional counseling programs, these things capture our attention. Jill also mentioned that she has felt better for the last five days, but then she quickly dismissed that observation as irrelevant. How easy it is for Jill and her counselor to overlook this. After all, the change may be nothing more than a "flight into health" or merely a fluke. It certainly doesn't seem significant, especially when compared with six months of depression.

When the counselor used exception-finding questions, Jill revealed that she had been sleeping better the last five days. Her increased sleep had allowed her to feel a little less depressed. She even made it through a whole day without crying. The counselor continued to explore what had allowed Jill to sleep a little bit better and discovered that she had walked to work the last five days because her car had broken down. By understanding exceptions to her problems, Jill's counselor was given several important clues to help treat her depression. Jill continued to walk to work and even explored new forms of physical exercise that helped her to continue to sleep better and feel less depressed.

While it may seem hard to believe, every problem has an exception. No problem occurs all the time, and no matter how small the exceptions to the problem may be, they suggest possible solutions. We all have preconceived ideas about how our clients' problems should be solved. Accordingly, we employ a limited range of solutions that often don't work. In doing so, we ignore exceptions to the problem, especially when they don't fit our expectations of what the solution should be. Exceptions are then seen as inconsequential, haphazard, or simply too inconsistent to be useful.[3]

In a brief-therapy model, the client and counselor must work together to uncover and understand exceptions. John Walter and Jane Peller note that when the client and counselor work together to elicit and amplify exceptions, the client is helped to gain control over situations that seemed out of control.[4] Learning to understand exceptions and make them happen more often is an effective means of helping people find solutions to their problems.

7. Cooperation Is Essential

What Do You See?

Take a few minutes to observe this picture before you read on. What do you see when you look at this picture? Perhaps the profile of a regal American Indian with a dark-colored headdress? Perhaps you see an Eskimo bundled in warm clothes, walking into a dark storm? Whether you see an American Indian, an Eskimo, or maybe even both, this picture illustrates an important point. When two people look at the same picture, are involved in the same relationship, or observe the same event, they may view it very differently. One person's perception of reality may vary greatly from another's, to the point that two people describing the same situation see entirely different things.

Does this mean there is no objective reality? Certainly not. As you look at this picture, you may see an American Indian or an Eskimo. While the perception is very different, there is also an underlying objective truth common to both. Both the American Indian and the Eskimo are Native American people and may be of a related heritage. The Bible provides objective truth from which each of us is instructed to live; however, we also recognize that experiences, culture, and upbringing may influence how we see life, people, and relationships.

Those of us in the helping professions are challenged each day to see and understand how those we help see their world. When we are unable to see as our clients do, or when we are unable to convince them of how we see their reality, we may label them as uncooperative or even resistant. I am humbly reminded of a client I saw early in my training experience, a middle-aged woman involved in a painful separation. In my naïveté, I was convinced that her marital problems were reenactments of her earlier relationships with her mother and father. While there were many signs to indicate this, my client did not agree with my diagnosis. In fact, she resisted any exploration of this area and became uncooperative. When I moved to a different office and transferred the client to another counselor, I learned something interesting about the client's reality. She was communicating that her past experiences were much too painful to explore. She wanted specific help with her present relationship. I wasn't listening to this because I was too busy with my own diagnosis of her problem. The new counselor worked to join with her and understand her perception of the world in order to focus treatment on the areas that the client wanted to change. As she did this, she became cooperative and made significant changes.

Our clients are *always* showing us how they believe change occurs. As we work to join them and understand their thinking, we are much more likely to elicit cooperation.[5] This is very different from the approach that many of us practice, the approach that says, "I love you, and I have a wonderful diagnosis for your life."

8. People Are Resourceful

Traditional models of counseling talk about deficits, pathology, and weakness. We look for faulty belief systems, inadequate coping skills, pathological relationships, poor attachments, and dysfunctional families. After identifying our client's deficits, we work to rebuild, reconstruct, and create.

While problems often exist, each person has unique gifts from God, no matter how they are tainted by sin. On a practical level, this means that each person has strengths that can be used to help overcome problems and difficulties. Brief therapists are keenly aware of the strengths that each person brings to the treatment. Brief therapists maintain a positive focus, always looking for these strengths. By identifying strengths and remaining positive, counselors and clients can develop further exceptions and promote change.

This assumption probably sounds tainted by humanistic philosophy and seemingly inconsistent with a Christian worldview. Let's contrast this assumption with similar assumptions proposed in the brief-therapy literature. For example, John Walter and Jane Peller assume that people have *all* the resources they need to solve their problems.[6] We see this differently. Because all people have been made in the image of God and because we all have access to the general revelation addressed in Romans 1, we believe that God has given each of us *some* resources from which we can draw. None of us has all of the resources we need, and each of us desperately needs God's perfect power to make these resources complete. Some people are very aware of these God-given resources and use them readily. Other people experience difficulty recognizing and using the resources God has given to them. As helpers, we work to help people understand their resources and learn how to access them. Most important, we work to help them understand their ultimate need for God.

By recognizing people's resources and strengths, do we overlook sin and psychopathology? By no means! This is neither responsible nor consistent with our faith. Instead, Christian counselors who use brief therapy know that "all have sinned; all fall short of God's glorious standard" (Rom. 3:23). We do not ignore sin. However, in the midst of sin, we are still reminded of the unique gifts God has given to his people. The Christian counselor doing brief therapy is also aware of psychopathology and makes careful choices about interventions based on these assessments. However, brief therapists may find it necessary to prioritize the problem to be addressed, especially if it is not related to the issue for which the client comes to counseling. While we are aware of psychopathology, we choose to focus on one piece of the puzzle. What remains important is a positive perspective that recognizes individual strengths and is responsibly aware of limitations so that exceptions can be found and change can occur.

9. Clients Define Their Goals

Do you remember Al Ego, the counselor introduced at the beginning of the chapter? As he meets with Jill for her first session, he diagnoses her condition, develops a treatment plan, and then sets out to change her internal representations of the self and her self-objects. Al is a well-trained and competent counselor; however, his goals may not match Jill's. As they work together, Al and Jill may end up at a place that is very different from what Jill intended. Bea Brief, on the other hand, explores Jill's goals with her. Jill describes her desire to sleep better, function effectively in her job, and find a church where she can meet other people her age. Bea helps Jill set goals that are achievable in a short amount of time and then works with her to find specific ways to accomplish those goals.

Traditional models of therapy give responsibility and control to the counselor. We assess problems, diagnose conditions, and then set out to find what is best for our clients. In doing so, we engage in a process that is strikingly similar to traditional medicine, in which a physician consults, runs tests, and then prescribes treatment.

Solution-based models of brief therapy take a noticeably different stance. Instead of putting the counselor in control, this model encourages the active participation of the client. Counselors work with clients to develop clear goals and then help them find ways to achieve their goals. In short, the client becomes the expert, on both the problems and the future solutions.

This assumption allows our clients to tell us what is meaningful and important to them. We assume the position of learners, allowing the clients to teach us about how much change is necessary and what amount of change will be helpful to them. By allowing our clients to set goals, therapy is then a goal-focused endeavor with the client in the driver's seat. If clients who have several problems decide to focus on only one area, we work with them on the area they choose, realizing that change in one aspect of life may lead to change in other areas. When we see other problematic areas in our clients' lives, we may point them out, allowing our clients to decide which goals are meaningful and necessary for them at that time.

SUMMARY

Theological, theoretical, and philosophical assumptions form the basis for many of the decisions we make each day. In fact, we rarely make a choice, engage in a behavior, or utter a word that isn't influenced by our basic assumptions. Because of this, we must understand the assumptions from which we operate. Not only do they theoretically undergird our work, but they actively influence the choices we make. By not understanding our assumptions, we easily fall prey to errors in logic, inconsistencies, and most important, actions and words that may contradict the clear teachings of Scripture.

This chapter has described a few of the working assumptions that undergird a Christian, solution-based model of brief therapy. We work diligently to test our psychological assumptions against God's inherent and infallible Word. Discovered truth must always take second place to revealed truth. In chapter 14 we will further discuss the theological assumptions that are the bedrock of our clinical work.

Many other relevant underpinnings are no doubt worthy of attention. We are still working to understand these assumptions and their implications. Because of this, they may change or be modified. Even so, we believe that they represent an important starting place as we think about the process of change and about ways to bring about change that are meaningfully Christian. We also hope that these assumptions have challenged you to look at people, their problems, and their solutions in a different light.

7/ THE FIRST SESSION

O Lord, teach me to do Thy will; teach me to converse worthily and humbly in Thy sight, for Thou art my wisdom.

THOMAS À KEMPIS, *The Imitation of Christ*

One of the more difficult things about learning and understanding counseling techniques is applying them. This chapter will help you practice some of the underlying assumptions and techniques discussed in the previous chapters.

In many ways, the first session is the most important session in brief counseling. For some clients this may be the only session as there seems to be a fairly large dropout rate after a first session. Other clients may need only one session.[1] Whether you see a client for one session or several sessions, what you do in the first session is crucial.

In the first session the counselor needs to hit the ground running. This is not simply a time to get to know the client and begin to establish rapport, even though these are important. Rather, the first session is a time when change begins to take place. It is also the time when clients learn what the counseling process will look like. In the first session counselors must be very active and engaged because it is their job to make sure the session stays on track.

Each of us will handle the first session differently. But we want to give you a sense of what the first session might look like. The interventions that we suggest have been helpful to us and hundreds of our clients. You will quickly see that what we do is not strictly cognitive-behavioral, MRI, or solution focused in its approach. Instead, this session utilizes aspects of each approach along with pieces from other clinical perspectives. That is why we have chosen to call this approach solution-based.

What is presented here is not meant to be a model you rigidly apply. Rather it is a model that we hope will stimulate your own creativity. It is up to you to adapt it.

As you read through this chapter, you may find yourself saying, "How can I accomplish all this in one session?" You can't! We have opted to give a comprehensive overview in this chapter rather than describe a process that can be covered in a certain amount of time. None of us will cover all of the suggested topics in one session. But we can make sure that we have all of this information within the first *two* sessions. The specific information that we obtain in any particular first session will depend on the situation. If a client is obviously depressed, we will inquire about suicidality in the first session, since suicidal ideation is common with depression. However, if a client wants help with parenting skills and clearly is not depressed, suicidality may not even be considered.

This chapter does not discuss the subject of diagnosis in depth. In some senses it is beyond the scope of where we are going. However, it is a topic that every counselor must understand. Many brief therapists consider diagnosis to be a concept that is, for the most part, not very helpful because it encourages a pathology focus or labeling. However, the reality is that when counselors work with insurance reimbursements, they must give a diagnosis. In our counseling practice we provide a diagnosis for the clients we work with, not only for insurance purposes, but also because it can provide an explanation for what is wrong. In addition, diagnosis can identify specific things that hinder a client's effectiveness, and it can provide avenues for intervention.

This chapter is structured somewhat differently from the others so that we can give a realistic example of how our approach works. We will discuss each category that is included in a first session and provide a sample dialogue to illustrate the specific category. The dialogue used here is reconstructed from a combination of actual cases. While it does not report one specific case, all of the dialogue is an accurate representation of situations that we have encountered.

THE INITIAL CONTACT

Before you actually see the client in your counseling office, you have some initial contact, usually on the phone. During this initial contact, let clients know how you approach the counseling process and what they can expect out of it. Also take time to gather some minimal background information. You can help clients begin the change process even before they come into your office by asking them to think about what change will look like for them.

THE FIRST SESSION

Review of Disclosure and Confidentiality

When a client comes to a counseling session, we review our disclosure statement and our approach to confidentiality so that the client enters into counseling informed of the limitations. Clients are assured that what is discussed in counseling is confidential. The only exceptions to this are cases where we suspect abuse or neglect (to a child, an incapacitated person, or an elderly person) or we judge that clients may hurt themselves or someone else. If we suspect abuse or neglect, we are obligated to file a report with the state. If we judge that clients may cause harm, we take whatever action is necessary to prevent that.

The laws regarding confidentiality may vary from state to state. Also, the legal requirements for a minister or a church counselor may be different from the requirements for a licensed professional counselor. However, whatever capacity counselors are working in, it is their responsibility to be aware of the limitations and to inform their clients of them. If counselors do not do this, they may be violating the law. In addition, if clients are not aware of these matters, they cannot make an informed decision as to what they want to talk about.

Goal Identification

After handling the administrative details, we begin to identify the termination criteria. Helping clients clarify their criteria for ending counseling influences the treatment plan. This can be done through a variety of questions that are geared to focusing the client on the process of change and the future, such as:

- What do you want to see different as a result of counseling?
- When we have finished, what would make you say that this was worth your time?
- What needs to happen for you to no longer need to come for counseling?
- When the things that brought you here today have changed, what will you be doing differently?

This approach of immediately identifying the end product of counseling is a significant distinction that sets brief therapy apart from other types of counseling. In most approaches, the initial emphasis is on identifying the problem, which is important for the counselor to understand. However, when counselors immediately work to clarify what *change* will look like instead of what the *problem* looks like, they begin to shape the client's perspective. This allows the client to view the situation somewhat differently. This is the first small step in the change process. For people to change the way they do something, they need to change the way they view it.

Let's look at how this works with a client. Rhonda is a forty-three-year-old woman who sells pharmaceuticals. She was referred to counseling by her pastor because of an increasingly severe depression. Rhonda is married, but she and her husband have no children. She is active in her church and periodically has held a variety of leadership positions. When Rhonda called to set up a counseling appointment, she sounded very depressed and said that she was having a difficult time getting anything done.

> *Counselor:* So tell me, Rhonda, what do you want to see different as a result of the counseling process? What will help you say that this experience was worthwhile?
>
> *Rhonda:* Well . . . I won't feel the way I do now.
>
> *Counselor:* What will be different?

Rhonda: I'll feel more energetic. Umm, I'll look forward to going to work. Probably, I'll have a new job.

Counselor: When this happens, what will you be *doing* differently?

Rhonda: I'm not sure.

Counselor: What do you think your husband will notice is different when you feel more energetic?

Rhonda: I might want to get out of the house. I might even be more interested in doing things with him. Right now, I mostly sit home.

Counselor: So at the end of counseling, you'll be feeling more energetic. Also, you'll be spending more time going out with your husband. What else will be different? What will be a sign to you that we have accomplished what you want?

Rhonda: Well, for one thing, I'll be able to interview successfully, and I'll get a new job. I just quit my job after being there for six months. It took me quite awhile to get it too. But I just had a difficult time remembering things. I couldn't memorize the information I needed to do the sales presentation. This didn't work real well for someone who's been in sales for twenty years. The last time I was out job hunting, I kept getting the feedback that I looked tired. They didn't feel I had enough drive to do the job. In the past, I've been quite successful in sales. Getting a new job or meeting my quotas has never been a problem.

After this short exchange, the treatment plan is beginning to emerge. Rhonda has stated and the counselor has helped her clarify that a successful end to counseling will involve feeling more energetic. The ways that this will be noticed include increased interaction and activities with her husband, being able to interview for and find a new job, and being able to come across as energetic during a job interview.

For some clients, interviewing and finding a job may be a questionable goal for counseling. It is definitely something that the counselor cannot control. In Rhonda's case, however, it was a very realistic goal. She has been a successful salesperson in her field for a long time. During that time she had also developed a number of contacts, so getting a job interview should not be difficult for her. The problem is that Rhonda's current level of functioning is interfering with her being able to accomplish what is reasonable for her.

In addition to beginning to set some goals as a result of this short exchange, the counselor also has gathered a good deal of other clinical information. Rhonda shows some of the classic symptoms of depression. She appears to have a decreased level of energy, is isolating herself from people, and may be experiencing problems with concentration or with short-term memory.

Assessing for Pre-Session Change

As we discussed in chapter 5, it is common for change to occur even before the client shows up for the first appointment. Pre-session change is a phenomenon that has been noted in the research on brief counseling.[2] It is important for the counselor to follow up in the first session by inquiring about any such change.

> *Counselor:* When we talked on the phone, I mentioned that people often notice things changing a little after the counseling appointment has been made. I wonder if you noticed anything.
>
> *Rhonda:* I did begin to feel a little more hopeful that I would be able to get this thing resolved.
>
> *Counselor:* That's great! What happened when you were able to notice that?
>
> *Rhonda:* Well, for one thing, I sent my résumé to a company. I may be able to get an interview for a different job.
>
> *Counselor:* Really? How were you able to do that?
>
> *Rhonda:* I figured I could take the risk since I already had this appointment set up. I guess having set the appointment gave me some hope, and I figured that by the time I had the interview, we might have made some progress anyway.

In Rhonda's case, as is typical, the pre-session change was not dramatic. However, it was the first small step in the overall process. Any change, no matter how small, should be reinforced by the counselor. It is common for clients to come into counseling at a contemplation or preparation stage. When you reinforce small changes, it helps clients to move ahead.

Exploring Attempted Solutions

Attempted solutions are the things that the client has done in an effort to solve the presenting problem. These are important because they represent what does not work and therefore what the counselor wants to avoid repeating. In addition, attempted solutions provide useful information for determining secondary interventions or tackling problems from a problem-solving approach. Our first thrust in problem resolution is usually focused on developing solutions. However, if this approach is unsuccessful, we will usually switch to a problem-solving approach and attempt to help the client do something that is different.

Some clients do not respond well to a solution-focused perspective. Some people have a need to talk about the problems. Their outlook causes them to feel that not talking about the problem is to be superficial or to minimize their difficulties. For others, their personality structure is such that they do not respond well to developing solutions. For all of these people, it is more appropriate to begin with a problem-solving perspective, then help them turn their focus to developing solutions. In this case it is more helpful if the counselor and the client approach the situation from a problem-solving perspective, as discussed in chapter 4.

Exploring the client's attempted solutions provides useful information for both the present and the future course of counseling. The way the client deals with attempted solutions gives clues as to whether a solution-based or a problem-solving perspective will be the most productive. Also, understanding the attempted solutions gives the counselor important information in case it becomes necessary to shift from a solution focus to a problem focus later on in the counseling.

> **Counselor:** Tell me, Rhonda, what are some things that you have done to try to solve this problem?
>
> **Rhonda:** Well, I called you.
>
> **Counselor:** I appreciate that. But I was wondering what you did to

help the situation before you got to the place that you felt you needed to call someone.

Rhonda: First, I asked my pastor for advice. He was the one who suggested that I call you.

Counselor: Did that help?

Rhonda: It helped some. It got me over my fear of talking to someone. But that was all it accomplished. My pastor has done some counseling before, and he thought that where I am required a professional.

Counselor: Was there anything else that you tried to make yourself feel better?

Rhonda: I tried talking to my husband and also a friend at work. Neither of them had anything helpful to suggest. And I thought about reading some self-help books, but I didn't get around to that. Oh, also, I went to my doctor about a week ago to see what he might suggest. When I told him how I was feeling, he recommended that I try an antidepressant. I've been taking it a few days now.

Counselor: Any other ways that you've tried to solve these difficulties?

Rhonda: The only other thing I can think of is what I told you about already. Even though I didn't feel like it, I decided to send my résumé to a company I heard about. I got the idea that they have a sales position open. I probably won't get the job, but I figured it couldn't hurt.

Notice how often the counselor had to ask the same question to get the desired information. At three different times and in three different ways the counselor asked Rhonda about her attempted solutions to the problem. This is not unusual since frequently clients are not used to thinking in terms of their attempts at problem solving. In addition, they may consider their efforts as inconsequential to counseling. It is important for the counselor, though, to be persistent in gathering this information.

This short exchange with Rhonda yielded valuable information. Most of her attempted solutions focused on passive maneuvers such as asking others for advice. Because of this, the counselor needs to be very careful about giving advice because this may replicate what Rhonda has already unsuccessfully attempted. Initially, any attempted solutions should be action oriented.

Since Rhonda was able to apply for a job, which is a reasonable maneuver given her current situation, it is evident that she is not totally passive. The counselor will want to applaud this action.

Finally, Rhonda revealed some important information before the counselor had directly asked about it. Obviously, it is essential that her counselor know about the antidepressant medication, including what she is taking, the dosage she is taking, what prompted her physician to prescribe it, and what the potential side effects are.

Determining Spiritual Resources

Christian counseling, whether it is brief or long term, cannot be done adequately without an understanding of the client's spiritual development. Chapter 2 reminded us that God has given us the ability to change. He has given us spiritual resources to help in the change process. It is important that we help the client discover what those resources are. This might include determining whether clients are born-again, what this means to them, and the degree to which they make use of the resources they have in Christ.

Clients come to us with different levels of spiritual maturity. Some are very active in their local church; others are on the fringe. Some struggle with including God in everyday life; others see him as a natural part of life. Some pray regularly and read the Bible; others don't.

To get a good understanding of clients' spiritual resources, it is helpful to understand their involvement in church. Do they attend regularly? Are they involved in a class or small group? In what ways do they serve in their church? Answers to these questions give information that can be used in helping clients to change.

It can also be helpful to find out what clients' spiritual lives look like away from church. Are they involved in regular Bible study and Bible memory? Do they have an accountability group? Are praise and worship a part of their life? How do they attempt to grow? What are other sources of fellowship for them?

Christian clients' spiritual lives are frequently important to them. Unfortunately, in many counseling approaches, the client's spiritual life is an area that is ignored. But, for effective *Christian* counseling, it is an area we should address. Many Christians look for a Christian counselor because they want a spiritual perspective as well as a psychological perspective on their situation.

When Rhonda came for counseling, she was referred by her pastor, who had attempted to help her. Consider the way the counselor addressed spiritual issues with Rhonda, and see how this can help in developing later interventions.

> *Counselor:* Tell me a little bit about your involvement at church.
>
> *Rhonda:* Well, my husband and I have been going to our church for a number of years. We first started going there after we became Christians. We used to teach Sunday school, but we don't right now. Most of our friends are at church, though.
>
> *Counselor:* Sounds as if you are pretty involved there.
>
> *Rhonda:* Yeah, we are. Our friends have been a big prayer support.
>
> *Counselor:* Are you involved in a small group or class?
>
> *Rhonda:* Yes and no. Our Sunday school classes are electives, so my husband and I go if the topic catches our interest. We used to be in a small group, but it broke up. We do have some friends that we were thinking of beginning one with again. These are people who know us pretty well and who we have a lot in common with.

In Rhonda's case it could be very helpful to encourage her to increase contact with some of her friends from church. It is a natural source of personal support for her. With her depression, she is tending to isolate herself from others. Directing her back toward fellowship with other believers is an intervention that can begin to address this problem.

History of the Problem

The history of a client's problem includes when it began, what specific symptoms the client is experiencing, how the situation is a problem for the client, any significant environmental factors about it, and the specific reason the client is seeking help at this time. It is also important to determine whether the client has ever experienced a similar problem before.

In many approaches to brief therapy, the counselor either ignores or treats lightly the history of the current problem, focusing instead on the client's current functioning and coping mechanisms. When a counselor approaches the client in a manner that downplays the history of the problem, important information can be ignored or overlooked. A recurrent or chronic problem may have to be handled differently from a onetime or acute situation. Reviewing the history will also help determine whether or not this is a crisis situation and thus needs to be dealt with in a more directive manner.

Suicidality or Homicidality

It is the counselor's duty to make sure that clients are not going to hurt themselves or someone else. If a specific client falls into one of these categories, then the counselor is obligated to take appropriate measures to attempt to prevent any harm from occurring. In the course of the session, Rhonda reveals to the counselor that she felt that life was hopeless and that she would not be upset if she got hit by a car. However, she was adamant that she would not do anything to take her life. The thought of harming someone else had never crossed her mind.

Exceptions

Chapter 5 discussed the significant role that exceptions play in a solution-based model. In exploring for exceptions, you should be looking for times when the problem was not present or was present to a lesser degree than the client is currently reporting. This information is essential in developing solutions that work and are effective for a specific client.

When clients seek help, they are usually focused on the problem that brought them to counseling. They are motivated by something that is not working and does not feel very good to them. Usually they are not focused on times when the problem is better. Thus, it can become difficult for them to start to think in terms of exceptions.

One way of helping the client make this shift in thinking is to do a small amount of education before asking about times when the problem is different. This can even be done in a casual manner.

Counselor: Rhonda, I know you realize that we are sinful people. As it says in Romans 3:23, "All have sinned; all fall short of God's glorious standard." Therefore we don't do things perfectly. At the same time, as Paul says in Romans 7, we can't always do the things that we want to do. But in spite of this, by God's grace, there are times when problems are not as bad as they are at other times. Or we might find ourselves feeling just a little better, in spite of everything. We may even be able to get some small thing accomplished. When have you experienced times like that?

By phrasing it in this manner, the counselor is educating Rhonda to the principle of exceptions. In addition, the counselor is assuming that there actually are times when Rhonda has responded differently. This places Rhonda in the position of having to identify those times. Thus, instead of talking about the extent of the problem, the job becomes finding the exceptions to it.

Another important factor in identifying exceptions is to look for little things that are different. When a client finds that a depressed mood is somewhat better for a half an hour, that is an exception. Because half an hour may not seem like much in the course of a week, the client could easily overlook it. However, even though it is small, it is an exception. In brief counseling, then, the counselor has to help the client identify these small things.

After a small exception has been identified, the counselor then needs to emphasize it, and if possible, expand it. This is done by examining the particulars, such as what caused it to happen and how often it has occurred. In doing this, it is essential for the counselor to give the client the credit for causing the exception. When a situation or exception is caused by a client, then it becomes something that is in the client's control to duplicate. The key word for placing an exception in a client's control is *how.* "How were you able to do that?" is a question that reinforces the client's control and power. Let's consider how small exceptions and the principle of giving the client control worked with Rhonda.

Counselor: As I mentioned, frequently people find that there are times when the situation is different, when they are feeling just a little bit better. It might last for only half an hour, but for that time their mood is somewhat brighter. When have you noticed that?

Rhonda: I don't know. It doesn't happen very often. Sometimes, I've felt that things weren't quite as hopeless when I go out for a walk. That doesn't happen very much, though.

Counselor: Really? How are you able to do that, feel better when you walk?

Rhonda: That's usually when I can shake off all this worry about my job situation and think of something different.

Counselor: That's great! I'm encouraged that you have been able to find something that helps you some. Many people in your situation wouldn't be able to do that. Since you've found something that helps you a little, be sure to keep doing it.

It is essential for the counselor to be very tuned in to looking for exceptions. At times the counselor may even notice exceptions that the client has missed. When this happens, the counselor needs to point those out to the client. Frequently this will occur when the client is recounting a specific event, and the information appears to slip out without the client's realizing the significance of it. Look at how this happened with Rhonda and what the counselor did with it.

Counselor: You mentioned earlier that work was getting to the place that you couldn't stand it anymore. Fill me in on that, will you?

Rhonda: As I said, it took me several months to land this job. I kept getting brushed over every time I interviewed. Everyone kept saying that I looked as if I had no energy. I was worn out. When I got my previous job, I tried really hard to come across different. That worked for a while. But when I kept having problems memorizing the product information, I realized that I didn't have much of a chance there. That's when I decided to call another company I had heard about, a company I had some previous connections with.

Given Rhonda's lack of motivation due to her depression, it is somewhat unusual that she would pursue another job. It is even more surprising that she would initiate it. This is the type of information that the counselor needs to highlight for her.

> *Counselor:* Just a minute. You called this company on your own?
>
> *Rhonda:* Yeah, and I was able to get an interview. In fact, it sounds as if it might work out.
>
> *Counselor:* How were you able to do that? I mean, call the company. It sounded as if you were pretty low. I would have expected that to be something that was pretty difficult to do.
>
> *Rhonda:* It wasn't that big a deal. I knew things weren't going to work at my present job. So I had to do something. I heard about this prospect through the grapevine and decided I had nothing to lose. Since I already had some connections, I just called.
>
> *Counselor:* Well, it may not feel like a big deal, but I think it's important to pay attention to the positive steps that you are taking to solve your problem. Sounds as if you've taken some steps forward.
>
> *Rhonda:* Maybe. It really isn't that big a deal. I haven't gotten the job yet.

Even though Rhonda is not ready to attach much significance to the event, it is important to emphasize the positive steps that she has taken on her own. This reinforces the concept of exceptions for clients. In addition, it increases the likelihood that clients will start noticing exceptions on their own.

Client Status

In the first session you need to assess whether the client is open to change or is in your office because someone else thinks he or she should be in counseling. Factors that help you make this determination are the client's level of involvement in the session, the reason he or she came to counseling, and the stated goals. More specifics about determining whether the client's status is that of a *visitor,* a *customer,* or a *complainant* will be given in the next chapter. However, to be effective in brief counseling, you should have some sense of your client's position in the first session. You will use different methodologies with clients who are customers than you will use with those who are visitors or complainants.

Rhonda is clearly open to change; she is a customer. Her goal is relief from depression and an increased level of functioning. She came to counseling because she recognized her need and wanted help. In addition, she was motivated to follow through with whatever she needed to do in order to bring about this change.

First Small Step

Change should begin in the first session. This can occur in several forms. Change can begin when clients see situations from a different perspective and react to the situations differently. Change can even involve describing a problem in a new manner. Change can come in a wave, in a steady stream, or in spurts. But no matter what arena it begins in or how rapidly it comes, all change has one thing in common: It begins with one small step. It is essential for clients to realize this principle if they are to optimize change for themselves. Most people come into counseling looking at the end product. They see the situation they are in and envision what life will be like without their particular problem. This is necessary for setting goals; however, the end of the problem is not where the client begins to develop solutions. The client needs to begin with the first small step in the journey of solving the problem.

In the first session the counselor must make sure that the client is able to identify and communicate what the first small step in the change process will look like. This may sound like a simple thing to do. However, the problem is that most clients tend to think too big. For example, a counselor asks a client, "What is the first small indicator to you that you have begun to get over your anxiety?" The client replies, "I won't feel nervous all day long." This is not a small step. Depending on the client's level of anxiety, it could be halfway to solving the problem. In this situation the counselor could reply, "This sounds like a pretty big step. What would be the first *little* thing that would tell you that you have begun to change?"

Small steps should be something that the client could potentially do immediately. They should be within the client's behavioral repertoire and potentially applicable at the present time.

Some clients find it difficult to conceptualize this idea of a small step in the change process. When this occurs, it can be helpful to suggest that they look through someone else's perspective. This can be done with a simple question such as, "What would your friend say would be the first small indicator that you have begun to change?" By helping clients view the situation, frequently they can become more objective. In Rhonda's case it was helpful to look through the eyes of her husband.

> *Counselor:* As you look at your situation, Rhonda, what would you say would be the first small indicator that you are beginning to feel better?
>
> *Rhonda:* I don't know. Umm, maybe I would go for a while without being depressed.
>
> *Counselor:* Well, that would be our goal. But what would be the first small step in that direction? What would be the first little thing that would tell you that you were beginning to feel better?
>
> *Rhonda:* I don't really know.
>
> *Counselor:* Let me ask you this. What is the first thing that your husband would notice as you begin to get better? What would tell him that you have begun to change?
>
> *Rhonda:* He would notice that I was spending less time in the basement.
>
> *Counselor:* Less time in the basement?
>
> *Rhonda:* Yeah. I spend a lot of time in the basement doing nothing.
>
> *Counselor:* So one of the first things your husband would notice that would tell him that you were getting better is that you would be spending less time in the basement? Instead, you would be doing . . . what?
>
> *Rhonda:* Instead, I would be upstairs, maybe talking with him.

Notice in this exchange how the counselor quickly helps Rhonda shift from an undesirable behavior (spending time in the basement) to a more desirable one (talking with her husband). It is important, in effective brief counseling, that as much as possible the focus of change stays on desirable behaviors rather than on behaviors the client wants to avoid.

Client Strengths

Assessing for clients' strengths is an important component of the first session. This can give the counselor a sense of potentially effective strategies to use. Assessing for strengths can be done both directly and indirectly.

In directly assessing for strengths, simply ask the client about them. When you say, "Tell me some things that you are good at," it gives the client a chance to make a temporary mental shift from focusing on the problems. This very small and sometimes short shift can be a building block in the change process.

Observe the client to assess indirect strengths. Strengths can include the client's verbal and intellectual ability, motivation, past ability to change, a well-developed support system, or the client's personality style. Also include an assessment of the client's spiritual resources.

Rhonda had a number of obvious strengths. She was very motivated to change her situation. She also had some strong spiritual resources that she could easily access. In addition, she was able to understand and begin to use a solution-oriented approach to problem solving.

You can use a client's strengths in structuring the counseling session and in designing homework assignments, which will be described more fully in chapter 9. If a client is well educated or fairly verbal, you may find that using metaphors can be effective. With other clients it is best to be more concrete and specific. Some clients have a more difficult time identifying alternative ways of acting or handling a situation. You may need to give more specific suggestions to these people.

Base homework assignments on the client's strengths. The client who likes to read should have books assigned as part of the homework. A client who feels isolated but has a potential support system should be actively directed back to that support system. A client who is active in the church or has had a history of positive spiritual growth needs to expand those relationships. Build homework assignments on the client's spiritual resources.

Family History

Some brief counselors do not see a client's family history as important, emphasizing instead the client's current situation. These counselors view the past as either unimportant or a diversion that can be a time-consuming detour. However, a client's family history can hold significant information even though it may not be the primary point of the therapeutic intervention. The goal in gathering family history is to use the information to provide another platform for change in the present.

Asking about the family will often bring up information about the client's past in general. This is a good time to emphasize the client's resources. You might say, "As you look at what has happened to you, what are some of the resources that helped you cope?" When these kinds of questions are asked under the influence of the Holy Spirit, they can elicit a fresh and helpful perspective of God's faithfulness and the reality that "God causes everything to work together for the good of those who love God and are called according to his purpose for them" (Rom. 8:28). A careful and spiritual handling of a client's past can show God's hand.

Medical History

Determining a client's medical history is essential for providing comprehensive treatment. A number of medical conditions can cause, exacerbate, or mimic psychological problems. Assessment of a client's medical history should include inquiring about known medical problems, current medications used, and the date of the last physical exam. If the client has not had a recent physical, especially after the start of the current psychological problems, refer the client to a primary physician for a physical. Instruct the client to inform the physician of the current psychological symptoms so that the physician can work to rule out other related conditions.

Rhonda was referred to her primary physician to see if a complete physical would be appropriate. She had consulted her physician before coming for counseling and been given a prescription for an antidepressant. However, it had been a couple of years since she had last had a physical.

Given the level of her depression, it was essential to rule out any physiological basis for it.

Substance Use

It is essential to inquire about the use of alcohol or drugs, even when working with Christian clients. A history of substance use tells about the client's coping mechanisms as well as possible contributors to current problems.

Alcohol or drug use can complicate a counseling situation in several ways. Alcohol and depression are a problematic combination. People can be tempted to use alcohol as a way of dealing with depression. However, alcohol is itself a depressant. Thus, using alcohol can worsen a depressed person's problem. In addition, alcohol can cause some antidepressants to be ineffective.

Since drugs can contribute to both depression and anxiety problems, it is important to inquire as to a client's habits in this area. Ask about the client's use of medications, including sleeping aids. The abuse of prescription or over-the-counter medications can be a significant factor in emotional problems. Yet medication abuse can be easily overlooked.

A final area to ask about is caffeine. Caffeine—whether it comes in coffee, tea, chocolate, or carbonated beverages—can be addicting. In addition, there is well-documented evidence that caffeine can be a major contributor to anxiety problems. Caffeine also has been shown to cause sleep disturbance. If a person does not get adequate sleep, the result can be depression. Caffeine can be easily downplayed as a contributor to psychological problems.

In Rhonda's case, a counselor could have been tempted to forgo asking about substance use since she is an evangelical Christian and active in her local church. However, there was important information to be gained from this line of inquiry.

Counselor: Rhonda, do you ever use alcohol or other substances?

Rhonda: Well, when I was in college, I experimented some with drugs. But that was before I became a Christian.

Counselor: How about alcohol?

Rhonda: Not now.

Counselor: Not *now?*

Rhonda: In the past I had a drinking problem. Then during that time just before I got my current position, I began drinking again. I was feeling so bad that I didn't know what to do.

Counselor: How often do you drink now?

Rhonda: Right now, never. I quit about three months ago. Up to that point I was drinking every other day. But I realized that it was only making me feel worse. So I decided to stop. I saw myself going down the same road I had been down before. Drinking had caused me too many problems before. I didn't want to have to deal with that again.

In Rhonda's situation, inquiring about substance use was extremely helpful. Even though she was not currently drinking, it is obvious that she is at risk to do so. If she were to begin abusing alcohol again, it could easily make her depression worse. In this situation, the counselor is wise to look for any signs that she may be drinking again. It would even be appropriate in a future session to inquire discreetly about her alcohol use.

Testing

Many short-term models do not advocate testing. It can be seen as superfluous or something that causes people to focus on problems rather than solutions. We have found that the limited use of psychological testing can facilitate a more accurate diagnosis and greater specificity in treatment planning. Testing is useful because it provides a good deal of information about the client in the beginning of counseling. Frequently the information gleaned from testing is information that an astute counselor could obtain eventually. But testing allows the information to be useful right from the beginning. Thus, testing helps the counselor to be more time effective. In our estimation it could take four to six sessions to gain the amount of information that we can obtain from testing.

Testing provides an objective client profile that helps the counselor in two ways. First, it prevents the client from successfully minimizing the severity of some aspects of the problem. Second, it prevents the counselor from missing important facts or dynamics about the client.

Another use of testing is in establishing a baseline for treatment. Tests can give a quick overview of clients' level of functioning. Repeating a particular instrument during the middle of counseling and then at the end can help highlight progress. Also, in some situations, testing can help you make a critical evaluation of clients' potential danger to themselves or to others.

In our clinic, testing instruments that have been particularly helpful are the Taylor-Johnson Temperament Analysis, the Beck Depression Inventory, the SCL-90-R (which is a symptom checklist), and the Minnesota Multiphasic Personality Inventory. Some of these, such as the Beck Depression Inventory, can be taken a number of times, usually at home, to chart progress and change. Even something simple like this can encourage growth, verify outcome, and facilitate the construction of an effective post-counseling treatment plan.

COMPLIMENTS AND HOMEWORK

Conclude the first session by complimenting the client's strengths and assigning homework. Emphasizing the client's strengths is an easy way of organizing a summary of the session. This naturally leads into a structured homework assignment.

Homework is an essential part of brief counseling. It keeps the change process moving faster because change does not have to be dependent on just what happens in the session. Clients spend a good deal more time away from each session than they do in session. Homework is a way of maximizing that time. Homework also gives more ownership of change to the clients because it makes them actively involved in the process.

Homework can involve a variety of things. It can include reading, observational tasks, or structured activities. At the end of the first session, homework tends to be somewhat lighter than after other sessions. One reason is that after only one session, you may not have a good sense of the client's level of cooperation. It is better to assign a small task and have it completed than to assign a more involved task and have it not completed. Even with homework, the emphasis should be on success.

As the counselor concludes the first session with Rhonda, notice how her strengths are used to structure the homework assignment.

Counselor: Rhonda, I want to thank you for your cooperation here today. I'm sure that it was not easy to come.

Rhonda: Well, I've gotten to the point that I really need help. If I don't change the way I'm feeling, my husband and I are going to have some big financial problems.

Counselor: I realize that. Yet I also recognize that coming to a counselor is not always easy. I've been impressed with some of the steps that you have already taken to change this situation. It shows that you are really motivated. Many people in your situation would not be able to go out and set up a job interview.

Rhonda: I felt I had to make progress.

Counselor: Still, at a time when you were feeling very low, you took some steps to begin to solve the problem. I want to encourage you to keep it up. Cultivating that type of attitude will contribute to your feeling better. Also, I've been impressed with how significant the prayer group at your church has been to you.

Rhonda: Thanks.

Counselor: Now here's something that might be helpful for you. Would you be up for a little homework?

Rhonda: I guess so. Though I have to warn you I don't have as much drive as I used to.

Counselor: That's fine. You should have no problem accomplishing what I have in mind. In fact, it may be too easy. It definitely will be easier than getting a job interview.

Rhonda: Let's give it a try.

Counselor: I want you to notice something. When you are at home and you find that you are spending time in rooms other than the basement or that you are with your husband, I want you to pay attention. At those times ask yourself, "What's different?" See if you can notice what it is that helps you do this. What makes it possible for you to be with him or in a different part of the house? Even if you are doing it for just a few minutes, ask yourself that question. Your answers will give us some important information. How does that sound?

Rhonda: I should be able to do that. But don't expect me to have any profound answers. I don't get out of the basement much.

Counselor: That's fine. Just notice the times that you are out, and ask the question. Also, two or three times next week, I want you to read a specific passage of Scripture. I'd like you to read Philippians 4:8, where Paul talks about fixing your thoughts on "what is true and honorable and right." Then notice the times when this passage could help you.

As mentioned earlier, the first session involves obtaining a good deal of information while at the same time beginning the process of change. Out of necessity, some information gathering will be delayed until the second session. The specifics will depend on the situation and what is crucial for the counselor to know right away.

What cannot wait until the second session is for the change process to begin. If counseling is going to be successful and time effective, change begins in the first session. This is accomplished through setting goals, determining what termination will look like, identifying small steps, emphasizing exceptions, and assigning homework. Educate the client about how change will occur or what change will look like, and allow the client to educate you. In addition, indirectly educate clients by your attitudes and expectations of change occurring.

The second session is the time when you will obtain the information that you were not able to get in the first session. However, you will approach the second and subsequent sessions in ways that are somewhat different from the way you approach the first session. This is primarily because these sessions are not as structured as the first session is. Before we deal with how to handle the different demands of these sessions, we want to consider the essential and often neglected subject of treatment goals and how to keep the counseling process focused.

8/ DEVELOPING *and* MAINTAINING *a* CLEAR FOCUS *in* TREATMENT

Hope deferred makes the heart sick, but when dreams come true,
there is life and joy.   PROVERBS 13:12

Imagine that you decided to go on a weeklong fishing trip. The first thing you do is check with your friends to see if anyone knows of a good location. Sure enough! Your next-door neighbor tells you of a great spot, about an hour away, where you are guaranteed to get your limit. So you pack your gear and head off. However, in your exuberance, you never bothered to ask the neighbor for directions. But that's okay. You have an idea of the general direction you have to head. Who needs to know where to turn? Besides, great fishing places are easy to recognize, so you'll just know the spot when you see it.

Attempting to counsel without clear treatment goals is a lot like trying to find the fishing spot without directions. Sometimes it is possible to get there just on instinct. And in this journey you may even go down some very interesting roads. However, it will take a lot longer to get to the final destination. And when a counselor decides to take the long way, the client is the one who suffers. This is certainly unhealthy and, in some cases, can border on being unethical. Well-developed goals tell the counselor and the client where the counseling process is heading, how to get to the client's destination, and what it will look like when that destination has been reached.

Initially, you might respond that all counseling is goal focused. When people say that they want to get along better with a spouse or child, that's a goal. When people say that they want to develop better self-esteem, that's setting a goal. When you seek to help clients work through transference issues, that's working from a goal. Yes, all of these are goals. However, they are significantly different from the types of goals that focus treatment and keep the counseling process brief.

The concept and methods of focusing treatment by means of clearly defined goals are not particularly difficult. However, this is an aspect of brief counseling that many therapists neglect to develop sufficiently. Insoo Kim Berg observed, "Of the hundreds of cases I have consulted on, supervised, and taught about around the world, the most common reason for therapists, counselors, and social workers to feel 'stuck' is related to unclear goals."[1]

In developing clear treatment goals, you need to keep three things in mind:

1. The person with whom you are working
2. Why you are working with that person
3. What change will look like in that person's situation

Initially, these criteria for clear treatment goals may appear to be obvious. After all, you have spent a good deal of time learning how to do these very things. However, in a brief-therapy approach, these three perspectives can be significantly different from what they would be in a long-term approach. It is these three concepts that, when implemented from the beginning, direct the treatment and keep brief therapy just that—brief.

THE PERSON WITH WHOM YOU ARE WORKING

Solution-based therapy views the client in a way that is particularly useful for helping to keep the counseling process on target. Clients are viewed as fitting into one of three categories: *visitors, complainants,* or *customers.* Each one of these categories describes a different motivation for entering treatment. Knowing which one of these categories best describes a particular client will influence the entire course of therapy.

Visitors

Visitors are people who come to counseling because someone else wants them there. Frequently, visitors do not see the issue that brought them to the counseling office as significant, but someone else does. Visitors do not have change as a goal since they do not see a problem with the situation. Their goal is to get someone else off their back. Suppose the following happened.

Mark and Janet have been married for three years, and they do not have any children. They are both active in their local church, which gives them many interests in common. All of their friends think that they are well suited for each other and that they get along extremely well. However, recently, things have been less than harmonious at home. When Mark and Janet come to your office, Janet states that she is tired of Mark's over-controlling nature. "All he does is tell me what to do," she says. "I'm beginning to feel that I'm incapable of making any decisions for myself."

When you ask Mark about his perspective on the situation, he states, "I don't understand what the problem is. I came here because Janet threatened to leave me if I didn't. As far as I'm concerned, we've got a great relationship. I make suggestions to her only because it's my job as the head of the house to make sure things get done right."

In this situation Mark would be classified as the visitor. The only reason that he appears to have come is Janet's insistence and threats. To begin to address his tendency to be overcontrolling is not likely to get anywhere because he does not see it as a problem. Mark is not a customer for changing this part of his behavior. For treatment to be effective with this couple, the counselor must establish goals on which both Mark and Janet can agree. In situations such as this, the counselor's job is to find out exactly what Mark would want from the counseling process.

By concretely identifying what Mark would want, the counselor has taken one of the first essential steps in brief treatment. What Mark wants out of counseling then becomes part of the treatment goal. This narrows the direction of the succeeding course of counseling, thus enabling the counselor to work in a briefer manner than in other methods of counseling.

Generally the first task with any visitor is to engage this person in treatment. Initially you do not want to give a visitor much in the way of homework. Because of the lack of investment in change, visitors are not likely to follow through with it. To assign any would be setting up failure and establishing a pattern of noncompliance. The most a visitor should be assigned would be a simple observational task: "Notice when things go a little bit better next week. Try to spot a couple of times when the two of you get along better." This is the type of task in which the visitor can be involved.

Another method of engaging visitors is to compliment them for their involvement. Their willingness to come to counseling, especially when they do not see any problem, should be recognized. Doing this as soon as you realize that the person is a visitor is a way of engaging an otherwise unwilling participant.

Complainants

The second category of person who will come to your office is the complainant. Complainants are not there because of specific problems they have, and they do not come to counseling at the insistence of someone else. *Complainants come to counseling because the behavior of another person is causing them problems.* "This client is bothered by the problem but does not see himself as part of the solution. He can describe the problem in great detail, including its patterns, its origins and what should happen but for some reason he cannot see himself taking steps to solve the problem." [2] A classic example of a complainant is the person who is married to an alcoholic. Frequently, these people seek help because of the spouse's drinking. In this situation complainants often have a good understanding of the drinking pattern and even when the spouse is able to abstain. However, these complainants come for help with a *spouse's* problem, not for help with their reaction to it.

One problem in dealing with complainants is fairly obvious. As a counselor, you cannot effectively help someone to change when that person is not coming to you for help. With complainants, the task becomes working with them to develop goals that are in their control. Sometimes this can be accomplished by directly pointing out this problem and asking the client for suggestions in solving it.

John Walter and Jane Peller suggest three additional strategies for dealing with the complainant who asks for help. One way of effectively managing this situation is to discuss what the future might look like if the desired change does not occur. Second, you could explore some hypothetical solutions to the problem. Or finally, you can explore what is behind the client's attempted solutions.[3]

Customers

Customers come to treatment because they have a problem or several problems that they want to resolve. Customers are self-motivated and want to change. They know why they are coming to treatment and generally have some idea of what they want to get out of the process. According to Berg, "The client, both verbally and nonverbally, indicates that he is at a point of wanting to do something about the problem."[4]

In working with clients who are customers, follow this general principle: Sell customers only what they want to buy! When clients come to you for treatment of depression, do not look for parent-child issues or control issues. Instead, focus on treating the depression that prompted them to seek help. Or if clients who are clearly personality disordered ask for help with panic attacks, treat only the panic attack.

Imagine that a thirty-five-year-old man seeks help because he is not getting along with his wife. In the course of treatment he is told that he has problems with unresolved issues from his family of origin that he must take care of before he can have a better relationship with his wife. So before he begins to learn general relations skills and ways of being more empathetic, he has to take care of these unresolved issues. This shifting of focus can be a psychological version of the old bait-and-switch sales technique. Most of us would not be happy if we went into an appliance store and the salesperson attempted to sell us a television that was three hundred dollars more than the advertised model that we came into the store to buy. Yet in counseling, we often expect clients to accept something that they did not initially want. In some situations, encountering resistance can be the by-product of not treating clients for the issues for which they are customers.

It should also be noted that clients who are classified as customers would roughly correspond to either Prochaska's preparation or action stages initially. As counseling progresses, they would likely move into the maintenance stage.

WHY YOU ARE DEALING WITH THAT PERSON

During the first session with your client, it is essential for you to answer two questions: "Why is the client coming for help at *this* particular time?" and "How is this situation a problem?" The answers to these two questions will greatly help you to narrow the focus of treatment and work in a more time-effective manner.

In addressing the first question, you need to know what prompted the client to seek help now instead of two weeks ago or instead of two weeks from now. When you clarify the reason the client is seeking help now, you gain important information about the client's coping mechanisms and view of what the problem is. A woman may have experienced periodic bouts of depression for a number of years. But she seeks help now because she has been staying in bed for the last two weeks, unable to go to work. The depression, while it was unpleasant, was manageable until it began to interfere with work. In this situation, understanding the precipitant for seeking counseling gives you direction for the initial treatment. For this woman it was essential to get back to work. She could deal with her emotional responses later.

The answer to the second question—"How is this a problem?"—will assist in further isolating the focus of the treatment. The question helps you shift into the client's framework rather than proceed with treatment on the basis of a false assumption. It is easy to think that you know why something is problematic, and yet you may be mistaken.

A pastor comes to you for help because he is having trouble with a woman he has been counseling. All of a sudden she is leaving notes and gifts on his desk at the church. She has also begun periodically calling him at home for help when a new problem overwhelms her. When you hear these details, it is easy to assume that the pastor wants to learn how to manage this woman so that she will not be so invasive. However, when you ask the pastor how this situation is a problem, he tells you he can't sleep, can't concentrate, is having stomach difficulties and general anxiety symptoms. The problem was not the woman's behavior. The pastor knew how to manage that. The problem was the anxiety reaction that he was experiencing. Not only did he not understand why he reacted this way or what to do about it, but he also wanted to make sure that he did not respond this way to future counseling situations.

Clarifying how a particular situation is a problem is essential for focused treatment. Without this clarification, you run the risk of attempting to treat things that are not necessarily the main problem or are not what the client wants treated.

WHAT CHANGE WILL LOOK LIKE IN THAT PERSON'S SITUATION

Once you have determined whether you are dealing with a customer, a visitor, or a complainant and have determined what the client wants to accomplish, you are ready to set goals for the counseling process. Goal setting is a skill that is not often taught in counseling courses. However, if you are going to operate in a time-effective manner, goals become essential. Goals are the road map for the counseling process, and they let you know when you have reached the destination.

Goals are specific objectives that you and the client develop to define what the end product of treatment will look like. Clearly defined goals answer the question, How will we know when the client is done with counseling? Effective goals communicate what the client wants to change and sets up ways to recognize when the client has accomplished the goals. Effective goals are *observable, attainable, specific, measurable,* and *positively focused.*

Observable

When a goal is observable, it is stated in such a way that the counselor and the client can see change. Observable goals define what the client will be doing differently as a result of counseling. When goals are stated in terms of observable behavior, it becomes much easier to determine when change has occurred. If goals are stated in terms of internal feelings and perceptions, change becomes very difficult to measure.

Suppose a couple's goal is to enjoy each other. You have to do some guesswork as to whether or not the goal has been met. Unless you are skilled at mind reading, it can be difficult to determine whether the couple is actually enjoying each other or putting on an act. However, when the couple sets the goal of being able to go out on a date without arguing, it becomes much easier to determine whether or not the goal has been met. It is possible to observe whether or not they have gone on a date. And they can report whether or not they had any arguments.

Sometimes it gets difficult to state goals in terms of observable behavior. The DSM-IV *(Diagnostic and Statistical Manual-IV)* lists one of the criteria for depressive disorder as a subjective feeling of depression. Frequently, people who are depressed will acknowledge this experience. So how do you set a goal that is observable when the client legitimately wants to change a feeling? One way is to state the goal in terms of the client's report. Thus, the goal could be that the client consistently reports feeling hopeful and encouraged. By stating the goal this way, the client's report becomes the observable behavior.

Attainable

The second characteristic of effective goals is that they are attainable. At first it would appear that this characteristic does not need to be pointed out. After all, why would someone set a goal that cannot be attained?

We don't intentionally set unattainable goals, but sometimes we or our clients have unrealistic expectations. When clients say that they do not want to feel depressed anymore, that is somewhat unrealistic. People experience mood changes in the course of daily living. At times we all feel mildly depressed. To expect never to feel depressed is an unattainable goal. When a counselor decides that a sixteen-year-old boy should always agree with his parents' decisions, the counselor has set an unattainable goal. Sixteen-year-olds will never completely agree with their parents. Individuality and forming one's own opinions are part of the growth toward independence.

When fourteen-year-old Ron first came to counseling, he was brought by his parents. They came because of numerous problems in his behavior. He had frequently been sent to the principal's office for fighting in school. Often when he was not fighting, he was not in school. When he was not in school, he was at home or at a friend's house, usually getting into trouble by smoking and stealing.

Quickly the goals for Ron became that he would attend school and remain in class instead of getting sent to the principal's office. When he was not at school, he would be at home or at friends' houses that had been preapproved by his parents. In addition, he would become involved in a hobby of his own choosing. Finally, there would be no more incidents of theft or fighting.

All of the goals that were mentioned were well within Ron's ability to accomplish. He could easily go to class, refrain from fighting, and fulfill the other expectations. In addition, it was very easy for his parents to determine whether or not he had accomplished them. He either went to school or he did not. When he was at school, he was either in the expected place or he was in the principal's office. Progress toward these goals was not only attainable but also easy to measure.

Specific

The next element in setting effective goals is to make sure that they are specific. Specific goals are those that communicate exactly what the end product will look like. Unfortunately this can be one of the more difficult characteristics for you to achieve. When clients come into the office and state that they want to feel better, they are not setting a specific goal. "Feeling better" can mean a wide variety of things, depending on who is saying it. Even stating that a person does not want to be depressed is not much more specific. You need to know what feeling better or not being depressed looks like to *that* person. A depression-free state can look different in different people. For a goal to be specific, it must communicate exactly what the client will be doing when he or she has achieved the goal. Take a look at the following goals, and try to decide which ones are specific and fit the criteria that have been given.

- At the end of counseling, the client will have a better relationship with her parents.
- In two weeks the client will report having calmly talked with her parents instead of arguing when she disagreed with their decision.
- When counseling is over, the client will know new ways of getting along with her parents.

It is easy to see that the first goal is not specific enough. A "better relationship" can mean a variety of things, depending on who you ask. For the client, a better relationship may mean that her parents give her a later curfew and not ask her where she is going. On the other hand, her parents may define a better relationship as having their daughter accept their rules without questioning them.

The second goal is specific. This goal spells out the change that is to occur in terms of observable actions. It would be very easy to determine whether the client has met this goal because there are two specific tasks built into it. First, there is the client's report. Either she does or doesn't give the counselor the information. There is no room for misinterpretation. The second way to determine whether or not this goal has been met depends on the client's actions at home. The client will know when she is disagreeing with her parents. From that point it will be very easy to determine, by her arguing or lack of it, whether or not she has met the goal. In this situation, her parents will also likely be able to tell whether the goal has been met.

What about the third goal? At first glance it may seem that it is specific. However, "knowing something" can be a vague goal because it can be open to different interpretations. It is also very difficult to determine whether a person actually knows how to do something if there is no specific standard by which to judge this knowledge. To make this goal a specific one, you would need to include some way to measure the goal.

Measurable

The fourth criterion for treatment goals is that they need to be measurable. A measurable goal is one that quantifies what the change process looks like. It states *how* you will know that an acceptable level of change has occurred. At this point you may be asking, "Can we really measure change?" And the answer to that question is a definite yes—if you conceptualize the change in measurable terms.

Consider the situation of Martha, a fifty-seven-year-old woman who came to counseling because she was almost incapacitated by fear and anxiety. Ever since she was the victim of a purse snatching two years ago, she has had periodic episodes of extreme anxiety. She would begin to shake, her breathing would become rapid, and she would become very confused. When these anxiety attacks would occur, Martha was barely able to speak. These attacks became so frequent that she was afraid she would have to quit her job. How would you set a treatment goal for her in measurable terms?

Before setting treatment goals for Martha, you need additional information. First, you need to know how often these panic episodes are occurring. It could be twice a week, twice a day, or twice an hour. Second, you need to know something about the intensity of the attacks. A simple 1–10 scale can be helpful for measuring the severity of Martha's attacks . In this situation, you could have Martha subjectively rate the severity of her attacks, with 1 being very mild and 10 representing incapacitation.

A treatment goal for Martha could focus on reducing the frequency of her anxiety attacks. A measurable goal could be that Martha would report that her attacks had decreased from two a day to only twice a week. Another goal, focusing on the severity of her attacks, could be that Martha would report that they decreased in severity from an 8 to a 2. And at a 2 they were mild enough that the anxiety presented only a minor nuisance. When the goal is stated in measurable terms, it becomes possible to measure change.

Positively Focused

The final criterion for effective treatment goals is that they need to be positive in focus. A positive focus is not a goal that is optimistic rather than pessimistic. Rather, a positive goal is one that is linguistically positive, stating what the client will do, as opposed to what the client will refrain from doing. To state that a client will begin doing specific tasks that have been identified with feeling cheerful is a positive goal because it indicates what the client will do. To state that a client will no longer feel depressed is a negative goal because it indicates what the client will not do.

The very act of stating that a client will not be doing something is a way of reinforcing the undesirable action. When you are on a diet and you want to control the amount you eat, you can focus on not eating. And what happens when you do this? You are constantly thinking of the food that you are not supposed to eat. This constant focus frequently makes the desire for the forbidden stronger. A more effective strategy would be to plan out the type of eating patterns and specific foods that you would eat to get to your goal.

Walter and Peller make a strong argument for stating goals in this manner. "The reason for stating the goal in a linguistically positive way is that we want the client to be developing a representation of the goal in his or her mind and experience. This can be a visual representation, it can be words or sounds, it can be feelings or sensations. The representation will likely include some or all of these sensory modalities. The critical piece is that the representation has to be something rather than the absence of something."[5]

To review, remember the five criteria of effective treatment goals. Goals can help keep treatment focused and help the client achieve the desired results when they are observable, attainable, specific, measurable, and positively focused. Take a minute now and review the following goals. Determine which ones fit all the criteria.

1. The client will develop appropriate modes of expression.
2. The client will initiate talking with three different friends for at least fifteen minutes as a way of changing her patterns of social isolation.
3. The client will report that on five specific occasions he has not yelled at his mother.
4. When in a situation that had previously provoked a panic attack, the client will use the relaxation techniques that have been learned.

If you said that numbers 2 and 4 fit the criteria for acceptable goals, you were right. If you thought that either number 1 or number 3 fit the criteria, go back and review the description of the types of goals that help to focus treatment. Goal number 3 might look as if it fits the criteria, but remember that effective goals identify what clients *will* be doing, not what they won't be doing.

BRIEF INTERVENTIONS

After you know who you are working with, why you are working with this person, and what change will look like in this person's situation, then the task becomes making sure that the counseling process stays on track. You can do a number of things to make sure you stay on track. These are not necessarily unique to a brief and focused approach. However, these techniques are consistent with this approach and facilitate effective brief counseling. We have found that these interventions or modifications of them can be useful tools in the change process.

Jerry Gale, who has written about the linguistic analysis of counseling, reviewed the work of O'Hanlon and Wilk as well as the work of O'Hanlon and Weiner-Davis. In reviewing *Shifting Contexts: The Generation of Effective Psychotherapy* and *In Search of Solutions: A New Direction in Psychotherapy,* Gale found ten interventions that were used with brief, solution-oriented counseling.[6] I list these ten interventions here and make brief observations about each one.

1. Speaking the client's language. This intervention describes the counselor's use of the client's spoken language (words, phrases, or metaphors) and paralanguage (emotional tone). When counselors speak the client's language, the client feels understood.

2. Presupposing change. This technique employs questions that assume change will occur. These types of questions ask *when* not *if* change occurs and assumes that change can be past or future focused. When a counselor asks, "When did you get angry back then?" it implies that there are times *now* that the client does not get angry. Asking, "When you have more confidence, how will you recognize it?" implies that the client will get to the point of having more confidence.

3. Multiple-choice questions. This technique uses questions that have imbedded in them possible answers that move the client in the direction the therapist would want to go. A mother has previously indicated that she feels calmer when she prays, takes a walk, or reviews a specific Scripture passage. In discussing the mother's tactics in managing her anger at her daughter, the counselor could ask, "The next time you begin to feel angry at your daughter, do you want to pray or review your Scripture passage?"

4. Therapeutic interruption. This intervention is designed to redirect the conversation toward a goal-directed solution. When a client says, "When I was in that situation, I felt extremely depressed. It was as if I was revisiting my childhood all over again. If that happens again, I—" the counselor intentionally interrupts the conversation and says, "Situations like that can be upsetting, but now tell me about a time when you were in a similar situation but did not feel depressed." This interruption serves the purpose of steering the conversation in a more constructive direction that leads toward the goal.

5. *Normalizing the problem*. This intervention describes the problem as a natural and normal occurrence rather than something pathological. A mother becomes depressed when her eighteen-year-old daughter goes to college. Initially the counselor empathizes with the mother's feelings. But then the counselor normalizes the situation by saying that the client is going through a common developmental adjustment. And in addition, many others in her situation would feel the same way she does.

6. *Summarizing with a twist*. This intervention summarizes a conversation but turns the summary into a solution-oriented direction. When the client understands that the summary is an equally valid way of looking at the situation, change can occur. The client can then define the situation differently. This new definition allows the client to act differently in the future. The counselor might say, "So yesterday you and your wife were upset with each other, yet instead of continuing the argument, you were able to stop it. That's great! What's also fantastic is that later you and your wife were able to pray together, when usually after a disagreement you two go for a day without speaking to each other. How were you able to do that?"

7. *Utilization*. This intervention is the process of accepting the client's perspective rather than rejecting, disagreeing with, or resisting how the client describes a situation. This technique helps the client move from a comfortable position to the goal. When a husband states that he nags his wife because he loves her and wants the best for her, utilization would dictate that the counselor accept that explanation rather than explain the husband's actions in terms of passive-aggressive behavior.

8. *Providing obvious solutions*. In this intervention the counselor offers commonsense suggestions. These can be suggestions for new behaviors or alternative ways of doing things. While brief counseling encourages clients to develop their own solutions, sometimes clients honestly don't have a clue about what to do. A sixteen-year-old boy and his father are in constant conflict over getting the chores done at home. The father wants them done before he gets home from work at six o'clock. When the chores are not completed by then, he says that his son is being lazy and uncooperative. The son claims that he does not have time to do them

because he doesn't get home from football practice until five o'clock. The father is frustrated and at a loss as to how to get past this deadlock. At this point the counselor can suggest that the father sit down with his son and negotiate an alternative time frame that will work better for both of them. This may seem like an obvious intervention for the father to attempt. However, sometimes clients are not aware of obvious options. You need to be sure that you don't fall into the trap of giving advice. However, when clients don't know what to do, pointing out the obvious can be helpful.

9. *Introducing doubt.* This intervention raises a question about the client's assumption or belief. When you help the client to find exceptions to problems or to see the situation differently, you create doubt. This doubt about previously held beliefs and explanations helps the client to move ahead. A wife complains that her husband is controlling and will not let her make a decision on her own. You create doubt when you suggest that the husband is well meaning though possibly misdirected in his efforts, that his control is his way of trying to protect her and express his love. This allows the wife to consider alternative ways of responding to her husband's actions.

10. *Future focus.* This final intervention directs the client toward what the future will look like when change has occurred. A future focus includes the use of assumptive language, in which it is assumed that change will occur. In this intervention, counselors talk about *when* change happens rather than *if* it happens.

> *Counselor:* Bob, you said that you want to feel more confident in making decisions at your job. What will you be doing differently *when* that happens?
>
> *Bob:* I guess I might go up to my boss and make a suggestion about an improvement that I think we need to make.
>
> *Counselor:* What do you think your boss will notice *when* you develop this type of confidence?
>
> *Bob:* Well, he'll probably notice that I'm not asking him as many questions. Instead, I will go ahead and do what I know needs to be done.

A clear focus for treatment is essential for working in brief counseling. This focus comes from defining who you are working with, why you are working with that person, and what change will look like for that person. The task then becomes structuring the counseling to match these characteristics. Defining change in terms of specific, well-developed goals also helps to maintain focus. Finally, it is important to use interventions that are consistent with a brief approach to counseling.

Keeping counseling brief but effective is a mind-set that determines how the process will unfold. The goals and structure that facilitate the process need to be consistent from one session to the next. In the next chapter we will address how to keep this mind-set going in the second and subsequent sessions. This includes not only what occurs in session but also what happens between sessions and after the counseling is over.

9/ AFTER *the* FIRST SESSION: KEEPING CHANGE GOING

*Long-standing custom will make resistance, but by a better habit
shall it be subdued.*   THOMAS À KEMPIS, *The Imitation of Christ*

It is one thing to begin the counseling process; it is another to keep it
going effectively. The first session is fairly structured in that there is specific
information that you need to gather. If you have reasonable counseling
skills, connect well with clients, and are thorough in gathering the
necessary information, your chances of having a successful first session are
good. What becomes a challenge, then, is continuing this process through
several sessions.

This chapter will look at a variety of ways to promote change as the
counseling process continues. To do this, we will consider the different
scenarios clients present when they come back to sessions and ways
you can deal with them. Also we will look at general interventions, the
spiritual aspects of brief therapy, homework, and the termination
process.

EVALUATING CHANGE

To start out effectively, the second and subsequent sessions ought to begin
with two things. First, ask the question "What has changed or gone better
since the last session?" This simple question focuses clients' minds on

solutions and exceptions and sets the direction of the session. Second, review the previous week's homework assignment. When you assign homework, you need to follow up on it in the next session. If you neglect to do this, you give clients the mistaken message that homework is not important and is optional.

When clients return for the second or subsequent sessions, they will report that one of three things has occurred: positive change has occurred; no change has occurred; or the situation is worse. Your reaction and how you continue with the counseling will depend on the category into which the clients fall. No matter what the situation, your task continues to be encouraging the clients to find ways either to do more of what is working or to do something that is different.

Change Has Occurred

When clients return to a session and report that change has occurred, spend a significant amount of time affirming this. Reinforcing the positive change involves amplifying the details of the success and finding ways to congratulate clients for what they have done right. This is important even if the change is small and clients classify it as insignificant.

Reinforcing clients at the start of a session can set the tone for the rest of the time. Insoo Kim Berg and Scott Miller have found that "it is important to focus on successes in the beginning of the session. When clients have had an opportunity to discuss their successes during the beginning of the session, subsequent discussions of other, more serious problems seem to be less overwhelming and discouraging."[1]

Encouraging clients in their progress can come through a variety of statements and questions.

- Wow! That's fantastic!
- How were you able to do that?
- How did you know that would help?
- What gave you the idea to try that?
- That is great! How did it help you?

Whatever phrases you choose to convey your support and encouragement, communicate sincerely. Clients will be able to tell if you do not believe what you are saying. And if you don't believe it, chances are they won't believe it.

Also, when you reinforce clients, you need to let them know that what they did was significant, even if it was small. Clients can dismiss small change as either chance or insignificant in comparison with the problem. To facilitate change, you may need to educate them on the value of small change.

Finally, what you say to encourage clients should put the responsibility for the change in their control. If change is a result of circumstances or the counselor's actions, clients have less of a chance of repeating it.

When positive change has occurred, you can employ what Matthew Selekman calls "consolidating questions."[2] These types of questions can be particularly helpful for reinforcing positive change that has already occurred and for building on that change in the future.

Consolidating questions are questions that focus on the progress and the mechanics necessary to maintain the change. The following are a few examples of consolidating questions.

- What will you have to do to continue this progress?
- If you could see into the future, what changes do you think your wife will notice next week?
- If this were our last counseling session, what will have changed from how things are now? What will you have to do for that to happen?
- What do you have to do to prevent a setback?

One mistake that you can easily make is to move too quickly past this stage of reinforcing gains. If any significant and positive change has occurred from your perspective, you need to spend adequate time examining it. This examination is done by asking clients detailed questions about the situation. It includes isolating what happened and the chain of events leading up to the change. You may want to inquire as to who else noticed the change and what gave the clients the idea that this person noticed. This type of in-depth questioning can take a good deal of time, but it communicates to clients that you consider these details to be an important part of the progress. This questioning also changes clients' perspective and encourages them to approach the situation in ways that develop solutions.

No Change Has Occurred

When clients return to a session and report that nothing is different, your first task is to determine whether the reports are accurate. Sometimes small changes occur, but clients either discount them or do not notice them. When you focus on asking exception-finding questions, such as the ones discussed in chapter 5, you can sometimes spot changes that clients have missed. If this occurs, then you proceed to point out these exceptions and amplify them.

A specific method of assessing for exceptions is to ask clients whether they have seen a day or even a short period of time when things were better than they were at the previous session. In doing this, be sure to obtain detailed information about the exceptions because it will serve as building blocks for future change. Probe thoroughly for exceptions before you assume that things are not changing and you move on to another approach.

You can also assess for unnoticed change by using scaling questions:

Counselor: You mention that things haven't changed since the last time we met. As far as you can tell, nothing has changed?

Bill: That's right.

Counselor: On a one-to-ten scale, where would you put yourself right now?

Bill: I'd probably say a three. Yeah that would be right, a three.

Counselor: Last week when I asked you that question, you put yourself at a two. What's the difference? What helped you go from a two to a three?

In this example the client is identifying change even though he originally stated that nothing is different. Whatever the client identifies as contributing to the 3 is an exception and can be viewed as progress. The counselor's job now becomes amplifying that change. Even if the client rated things as a 3 due to a vague subjective feeling, that is significant. Most clients, when they think long enough, can identify some small reason for why the rating is higher.

Berg and Miller have observed that when clients report that no change occurred between sessions, it may be that the change was not dramatic or fast enough for them.[3] In this situation it is important to acknowledge and validate the clients' feelings. Subsequently, it may be necessary to educate clients as to the nature of change and the phenomenon of change occurring in small steps.

It is also important to realize that clients may have experienced negative events just before coming to the counseling session. If this has happened, it can influence their assessment of the whole week, even though they may have made progress. In this case it is again helpful to validate the clients' feeling but then tactfully begin probing for exceptions. When exceptions are identified in this situation, the result can be hope and encouragement for clients.

If it is not possible to generate any exceptions from the clients, the next strategy is to explore what kept things from getting worse. This can give important clues as to the clients' skills and coping strategies.

Twelve-year-old Rob threw temper tantrums of monumental proportions. When his mother brought him to counseling, the counselor suggested that both the mother and the son should be involved in working on this situation. When they came in for their second session, the mother reported that things hadn't changed. Notice what the counselor did with this report of no progress.

Counselor: So, last week the two of you had a blowup. How was it different from other times that happened?

The mother: (somewhat begrudgingly) Well, Rob did not get quite as angry as he has before. Also, his volume was lower.

Counselor: (to Rob) You mean you controlled things better than you had before?"

Rob: (sheepishly) Yeah, I guess I did.

Counselor: That's great! How did you manage to do that?

Rob: This time Mom didn't keep going on about things. She backed off and left me alone for a while. Then I was able to cool off.

Counselor: (to Rob's mom) Good job! I'm impressed! Usually when these things happen, the arguments keep on until something gets broken. How did you manage to stop things when you did?

The mother: I thought about what we said last week and decided to go into the other room for a while. I figured that Rob and I could talk about the issue later when we were both calmed down.

Counselor: Congratulations! You both did a great job of starting to change things. Now let's see how we can get that to happen again.

At times things really will not have changed between sessions. Barbara McFarland, who has implemented brief therapy with the difficult area of eating disorders, suggests four steps that can help you maintain perspective and decide what you need to do next.

1. Separate the person from the problem. Stay focused on the client's strengths and resources.
2. Do not take a position regarding the client's situation. Refrain from speculating about the client or making assumptions related to the lack of progress.
3. Check if the client's goal is the same or if it has changed. Begin to discuss specifically what difference the client wants to see as a result of therapy. If the client's goal seems to have changed, share your observation with the client.
4. Evaluate the client's stage of change more carefully.[4]

In implementing McFarland's suggestions, it is important to pay close attention to number 4. Clients who are in the precontemplation, contemplation, or preparative stages may not be ready to do anything yet. Be sure to work with these clients according to the stage they are in.[5] After assessing the situation from these perspectives, if you continue to be unsure of what to do, it may very well be time to implement one of the strategies suggested for getting unstuck (see chapter 12).

The Situation Is Worse

The third scenario is that clients come to the second session and report that things got worse. When this occurs, it may be time to do something different from what has been attempted previously. But before actually taking that step, reassess the treatment goals, and determine whether they are on track. In addition, you will want to make sure that these goals are reasonable and that the clients are not attempting to take too big a step.

When Rhonda, whom we met in chapter 7, came back for the second session, things had gotten worse.

> *Counselor:* So tell me, how have things changed since we met last? What's better?
>
> *Rhonda:* Nothing. I haven't heard from that job that I interviewed for. On top of that, I just feel rotten. I still hang out in the basement. And I don't feel any better. If things don't get better soon, I'm going to just give up. When I left here last week, I had some hope. I thought everything would change. But, boy, was I wrong. It seems that things are worse than ever.
>
> *Counselor:* When you say "everything," what do you mean?
>
> *Rhonda:* I thought that I would be more energetic, that I would be able to land at least two more job interviews, that I would maybe have a job offer—
>
> *Counselor:* (interrupting her rapid-fire list) Wait a minute. Those are all great things. But do you remember the homework that I gave you last time?
>
> *Rhonda:* Yes, but what does that have to do with anything?
>
> *Counselor:* Well, if you remember, I asked you to notice a couple of things and to review some Scripture. I asked you to do those things because change will happen one step at a time. Change comes in little pieces. The steps you take are very important, and they will build on each other. However, the steps are small. It sounds as if you are expecting too much.

Rhonda was attempting to do more than was reasonable. That set her up for feeling that things had gotten worse.

However, sometimes things do get worse. The process of change is not a smooth upward climb. Most people experience peaks of progress and valleys of setbacks. When clients are aware of this, they may be able to handle the setbacks better.

From Berg's perspective a setback is an internal reminder of the need to remain vigilant.[6] When you reframe the situation like this, then a setback has the potential for becoming a useful learning tool rather than a failure.

When a setback does occur, an effective strategy can be to focus on what the client did to keep the situation from getting worse than it did. Ask questions like these:

- How did you stop the argument from getting worse?
- When you had the panic attack, what did you do to end it?
- What helpful things did your wife do when you were feeling so down?
- When you got angry, what would your husband say was different about this time?

Questions like these help clients know that they are making progress in spite of setbacks. In reality the way that clients handle the inevitable setbacks can be a measure of the change that is occurring. Using this approach also helps clients to identify problem-solving strategies that work for them.

Some of these questions appear to be very similar to those you might ask when clients are reporting that positive change is occurring. In actuality they are. However, the repetition of questions can be a learning tool for clients. Having to think through the same grid can be a part of reshaping how clients view situations and thus facilitate their ability to develop solutions. In addition, it is helpful for clients to be forced to explain occurrences. The more they do this, the more likely they will be to develop plausible solutions and explanations. This then develops their repertoire of problem-solving skills.

When things are worse, reevaluate the situation. If the client is experiencing only a minor setback, then it is reasonable to continue with the same approach, at least for a time. However, if things are significantly worse, then it is time to review your goals and consider shifting approaches. Don't continue doing what doesn't work.

TECHNIQUES THAT PROMOTE CHANGE

You have been exposed to a number of basic techniques up to this point. However, we all know that clients are infinitely varied. And no matter how skilled you are or how hard you try, what works for one client may not work for another. We offer some additional techniques or variations on techniques that you have seen. We hope that this will help as you adapt to unique clients and situations.

Modified Scaling

We have talked about scaling as a technique for promoting and measuring change. In addition to the 1–10 scale, you can use another method of scaling. In some situations it can be more effective to use a scale that is based on percentages. When you do this, 100 percent represents the goal that the clients are attempting to attain. Clients feel that they make more progress when they see it move from 20 percent to 90 percent than when the progress moves from a 2 to a 9. However, for some clients change comes very slowly and in extremely small steps. When this occurs, it can be difficult to measure the change on a 1–10 scale. On a percentage scale you can more easily measure the very small steps and thus reinforce this change.

Reinforcing Change

At times, your main focus may not be facilitating change. Instead, it may be reinforcing the change that has already occurred. In this situation a helpful tactic may be to review what has been helpful and have clients identify what they want to continue in the future. Notice how this works with a family.

> *Counselor:* You have all been making good progress. What helpful things would you want to continue in the future? What things will help you all get along as well as you have been doing recently?

> **The father:** I guess one thing that I can do is make sure that we continue to have family meetings. We always seem to get along better when we do that.
>
> **The mother:** The next time I feel uptight, I'm going to take a walk. The last time I did that, everything mellowed out afterward, and we didn't get into another brawl.
>
> **The son:** If Mom and Dad can do those things, we won't have any problems.
>
> **Counselor:** What do *you* need to do to help the whole family get along as well as they have been?
>
> **The son:** I guess I could continue to take a time-out when I find myself getting upset. That seems to help everything go better.

Confusion Technique

Sometimes clients will give you contradictory information. They say that they want to change, but then they don't follow through. They state that a specific goal is important, but they can't seem to accomplish the necessary steps. When this situation occurs, the confusion technique can be a powerful intervention. "Confusion" may even be more effective than direct confrontation because it places the responsibility for solving the problem on the client.

> **Counselor:** We've been working together for a while now, and you've made good progress. But I'm confused about something. You were clear that you thought the next step was to get back into church on a regular basis. We've talked about ways that you can do this, and you've even identified some good solutions to the issues that kept you away. Yet no matter what we do, it doesn't seem that this next step happens. Help me understand this situation.

Early Warning System

In situations where there is excessive anger or other impulsive behavior, it can be helpful to develop an early warning system. Frequently, impulsive behavior is not as impulsive as it looks. Often it can actually be the result of a chain of small events. When this occurs, clients need to identify the specific links in the chain so that they can intervene at the earliest possible stage. Clients will have more success changing patterns when they intervene early than if they wait until they are on the verge of acting. Developing an early warning system is simply having clients identify the first small step in their chain and then planning an appropriate alternative action that will lead away from the buildup.

Rich had a history of explosive anger. When he got angry, which he did several times a week, he would usually end up breaking something. For him, it was extremely helpful to learn to recognize the signs that indicated he was beginning to get angry. After discussing the idea of early warning signs with his counselor, Rich noticed that when he was frustrated, he would begin feeling tension in his neck. He would also start to talk at a more rapid pace than usual. These signs usually occurred when he thought that someone was not understanding him. After identifying these signs, Rich began to walk away from situations when he noticed the signs occurring. After cooling down for ten minutes, he found that he could handle the situation in a more rational manner. When he began using this approach, Rich found that the times when he exploded had decreased drastically.

Give Clients Choice

Despite the fact that some clients want to change, they will react negatively to any specific suggestion that you give them. Sometimes all they need to become oppositional is to think that you are suggesting something. One way around this is to give them a list of options instead of making a direct suggestion. When giving clients homework assignments, you can say, "I would like you to read a specific book that could be helpful for you." Or you could say, "Do you think it would be more helpful if you were to read, discuss the situation with your spouse, or observe what you are doing differently during those times when you are not arguing?"

A Reminder of Comfort

With some clients, especially ones who have been traumatized or are extremely anxious, it can helpful for them to develop a symbolic reminder of comfort—something tangible that they can carry around with them and then pull out when they are upset. For this to work, clients must attach some symbolic meaning to the object, a meaning that speaks comfort to them. When helping clients decide on a specific object, steer them toward something that is small enough to carry around at all times.

The symbol can be

- a small rock that reminds the client that "Jesus is our rock"
- a handwritten note that says, "Those who live in the shelter of the Most High will find rest in the shadow of the Almighty" (Ps. 91:1)
- a small nail that is a reminder of Jesus' love for us, shown by his death on the cross
- any small object to which the client attaches significance and a special meaning

SPIRITUAL INTERVENTIONS

Integrating spiritual resources into the change process is an important component of how we work. The integration of the spiritual is not merely using a number of techniques that emphasize Bible reading, prayer, and Scripture memory, though we may use all of these methods. Rather, integration begins with our understanding of who God is and how he made people. Integration also involves basing our presuppositions for how we work on these understandings.

When we work from a spiritual basis alongside a solution-oriented one, we find ourselves dealing with spiritual issues in different settings. We can deal with spiritual issues in the counseling session as well as in our homework assignments. At times, we find ourselves using spiritual principles to develop solutions and promote change. At other times we may directly discuss spiritual problems in a counseling session as part of the change that clients want to make.

Spiritual Perspectives in Session

Christian counselors debate about whether or not it is appropriate to pray with clients. On one side, the argument is that prayer can create an unhealthy dependency or reinforce clients' denial. The other side of the argument is that prayer is a powerful spiritual tool that God has given us.

Mark McMinn, author of *Psychology, Theology, and Spirituality in Christian Counseling,* identifies another perspective on this debate. "'Should counselors pray with clients?' is the wrong question to ask. Instead, we ought to ask, 'Which forms of prayer should we use with which clients and under which circumstances?' If we focus too intently on the question of praying with clients in sessions, we overlook other important questions about prayer in counseling. For example, how often do we pray silently for our clients during a counseling session? How often do we pray for our clients outside of the counseling session?"[7]

Prayer is an integral part of the work we do. At times that means praying for the clients we are working with. At other times it means directly praying with the clients, with their permission. Prayer in session is an acknowledgment of both the counselor's and the client's dependency on God for wisdom and ultimately any lasting change that occurs. When praying a for client in session, it is important to understand the client with whom you are working. Praying with a particular client may not be the best thing to do. This depends on the client's personality structure and how he or she will interpret prayer.

Spiritual interventions in session can build on existing resources. Clients who are already involved in a local church should take advantage of the resources there to develop solutions. When clients are feeling isolated, involvement in a fellowship group may be an effective intervention. Sharing struggles in a safe environment other than the counseling office and knowing that someone will pray can be an important step in the change process. Accountability groups are another effective means of encouraging clients to stay on track. Some of the spiritual issues clients will bring up in a counseling session are beyond our ability to address; we are wise to refer clients to their pastors for help with those issues. On the other hand, some spiritual issues are within our training to address, and dealing with them is essential to the change process. In those situations you can use some of the solution-based techniques that we have suggested.

Ken: You know, I just don't feel very close to God anymore. My spiritual life is going down the tubes, and I don't know what to do about it.

Counselor: It sounds as if there was a time when you felt better about your relationship with God.

Ken: Yes, I suppose there was.

Counselor: Think back to that time. What were you doing differently? What allowed you to walk more closely with Jesus?

Ken: Well, it's hard to remember, but I suppose I was praying a bit more. I was probably reading my Bible, and I guess I went to church more than just once a month.

Counselor: Those are all important things. Which one of those would you like to see change first?

Ken: I suppose I would like to read my Bible. But you know, it's so hard.

Counselor: If you were to make just a small change in the amount of time you spend reading your Bible, what would you do?

Ken: I don't know. I guess I could start reading Psalms again.

Counselor: That sounds good. How many days this week would that need to happen for you to feel just a little bit closer to God?

Ken: I think it would help if I could do that even two days.

While most of our Christian clients will already be comfortable praying about their problem situations, they may need some direction about how they can pray differently. When Martha was in counseling for her depression, she expressed lots of resentment toward her husband, and that resentment was contributing to her depression. At one point, she mentioned that she was praying for her husband to change his habits. When the counselor suggested that she begin praying slightly differently, Martha saw some change.

Counselor: I'm glad to see that you are praying about your situation rather than trying to make your husband change. That would likely bring only more frustration and get the two of you battling. But could I make a suggestion? I'd like you to shift the focus of your prayers slightly.

Martha: I'm not sure I understand.

Counselor: Instead of asking God to change your husband, I'd like you to spend the next week thanking God for your husband and focusing on his strong points.

Martha: I guess I could do that, but what good would it do?

Counselor: I've found that when we have problems with other people, it is easy to get things out of perspective and to focus only on what they do wrong. Scripture is filled with examples of praying with thanksgiving for others. When you pray in this way, you can sometimes get a better perspective on the situation.

When Martha came back the next week, she reported having begun to pray as the counselor had suggested. And in addition, she noted, "I've found that my husband is easier to live with. I guess I was so focused on his irritating behavior that I forgot his qualities that I really like."

Scripture can also be an effective tool in counseling. However, we must be careful not to use Scripture to support our personal views or to coerce clients under the guise of God's directives. When used appropriately, Scripture in session can be used to educate clients as to new perspectives or truth that can help them. Scripture can also be part of God's change process for clients.

Outside of session, Scripture can be a means of promoting further change. An effective intervention that can be used with Scripture is the *stop-think* technique. Clients who are trying to change their thought processes use note cards to help them stop, think, and change their thinking. During a devotional time or a homework assignment, they write meaningful Scripture verses on one side of note cards. On the other side of the note card, they write the word *stop.* Clients carry these note cards with them so that when they find themselves thinking in ways that are not healthy, they take a note card and read (aloud, if possible) *stop.* Then they can turn over the card and read the Scripture verse that will help them focus on the Lord's truth.

We used this intervention with Jack, who was having some obsessional thoughts. When he was around his wife, Jack would fixate on the caustic comments she used to make. Even though his wife had made significant changes in this area, he would react as if she were still making these comments to him. After his counselor explained the stop-think intervention, Jack decided to try it. On the back side of the note card he wrote out Philippians 2:3-4. "Do nothing out of selfish ambition or vain conceit, but in humility consider others better than yourselves. Each of you should look not only to your own interests, but also to the interests of others" (NIV). He chose this verse to remind himself to focus on his wife's needs and perspectives rather than on his own hurt feelings. When he came back to the next session, he told the counselor, "When I agreed to try the card idea, I was a little skeptical. I wasn't sure that it would work. But I was surprised after I tried it. When I read the verse, I find that I start to pray for my wife. Since doing this, I've found myself feeling a little better about her. My feelings haven't changed completely, but they are getting better."

HOMEWORK

While chapter 7 discussed the use of homework in the change process, we want to expand that discussion by providing some practical examples. Homework is an integral component in a solution-based approach to counseling because it helps the counseling to progress at a faster rate. With the addition of homework, clients spend more time than just the counseling session working on solutions. Homework also implies that the clients are capable of making progress without you, the counselor, directing their every step. In addition, when homework is done outside of the formal counseling setting, clients have the potential to address important issues that may never show up in your office. Homework encourages clients to develop solutions in real-life situations.

Homework should be targeted to the specific situation the client faces and to the client's goals. In addition, homework should take into consideration clients' personality traits and interests.

As you prepare homework assignments for your clients, think of three categories you can use. Homework can be educational, helping clients learn new skills or gain new information. Homework can also be solution oriented, helping clients develop solutions to problems. Finally, homework can be more problem focused or paradoxical.

Educational Homework

Educational homework is a counseling supplement that aims at helping the client to develop new skills and knowledge. When a couple lacks the skills to communicate effectively, they can grow from reading books about communication techniques. In learning to manage anger, clients may find it beneficial to read a book that focuses on anger management. When clients read, they are working outside of the counseling session on solution development. And thus, they are investing additional time in the change process.

Educational homework can also help clients gain understanding. Suppose a couple comes into your office seeking help with their eight-year-old son. They are confused and frustrated by his behavior. Yet as they share the problems with you, it becomes apparent that some of the child's behavior is very age appropriate. In this situation, it may be beneficial for the parents to read about child development. In some cases, parents can learn to tolerate what was previously termed problem behavior if they realize that it is normal and will eventually change as the child matures.

All educational homework does not have to be reading. Clients can learn new skills and gain understanding by interviewing people. An effective strategy in learning conflict resolution can be to have a couple talk with friends and ask them what techniques they have found helpful in solving disagreements. Videos can also be effective educational tools. A powerful part of the change process for a couple can be watching and discussing a video about Christian marriage.

Solution-Oriented Homework

Solution-oriented homework is given to help clients notice exceptions to problems, identify solutions that they may not have been aware of, or reinforce positive change that is already occurring. Solution-oriented homework can be focused on one of these aspects, or it may actually address more than one at a time.

It is difficult to divide homework assignments into distinct categories. However, solution-oriented homework typically involves either observational tasks or assignments that emphasize some type of action.

With observational homework, you tend to ask clients to pay attention to some aspect in their environment.

- Notice the times when you find yourself at a 3 instead of a 2, and see if you can tell what helped you to be there.

- Pay attention to the times when your miracle is happening. Who is doing what at that time?
- See if you can tell when your spouse's/child's/parent's miracle is happening.
- Notice when you are feeling a little happier.

Action-type homework involves having clients do some specific task that is aimed at developing solutions and/or reinforcing change. One example is assigning the miracle question. Ask clients to imagine what it would be like if a miracle had happened and the problems that brought them into counseling have been resolved. They are then to pick a day and act as they imagine they would act if that miracle had actually occurred. If you are using this intervention with a couple, you can add a twist: Instruct them not to tell the other spouse what day they choose until they come back to the next counseling session, but they may try to guess what day their spouse picked based on the other one's actions.

A second example involves assigning a task after you have helped your clients identify exceptions to their problems. Give your clients homework tasks that ask them to repeat the exceptions and then observe what happens.

A third application of action focuses on maintaining change that has already occurred. Ask clients to speculate about what they must do to continue some changes that have already begun. Then assign them the job of implementing these maintenance tactics.

Problem-Focused Homework

The basic goal of problem-focused homework is interrupting problem-maintaining behavior. As a secondary result, clients usually gain a greater sense of their own ability to control some problems or aspects of their situation. The activity involved in the homework frequently helps clients realize that they really can do something about situations they thought were out of their control. Make sure that these kinds of assignments are designed to fit the particular client and situation. Problem-focused homework tends to be unproductive if it is haphazardly assigned.

An effective problem-focused homework task is the *coin flip*. Tell clients to flip a coin every day when they get up. If the coin comes up heads, they are to "have" their problem that day; if the coin comes up tails, they are to act as if they were problem free. That is, they are to make their choices and generally pretend that their problem has been resolved. Frequently clients come out of this assignment with a greater sense of the behaviors that have maintained their problems.

Another homework assignment that works especially well with couples or families is the *prediction assignment*. Notice how this can work for a family where Ben, the sixteen-year-old son, has been skipping school.

> *Counselor:* I have a task for all of you to work on this week. I want to see how well each of you understands the situation. Every night I want each of you to predict whether or not Ben will stay in school the next day. You need to write out your prediction but not tell anyone else what it is.

> *The father:* You want us to try to guess? Why would I do that? I want him to stay in school. If I predicted that he was going to ditch the next day, it would be like giving him permission to do it.

> *Counselor:* It might seem like that, but until he changes his mind for himself, Ben is going to skip school whenever he wants. The reason that I want you to predict is that I want all of you to get a better understanding of the situation. I want you to see if you can figure out why Ben ditches. I don't think you know all of the reasons yet. How about it, Ben? Are you willing to try this?

> *Ben:* Yeah, I guess so, but I bet I get an A on this one.

> *Counselor:* Now, there's a second part to this assignment. Every evening you have to get together for a few minutes, share what your prediction was for that day, and then explain what that prediction was based on. Do you think you could do this?

> *The mother:* (somewhat doubtful) I'm not sure what good it will do.

> *Counselor:* As I mentioned earlier, I want all of you to get a better understanding of why Ben skips school. This way you will have more information to help you decide how to handle it.

This prediction assignment, like many problem-focused interventions, can have some unexpected results. It is not unusual to discover that after this type of assignment the frequency of the problem behavior actually decreases. Asking Ben to predict his behavior makes what appears to be impulsive behavior much more preplanned. Also, when his parents have to give reasons for their predictions, they can become aware of how they contribute to the problem. This opens up another avenue for intervention. When you use interventions like this, be prepared to have to sell clients on the assignment. This homework may seem a little strange to them.

Another intervention that can be helpful is to *prescribe the problem*. When clients are having extreme difficulty overcoming a particular problem, this can be an effective intervention.

Marcie, a single woman, came to counseling for help with mild depression. When the counselor and Marcie saw little change in her depression after three sessions, her counselor decided to try a different approach. Marcie was instructed that each day during the following week, she was to pick a twenty-minute period when she was to work at being depressed. Her job was to be as depressed as she possibly could be during the chosen time slot. She needed to think of the things that would make her depressed and try to ignore any feelings that were not depressing. She would report on what she had learned when she came back to counseling the following week.

The next week at counseling Marcie expressed some different reactions to the homework. "I tried to follow your instructions," she explained to her counselor, "but it didn't work. No matter how hard I tried, I couldn't stay depressed for twenty minutes." In fact, something else had occurred. "When I tried to do the assignment, I got pretty frustrated with the whole thing," she continued. "I realized that this whole assignment was stupid! Why would I want to make myself depressed?" Then it hit her: "I guess that some things I was doing in the assignment are the things I do every day."

Marcie's reaction is a common one for clients after they have tried this type of homework assignment. Frequently they will recognize how they have been causing or maintaining their problem. Another reaction is to realize how absurd their situation is. This then can result in an increased motivation for change. Another typical response to this type of assignment is for the problem to begin changing, even though the clients may not express any understanding of the change. Whichever one of these results occurs, clients still take a step forward.

Exercise some caution when using this intervention with clients. It obviously is not an appropriate intervention in all situations. Clients should never be directed to engage in problem behavior when they are working on any sort of an addiction problem. To do that would only reinforce the addiction. Also, you should not use this type of intervention when clients are significantly depressed. In Marcie's case the depression was mild. However, if she had been severely depressed, this assignment could have made her even more depressed, which could be dangerous for her.

TERMINATION

Termination is a subject that you begin addressing during the first session when you ask, "What do you want to be different as a result of counseling?" If you have gotten a concrete answer to that question and if you and the client have set specific and measurable goals, then you will know when you are approaching termination.

Clients do not end counseling because they have been cured. Rather they end because they have gained the resources that they need to develop workable solutions for their situation. Sometimes they may have solved their problems. But other times something else may have occurred. They may have learned what the solutions are and how to accomplish them, but they just need a little more time to do that. Sometimes the clients choose to complete this last part of the journey outside of the counseling office.

When it is time to terminate the counseling, you should cover several things before you send clients out the door. This will bring the counseling process to a smooth close and provide some means for clients to maintain the progress that they have made.

1. *Review exceptions and summarize gains.* By doing this, you reinforce the means by which clients have changed. This is also the time to review any patterns that had previously maintained problems and to reinforce the "something different" that clients have done to interrupt this cycle.

2. *Reinforce client's strengths through compliments.* Compliments given at the end of a session can be a strong motivator for clients to build on their strengths and to continue to implement the solutions that they have developed.

3. Develop an aftercare plan. Clients need a plan for maintaining the gains that they have made. This plan should include a number of elements.

- clients' perception of progress they have made
- clients' identification of specific measures they want to use to continue progress
- warning signs that would let clients know if they were slipping into problem behaviors
- specific measures that clients can use if they notice problems resurfacing
- counselor's suggestions for ways to maintain progress; may include suggested reading

The termination of this period of counseling may not be the end of the counseling relationship. Rather, it may be the end of a phase of the relationship. For some clients the counselor becomes like their medical doctor, a person to whom they will return when they have some specific issue or problem with which they need help. Thus, brief therapy can span a number of years on an intermittent basis. Some brief therapists report experiences in which the counseling relationship lasted over twenty years.[8]

Finally, when terminating in brief therapy, clients need to know that they have the opportunity to return, even if it is for only one session, if they need help with new problems. Frequently sharing this with clients brings a response that says, "That's a relief to know that I can come back if I need to and not have to go through the whole counseling process again."

Keeping change going is not something that just happens. It takes planned and proactive interventions on your part. Whether you are assigning homework, helping clients do something different, or intervening spiritually, you need to be purposeful in what you do. When you invest in using the techniques suggested in these chapters, frequently the dividend is more effective and briefer counseling.

PART THREE

Practical Uses of Brief Therapy

10/ Adolescents: Sometimes It's Got *to* Be Brief

If it ain't broke, don't fix it.

If it works, do more of it.

If it's not working, stop and try something new.

THE CENTRAL PHILOSOPHY OF THE MRI MODEL

How can something so simple make so much sense? It may be hard to believe, but these simple axioms have helped provide an effective and useful set of guidelines for work with adolescents, even difficult adolescents. Some may call this approach simplistic, but before you make a decision, read this chapter, which will describe an integrated approach for MRI problem solving and solution-based counseling for adolescent clients and their families.

Most counselors would agree that working with adolescents is both challenging and rewarding. With the impinging demands of a changing body, the new importance of peer relationships, significant alterations in cognitive structures, and the complexity of the American family, our adolescent clients present a complicated and challenging package. Because many adolescent clients do not seek treatment on their own, motivation can be limited. Even when they are motivated, the motivation frequently appears for only a short period of time. This means that brief counseling is sometimes the only available option. In our counseling practice, we have found that an integrated, solution-based and problem-solving approach is a highly effective means of treating adolescent clients. Sometimes it is all that is needed to address the presenting issues. At other times it provides an efficient means of beginning the change process so that important developmental and family issues can be addressed.

Whether or not you work with adolescents and their families on a regular basis, these principles can help you. Before we jump in, let's brush up on some of the basics of good counseling with adolescents.

BACK TO BASICS

Successful work with adolescents requires a set of skills that is different from the set I (Matt) use with adults. Long silences, inactive nondirective therapy, and psychobabble just don't cut it with many teenage clients. Let's examine several of the basics of therapy with teens.[1]

Build Rapport

Without building some kind of relationship, it's all but impossible to bring about change with a teenage client. On top of that, if you are working within a brief model, you have to build that relationship fast. How do you do it? I have found it especially helpful to keep up on cultural trends and fads. By knowing about the music, clothing styles, and slang of this age group, it is much easier to form a relationship. In fact, if I don't know, I ask them to teach me about what they are wearing and what they like. Most adolescents love to educate an adult about what is "cool." Ask questions, listen carefully, and talk about things that are important to the client, and you will more easily establish a relationship, even with an adolescent who does not want your help.

Avoid Labeling

Labels are seldom helpful with adolescents. Tell a teenage boy that he is depressed, and a battle ensues. He resists, and you have engaged in a power struggle that is seldom productive to therapy or your relationship. Or tell an adolescent that she is anxious, and that anxiety becomes a handy identity, a new way to relate to those around her. In either case, labeling is seldom helpful or productive.

Use Humor and Self-Disclosure

I recently worked with a client who told me that anyone over nineteen was old and certainly couldn't understand her. After all, isn't everyone over twenty senile, forgetful, and unable to remember their teenage years? Maybe so, but I doubt it. Appropriately placed self-disclosure about my experiences as a teenager has helped immensely. Not only does self-disclosure help strengthen rapport, but it also provides valuable learning tools. Similarly, a well-placed and appropriate joke lets adolescent clients know that therapy can actually be enjoyable. They may even believe that adults are people too!

Avoid Doing More of the Same

We easily forget that our clients are a wealth of information about what does and doesn't work for them. To avoid doing more of what doesn't work, I try to understand what each adolescent client needs. Questions similar to the following help me to avoid doing more of the same:

- How can I be helpful to you?
- What actions by others have been helpful to you?
- What actions by others have not helped you?

WHY BE SOLUTION BASED WITH ADOLESCENTS?

Regardless of whether or not time and resources are limited, there are many reasons why a solution-based model is helpful with adolescent clients. First, with a focus on strengths, existing resources, and possibilities rather than weakness, pathology, and deficits, adolescents feel empowered and good about themselves. Think about the teenage clients you have seen. Perhaps they have been labeled as problems, deviants, rebellious, or whatever. When these labels are removed, adolescent clients are freed to find their own solutions and move beyond the confines of a stereotype and create a healthy identity.

In addition, the solution-based model allows for interventions at many levels in a client's system. Parents, teachers, and even probation officers can be brought into treatment in order to help the adolescent client. Even more important, by including others in treatment, especially parents and siblings, families can be strengthened. Solution-based treatment of adolescents and parents encourages all family members to take responsibility for their actions and make appropriate changes. Strengthening relationships is central to our work as Christian professionals.

ASSESS WHOM YOU ARE WORKING WITH

Perhaps the greatest challenge to working with adolescent clients is counseling clients who are ordered (by parents, schools, or the courts) to seek treatment. More than likely, they have no desire to be there. In fact, they may even tell you they'd rather be at the dentist than in your office. Without a willing client—a customer—the therapy hour can be long, excruciatingly long. Adolescents are frequently visitors, especially if they are forced or provoked to seek treatment. When I ask adolescents what brings them to my office for counseling, they often answer, "my parents," or "my car." The challenge then becomes to move them from visitor status to customer status so that solutions can be generated and treatment can begin.

Using Prochaska's model of change to gain perspective, it is helpful to remember that many adolescents are in a precontemplation stage. Two techniques have been especially helpful in moving adolescents from the precontemplation stage of a visitor to the action stage of a customer.

Empathize

Believe it or not, brief therapy does not preclude the use of empathy. Empathizing with clients' situations, no matter what they are, can be a powerful means of aligning and moving them toward becoming customers. When seventeen-year-old Jim was brought for treatment after his parents found he was using alcohol, skipping classes, and violating his curfew, I learned that his previous therapy had ended after one session. Jim was clearly a visitor. When I asked him why he thought he was in my office, he noted that it was because his parents forced him. As he talked, I empathized with his horrible predicament. He complained about losing his car. I replied, "It must be really frustrating not to be able to go and see your friends when you want." Later in the conversation, as he continued to complain about how awful his parents were, I responded, "You must be really angry at how your parents are treating you right now." These simple empathic responses, the kind learned early in training, helped Jim to trust me and eventually identify areas that he was willing to work on in counseling.

Find Something—Anything—to Work On

Adolescents are customers much more frequently than we give them credit for. However, they are frequently customers for things that we think they shouldn't be. Parents and even counselors expect adolescents to enter therapy and be a customer for their depression, their school behavioral problems, or even their "attitude problem." While these are all important things, I have never had an adolescent walk into my office and say, "I have an attitude problem that I'd really like to fix."

However, many teenage clients do reveal issues for which they are customers, but we often miss the clues. I am much more likely to hear statements like these: "I can't stand my teachers; they're always picking on me." "I wish my parents would leave me alone." While these may not appear to be the typical issues for which people seek help, they provide a useful place to begin therapy. By working with the issue that the client sees as the problem, you gain the client's cooperation, minimize the resistance, and begin to explore exceptions. Let's look at an example:

Client: I can't stand my parents. They're always nagging at me and making me follow all their dumb rules. I can't do anything with them around. I can't go out with my friends. I can't talk on the phone. I can't do anything.

Counselor: It sounds like it really makes you angry that you have so few privileges right now.

Client: Yes, it does. And I don't get it. I haven't even done anything to be here. This stinks.

Counselor: You sound really frustrated with your parents. I wonder if there is something you would like me to help change about your parents.

Client: Yeah, I'd love it if they would let me stay out later and see me as someone they can trust.

> *Counselor:* That sounds great. Let's talk about ways we can help your parents to give you that and see you in that way.

By finding areas for which the adolescent is already a customer and by working with those areas, change becomes possible. The client in the example given above was able to identify the fact that his parents gave him privileges and trusted him when he was going to school and coming home on time. These became important exceptions that helped generate solutions. Other questions that are helpful in helping visitors become customers include these:

- How can I be helpful to you?
- Is there a privilege you would like me to help you get back from your parents?
- How can I help you get your teacher off your back?

ENGAGE COMPLAINANTS

Linda, a forty-year-old mother of three children, enters your office and describes problems with her sixteen-year-old daughter. With frustration in her voice, she describes her daughter's late nights out with her friends, her waning interest in school, and her general disregard for family activities.

Linda is a complainant: She comes for therapy because she wants her daughter to be fixed. Complainants in adolescent cases—whether parents, teachers, or the courts—don't see themselves as part of the solution. We've all worked with complainants, and many of us struggle to meaningfully engage them in the change process.

I have found three critical tools that help me engage complainants and make them customers for some type of change.

1. Listen. Complainants usually have invaluable information to share about the adolescent client. I listen to complainants, build rapport, and compliment them on their insights and coping skills.[2] This helps them see that they are part of the change process.

2. Observe. After complimenting complainants on their insight and desire to help, I ask them to observe what is different when the problem is not occurring.[3] What are they doing differently? What is the adolescent doing differently? This simple task has helped turn many complainants into customers. Not only does it begin the process of generating exceptions to the problems, but it encourages complainants to examine their role in the maintenance of the problem. This task is especially helpful with parents who want you to "fix" their children.

3. *Explore attempted solutions.* If neither of these techniques helps change complainants into customers, ask the complainants to list all of the ways they have tried to solve the problem. Then encourage complainants to try something new. In this way, they become customers as they understand their failed attempts and are encouraged to think and act creatively to help solve the client's problem.

HOW TO HANDLE MULTIPLE CUSTOMERS

Once you have customers, the counseling process begins. As you think about the above examples, you may be wondering what you do when your client and his or her parents or other presenting adult are customers for different things. After all, an adolescent may be a customer to change his or her parents or reinstate a privilege. At the same time, the parents may be customers to change their adolescent. How can these divergent goals work together? Let's look at some tools that will help this make sense.

Explore the Miracle Question

The miracle question helps both parents and adolescents imagine a time in the future when problems are not occurring.[4] Not only does it begin to generate exceptions, but it helps clarify goals and allows each member to imagine what life will look like when treatment is completed successfully. I frequently begin treatment with the miracle question, hoping to plant the seeds of change. Later in therapy if clients experience difficulty generating exceptions or if they become especially pessimistic, I may return to the miracle question. Matthew Selekman provides a helpful sequence of questions he uses with adolescents and their parents to elicit and follow up with the miracle.

- Suppose that while you are asleep tonight, a miracle happens and your problem is solved. How will you be able to tell the next day that a miracle has happened?

- What will be different?
- How will you have done that?
- What else will be different between the three of you?
- Who will be the most surprised when you do that?
- Who will be the next most surprised?
- If I were a fly on your living room wall watching the three of you after the miracle occurs, what kinds of things will I see you doing together?
- If a sibling or friend were sitting here, what would he or she say is different about how you and your parents are getting along after the miracle?
- I'm curious, are any of these miracles happening a little bit already?[5]

By elaborating on the miracle and hearing the perspectives of as many people as possible, important members of the system are brought into the miracle and later solutions. This is done by asking as many questions as possible about the miracle from a variety of perspectives, both with the adolescent and with the parents.

Sometimes parents present for treatment without their teenage child. Quite simply, their son or daughter will not set foot in the office of a "shrink." Similarly, there are times when parents are unable to move from complainants to customers. In these instances, I have used a miracle-question variation that allows parents to envision a future reality that is free of the problem. It also reminds parents of the ultimate goals of parenting, to raise well-adjusted children who are able to function on their own and are engaged in a committed relationship to Christ. To do this, I ask parents who they would like their son or daughter to be in five or six years. What kinds of things would they like to see their child doing? What kind of person would they like to see him or her be?

Here's an example from a session with the parents of a seventeen-year-old girl who had run away from home, was experiencing difficulty at school, was abusing substances, and was having significant conflict with her father. The adolescent would not come for counseling, so her mom brought her reluctant husband to a session without their daughter.

Counselor: It's important that we look ahead and plan for the future. While things seem bad now, they may not always be this bad. By imagining how you would like Judy to be in five years, we can lay the groundwork for future change. I want you to think a minute. Who would you like Judy to be in five years? What type of person? What would you like to see her doing with her life?

The mother: I would like Judy to be working in a job that she likes. She has always done well in mechanical things. I would like her to have a job that helps her feel successful and raises her self-esteem. I would like for her to have graduated from high school and have a decent relationship with her family. I would also like for her to know Christ.

Counselor: Those sound like important things. Dad, where would you like to see Judy?

The father: I guess I would like the same things for Judy—to finish high school and get a job that she likes. But, you know, the kid is just no good. She smokes pot, and her word isn't worth anything. I'm just ready to turn her loose.

Counselor: It sounds as if you both want good things for Judy, a job, a high school diploma, greater self-esteem, a relationship with Christ. Did I miss anything?

The mother: No, that sounds good.

Counselor: You know, as I listen, I can tell how much you both love your daughter and how much you want to see her be happy.

The father: Yeah, I do love her. I just don't know what to do with her. She lies, and she's manipulative. My boys never gave me a lick of trouble. I don't know what this is about.

Read on to see how Judy's parents used exception-finding questions to help bring about change.

Ask Exception-Finding Questions

With both parents and adolescents, it is often difficult to move from problem talk to solutions. Parents want their children to change, and they want you to know how hard it has been for them. At the same time, adolescents want their parents and environment to change. Exception-finding questions are important tools used to interrupt problem talk. When the exceptions are amplified, they can serve as important steps toward solutions.[6] Exceptions may come in the form of actions, behaviors, attitudes, feelings, and even wishes. Here are some questions used to elicit exceptions:

Questions for Adolescents:

1. When the problem is not occurring, what are you doing instead?
2. What was different for you when you did it that way?
3. How did you come up with that idea?
4. What are your parents doing differently when the problem is not occurring?

Questions for Parents:

1. What are you doing differently when the problem is not occurring?
2. What will have to occur for that exception to happen again tomorrow or later this week?
3. If I were to ask your daughter [or son] what she would say the two of you would continue to do so that she could get along well with you, what would she tell me?[7]

Exception-finding questions not only assist both parents and adolescents as they look for meaningful exceptions, but they also allow family members to collaborate and interact in a healthy manner. They can find common goals, and by amplifying exceptions, they can make changes in the structure of the family as family members are encouraged to engage in more of the thoughts, feelings, and behaviors that lead to continued exceptions.

Exception-finding questions can be used with whomever presents for treatment. I have found them useful with both parents and adolescents in the counseling room at the same time, and I have also used them effectively with just a parent or a teenage client. Let's return to the session with Judy's parents and see how exception-finding questions were used to follow up miracle questioning.

Counselor: Not only is it important to plan for the future as we think about Judy, but frequently we can learn from the past. I want you both to think about times when things were better with Judy. What were you doing? What was different? Sometimes these things can be used to help with the problems you came in with today.

The father: Well, Judy has always been a deceitful child. She's by far the hardest I've raised of my three kids. If you can't take a person at her word, then you don't have much, do you?

Counselor: You sound hurt and frustrated. That can make it hard to remember when things were better. I want you to think for a minute while I check in with your wife. When do you remember things being better?

The mother: I remember lots of times. Things were much better in ninth grade. We all got along much better, and Judy seemed happy.

Counselor: Really, that sounds like a good time. What was different then?

The mother: Well, Judy was involved in sports in school. She really is a good athlete, you know. She was doing a little bit better in her classes then, and her brother was around. She really looks up to her brother, and her brother took her to church. Judy even had good friends that year, the kind we could trust.

Counselor: It sounds as if she had a really good year, and it reminds us of all Judy's strengths. What you were doing differently that year?

The mother: We were supporting her, I guess.

Counselor: How were you supporting her?

The father: That was a better year. I never missed any of her sporting events, except for golf. She knew that we were there for her.

Counselor: How else did you show your support?

The father: I really praised her when she was doing so well in sports. You know, I let her know that she was a good athlete and that I was proud of her.

Counselor: That's great. How did she respond to that?

The mother: She loved it. She always has responded well to positive feedback.

The father: But there's been nothing to praise her for during the last two years. I can't trust her. She's failing school, and she really hasn't done anything well enough to deserve praise.

Counselor: You sound frustrated. Sometimes it's easy to overlook the small things that people do when we're used to big things. I wonder if there's anything at all that Judy has done recently that would be worthy of praise.

The father: I can't think of anything.

The mother: Well, I can. She called last night when she knew she was going to be late, and she came home after being gone for four weeks. And you know, Jim, she's always done well at work.

The father: I suppose. She is one of my better workers. She's always fast and accurate, and with the turnover I've had in the last year, she's got a lot of seniority. In fact, I think the other workers look up to her.

Counselor: That's great. It sounds as if there are lots of things that Judy deserves praise for. I wonder what else you were doing differently that year that helped Judy to be successful?

From this, the counselor and the parents made a list of exceptions. Not only were the parents reminded of Judy's many strengths, but they also generated a list of things they could reinstate. Perhaps most important, Judy's dad was moved from a complainant to a customer. The negative interactions and his criticism of Judy were brought to light in a productive manner, and he began to see the need to maintain a supportive and open relationship with his daughter.

Exception-finding questions also have powerful effects with adolescent clients. I am reminded of seventeen-year-old Steve, who was brought to treatment by his parents because he had been suspended from school for smoking marijuana. Rather than taking a traditional approach to the treatment of substance abuse issues, exception-finding questions were used, and Steve discovered that he wasn't using marijuana when he was busy and "not bored." Homework focused on finding ways to stay "not bored," and Steve generated a top-ten list of things he could do when he was bored. After five sessions, spread out over the course of several months, Steve and his parents reported that he had not used marijuana or any other drugs for nearly four months. Much to his parents' amazement, Steve was also spending more time with his family and actually asked his younger siblings to spend time with him.

Use Scaling Techniques

From either exception-finding sequences or the miracle question, you can use scaling techniques to help adolescent clients and their parents attain their goals. Adolescents and parents may share the same scale. For example, both may agree that Bobby will move from a 3 to a 4 on the scale if he attends school two out of five days this week. However, adolescents and parents may also have different scales. For example, Suzie may agree to come home on time both nights of the weekend, moving her scale from a 6 to a 7. At the same time, her mother may agree to "let go" just a little bit more by not standing at the door waiting for her arrival, allowing her scale to move from a 5 to a 6. In either of these instances, the counselor acts as a negotiator, helping both parties to understand what they would need to do to move a point or even a fraction of a point within the next week. Remember, we are looking for small changes, not the whole miracle at this time.

Using scaling questions often includes negotiating privileges. For example, if Bobby would move from a 3 to a 4 by going to school for two out of five days this week, his parents would be encouraged to grant a privilege. In this case, Bobby may be allowed to stay out a half hour later on Friday night if he accomplishes this goal. Remember, small change leads to larger change. While Bobby may not be in school every day of the week, this is a change in the right direction, and it can be built on in subsequent sessions.

Chuck was "forced" to seek counseling after a series of behavioral problems at home. He failed the majority of his classes at school and was asked to leave his home for three days after having a fight with his father. His mother also suspected that he was abusing drugs and alcohol. After several sessions, Chuck moved from a visitor to a customer. In a session with his mother, the counselor used scaling questions to negotiate further change. When Chuck was asked what he would like to change about his mom, he noted that she needed to continue to "give him space." He said that she was a 6 on his scale, but she would move to a 7 if she would not ask where he was three nights this week. When Chuck's mother was asked about his progress, she stated that he was presently at a 7 on her scale. He would move to an 8 if he looked for a job and registered for summer school during the coming week. In subsequent sessions, each had worked to move up the other's scale, and significant change was reported.

Don't Give Up

Sometimes adolescents and parents are unable to generate exceptions to problems. Sometimes they are unable to identify or even imagine a miracle. What do you do then? How is change possible if no exceptions can be found?

In the chapter about the MRI problem-solving model of brief therapy, we discussed the need to understand the client's position or belief system. Sometimes it is necessary to mirror the client's position, however negative it may be, in order to generate exceptions and bring about change. When a negative view prevails and there is seemingly no escape from problem talk, you can use a pessimistic stance to help clients move forward. You can ask questions like these:

- It seems that things are really bad. How you have kept them from getting worse?
- What do you think will happen if things get worse?
- Who would suffer the most if that happened?
- What's one little thing you could do to keep things from getting worse?
- What could others in your family do?[8]

These questions allow us to join with clients in their pessimism while encouraging them to elaborate on the ways that they have kept things from getting worse. In doing so, they may see additional resources, and together you may be able to generate new exceptions.

DEVELOP INTERVENTIONS AND HOMEWORK

So what do you do with all of this? What else can help in these cases? Once you have used the miracle question, give homework to help ensure that change continues.

Pretend the Miracle Happened

One assignment that is especially meaningful allows adolescent clients to pretend that either their miracle or their parents' miracle has already happened. After adolescent clients have answered the miracle question, ask them to pick two days or two times during the week in which they will pretend the miracle has occurred. Also instruct them to notice how their parents respond to them when they do this. Are there any differences? Do their parents act any differently? In addition, instruct parents to look for times that the miracle is occurring. The counselor's job is to follow up, while noting and amplifying the changes that occur.

I am reminded of Gina, a seventeen-year-old client who came to counseling for a variety of issues, one of which was significant conflict with her mother and stepfather. When I asked the mother the miracle question, she replied that a miracle would have occurred if her daughter were to help out around the house and do her chores. Gina was instructed to surprise her mother and act as if the miracle occurred once during the week. Gina did even more: She not only did her chores, but she also did her family's grocery shopping. This was the beginning of a significant shift in their relationship.

Do Something Different

We started the chapter with these simple axioms: If it ain't broke, don't fix it; if it works, do more of it; if it's not working, stop and try something new. As you have read this chapter, you have learned a little bit more about brief therapy with adolescents. Now it's time to see how this simple axiom can be integrated and used to guide the treatment of an adolescent case.

Let's take a look at Tiffany and see how doing something different can be integrated with exceptions and miracles.

Tiffany, a fourteen-year-old, was brought to therapy by her mother, who was concerned about her low grades in school, defiant behavior at home, and consistent conflict with her stepfather. Tiffany's family had recently been homeless, and she was now living in transitional housing with her parents and three stepsiblings. In addition, there was a history of substance abuse, divorce, and significant family conflict.

Counseling could address many issues with this family, including the marital conflict, recent homelessness, previous substance abuse, multiple divorces, blended family relationships, etc. In talking to Tiffany and her mother, it became apparent that many of these things were not broken. While they had been problems at one time, this family had found creative ways to solve their problems, and they had used their God-given resources in constructive ways.

Instead of fixing what wasn't broken, treatment started by helping Tiffany and her mother do more of what already worked. When the counselor asked Tiffany the miracle question, she lit up and responded that if her miracle were to occur, she would have more peace and quiet at home, she would feel happier, and she would be spending more time roller skating with her friends. When the counselor asked the mother the miracle question, she said that Tiffany would be doing her homework and receiving passing grades and that there would be less conflict in the home. When asked about exceptions, Tiffany thought for a few minutes and then realized that there was less conflict when she was able to spend time with her mother. Much to her mother's surprise, she also told us that she felt more like doing her homework when she knew she would have time with her mother.

The counselor and clients built on the miracle sequence, and after the first session, Tiffany was instructed to pretend her mother's miracle was happening. Tiffany quickly responded that there was no way she could do her homework; however, she agreed at least "to pretend" to do her homework. In exchange, her mother agreed to stop checking in on her after school. In the second and third sessions, Tiffany reported that she had made considerable progress at school. She had made up incomplete grades, was ready to graduate to the ninth grade, and was thrilled that her mother had "stopped nagging" her. In accordance with the agreement made in the first session, Tiffany's mother agreed to build on exceptions, and she scheduled time with her daughter each Saturday morning. When asked what she needed to do to maintain all of her progress, Tiffany decided that she would remain focused on school, and she even devised a secret game she would play with a teacher with whom she had conflict. This game helped her to pass the class.

While Tiffany maintained progress in school, she still had considerable tension with her stepfather. Tiffany's stepfather was unable to attend a session, and when the counselor asked Tiffany and her mother about exceptions to the tension, neither of them was able to think of anything. We hit a roadblock.

If it's not working, stop and try something new. We switched gears and used a problem-solving technique. We generated a list of ways that Tiffany's stepfather had attempted to deal with her defiance. It became apparent that the theme of his attempted solutions was, "You must obey." Because this had not worked, the attempted solutions had become punctuated with anger, and Tiffany had developed her own set of angry responses. Her stepfather still refused to attend a session, so Tiffany and I discussed the need to do something different. Tiffany began to see the value of surprising her stepfather. I suggested that he really needed her help not to become angry. He just couldn't do it on his own, and for him to be successful, he would probably need her wisdom and experience.

Tiffany liked this idea. I instructed her to do something different when her stepfather became angry. To prevent herself from becoming angry, Tiffany sang to herself, went about her chores, and on one occasion poured her stepfather a cup of coffee. She enjoyed the challenge of doing something different, and he was so amazed that he came to the next session two weeks later. Not only did he report considerably less conflict between the two of them, but he also agreed to begin spending time with her doing things that she liked.

When Problem Talk Becomes the Solution

Sometimes solutions look different from what we might expect. In fact, some solutions look very similar to the techniques we were taught in graduate school. These solutions can be meaningfully integrated within a brief model. Sixteen-year-old Mark was brought to therapy by his mother because he "had an attitude," was angry and fighting with his siblings, and was "mouthing off to his teachers." In the first session, Mark's mom mentioned that his father had abandoned her and their five children when Mark was only five years old. She mentioned that she believed this was part of his problem. When Mark was asked about this, he promptly denied that he was angry, noting that he wanted nothing to do with this topic.

In the second session, the counselor used the miracle question, exception-finding questions, and scaling techniques to precipitate change. Mark worked to show less anger around the house. This was evidenced as he fought less with his siblings and began to come home on time. In exchange, he was given privileges, including the use of his car.

Once his behavior was stabilized and the conflict between Mark and his mother decreased, Mark was willing to talk about the anger he felt toward his father. Three sessions were devoted to issues related to Mark's anger, and one of the solutions he generated included writing a letter to his father, expressing his hurt, frustration, and loss. This turned out to be no ordinary letter. In fact, I was blown away that this angry adolescent, who initially resisted therapy, spent hours composing a well-developed and highly emotional letter to his father. Mark then mailed the letter to his father and later scheduled a time to meet with him and talk about his feelings. This story didn't end there. Mark also convinced his older brother to talk to his father as well.

Sometimes telling one's story, being heard, and expressing feelings are all important parts of an adolescent's solutions. We cannot overlook the importance of allowing our clients to be heard and validated. While this may at times fall into the category of problem talk, it may also lead to meaningful solutions. A distinction between problem talk and the need to be heard and validated is not easily distinguished. However, we must be sensitive to opportunities to allow our adolescent clients to tell their stories while remaining aware of opportunities to move them toward meaningful solutions. In this case, emotional expression, confrontation, and eventually forgiveness were important parts of Mark's solutions.

Brief therapy with adolescents requires creativity and flexibility. Through the use of the techniques of the solution-based and problem-solving models, effective and lasting change is possible. Believe it or not, change is possible with difficult and treatment-resistant cases. By building on strengths, adolescents and their parents feel empowered. Sometimes a few sessions of building on exceptions and amplifying change are all that is needed. In other cases, these techniques and ways of viewing change will lay the groundwork for more in-depth discussions of the underlying problems. In either case, we have found the techniques explained in this chapter a meaningful and helpful place to start when working with adolescent clients and their families.

Experiment with the miracle question, exception-finding questions, and scaling questions. If you become stuck, avoid doing more of what isn't working, and try something new. Most important, find a style that works for you. This will allow you to help your adolescent clients create meaningful changes in their lives.

11/ PROMOTING CHANGE
in
MARRIAGES

God is perfect, the ideal of Christian marriage is perfect, and the
means God puts at the disposal of Christian couples are perfect. Yet
there is no perfect marriage, no perfect communication in marriage.
The glory of Christian marriage is in accepting the lifelong task of
making continual adjustments within the disorder of human
existence, ever working to improve communication skills necessary to
this task and seeking God's enabling power in it all.

DWIGHT SMALL, *After You've Said I Do*

Counseling couples can be hard and frustrating work. In many approaches
to marriage counseling, the process begins with an in-depth exploration
of a couple's families of origin or a focus on identifying the couple's
respective expectations. At times, marriage counseling may even take a
look at the general functioning patterns of the relationship, including the
roles and unspoken rules by which the couple operates. All of these
approaches can be helpful.

However, a couple may need to change as fast as possible in order to
avoid irreparable damage to the marriage. With its emphasis on beginning change in the first session, a solution-based, brief approach can
begin to help a couple immediately. The initial interventions help
couples to identify what has worked in the past and focus on finding
ways to repeat the successful actions. This has the possibility of getting
change going right away.

Frequently couples engage in a pattern of mutual blame and shifting
responsibility. Their unspoken assumption is that if you, the counselor,
could decide who is to blame, then you could change the responsible
person and solve the relationship problems. This puts you in the position

of playing referee, a role you are better off avoiding. Sometimes, though, it does not matter who is to blame; things just need to change. A brief-therapy approach emphasizes changing things before the situation gets worse.

In this chapter you will see an example of how our approach to brief therapy works with a marriage. Marital counseling is frequently more difficult than individual counseling because you need to work with two people who often see their problems very differently. Also you will need to work with the interactional dynamic between spouses. In spite of these factors, a brief approach to marital counseling can be effective.

TEN SESSIONS WITH A COUPLE

This chapter will follow a couple, Brian and Lori, who are fairly typical of a situation you could face in a counseling situation. They initially came for counseling because of a significant increase in disagreements, because of general dissatisfaction with the relationship, and because Brian had recently begun to think about divorce as an option. They have been married sixteen years and have three children: a twelve-year-old son, a ten-year-old son, and a five-year-old daughter. Both Brian and Lori became Christians after they were married.

Brian and Lori's case will be presented from start to finish, in a total of ten sessions. Each section will discuss the basic techniques used in that session. While Brian and Lori are a composite of several different couples, the dialogue, interventions, and their responses are based on actual incidents.

Session 1

When Brian and Lori came into the counseling office, it was obvious that they had significant marriage problems. They made no attempt to hide their anger and punctuated it by sitting as far away from each other as possible. When their counselor asked them what they would like to see different in their relationship, Lori spoke first.

> **Lori:** When we were engaged, Brian made me feel that I was the most wonderful, unique, and intelligent person in the world. He was eager to be with me and excited about what I had to say. We were

good friends. Now it seems that Brian doesn't see me even when he's looking at me. Instead of talking with me, he talks to me or at me. And rather than being excited about what I have to say, he seems to endure it. I don't know where we went wrong, but I want to fix things. I just hope we can get our marriage back to where it used to be.

Brian: Early on in our relationship Lori complimented me on how I looked, on what I did, on who I was. She made me feel that I was someone special. I didn't love her just for who she was. I also loved her for how she made me feel when I was with her. But it didn't take long before I couldn't do anything right. I didn't dress right. I worked too long or too hard. I didn't talk enough or didn't say the right things when I did talk. I felt that she was trying to change me into a totally different person. Over time I began to feel like a failure. Now all I get from her is complaining. If things are going to get any better, she's going to have to quit being so critical.

From the start Brian and Lori present a unique situation. It is a challenge to help them determine their goals and get a sense of whether they are visitors, complainants, or customers. Lori gives the indication that she is probably a customer. While she is direct about her frustrations with the marriage, she also indicates that she is willing to do her part to change.

Brian, though, appears to be more of a complainant. His statements and the tone of his voice leave no doubt that he wants Lori to do the changing. He might be aware of his own contributions to the problems, somewhere deep inside. However, he is not willing to acknowledge this.

From the start the counselor is in a difficult situation. The two people are at different places as to their motivation to change. Since Lori is a customer and Brian is a complainant, the counselor has the difficult task of trying to deal differently with two people within the same session.

When you find yourself in this situation, you need to find some goals with which both spouses can agree. If you cannot identify a single goal that both can agree on, you may have to identify separate goals for each one. This puts you in the place of managing multiple objectives.

In Brian and Lori's situation the counselor chose to find some goal that

Brian could align with in order to keep him involved in the counseling. This was done by keying in on his complaints about Lori's criticisms.

> *Counselor:* Tell me, Brian, what would you be willing to do so that Lori would talk to you in the way you want?
>
> *Brian:* I'd be willing to do just about anything.
>
> *Counselor:* It's been my experience that couples can get into some pretty negative patterns with each other. Once one spouse does something, the other reacts, only making the first spouse react even more strongly, and off they go.
>
> *Brian:* That sure sounds like us.
>
> *Counselor:* There's a way you may be able to break that pattern if you are willing to try. If one person responds differently, even though the other started out wrong, the cycle can often stop. Would you be willing to learn how to respond differently to Lori if it meant that she would start reacting to you differently?
>
> *Brian:* It would be worth a try.

By this point, Brian may be starting to move toward being a customer. He is not necessarily a customer for the same thing that Lori is. But he may be a customer for getting her off his back. It is not necessary for each spouse to be a customer for the same thing, as long as their individual goals are mutually compatible.

At this point the counselor can move ahead with getting a sense of this couple's perception of the general state of the marriage. It is also time to begin the change process. Using scaling questions can be an effective technique for doing this.

> *Counselor:* I would like each of you to rate your marriage on a scale of one to ten. One would represent your relationship at its worst. Ten would represent how you would like it to be when you have finished counseling. At a ten, things would not be perfect. You would still have some disagreements, as all couples do. But the disagree-

ments would be manageable. You could resolve the differences and still feel that you really enjoyed each other. Where would you rate your marriage today?

Brian: I'd probably place it at a three.

Lori: I'd say the same. A three.

Counselor: Really? What makes it a three, rather than a one or a two?

Lori: For one thing we are coming here for help. Also, there are some times when we can get along. Like last Tuesday.

By having the couple explain their rating of the marriage, the counselor is able to identify an exception to their problem. Even though Lori mentioned last Tuesday only in passing, it is an exception. Quite possibly Lori or Brian may not realize its significance. So the counselor needs to stop the conversation in order to draw their attention to it and try to emphasize the mechanics that allowed this to happen. By asking them to explain what they did to get along better last Tuesday, the counselor can identify what already works for Brian and Lori. The counselor will also encourage them to do more of whatever works.

You may notice that in a solution-based approach, the counselor will frequently ask the same questions in different forms. This is not just to get the clients' perspectives. Rather it is a way of emphasizing some very key points to them. This technique allows the clients to hear themselves and realize what they are doing. As the sessions for Brian and Lori progress, look for the ways that the counselor does this.

By the end of the session Brian and Lori were both able to agree that they wanted things to be different in their marriage. Both were also able to agree that they each had to put forth effort to do some things differently. Brian was a little more reluctant than Lori was on this point, but he was willing to give it a try.

It is important for counselors to get each spouse's perspective of the circumstances. Each one will likely see the situation differently. The only way to develop workable goals is to find goals that each spouse can agree with.

As the session proceeds, the counselor identifies the fact that Brian has some severe personality traits that could make him difficult to get along with. He can be very self-focused and think that he rarely makes mistakes. For him, the problem usually lies with the other person. He often sees himself as the center of attention and does not understand why others do not realize how unique he is.

Note how this is handled differently in a brief-therapy approach. Brian is not coming to counseling for help with his personality problems. In fact, if the counselor suggested that he needed to work on these personality traits, Brian could easily terminate counseling. In this situation the counselor needs to stay very narrowly focused on the issues that the couple wants to change.

At the end of their first meeting, the counselor spends a few minutes summarizing the session. This includes complimenting Brian and Lori on their strengths both as individuals and as a couple. The counselor also points out the positive resources that they have brought to the counseling session. The counselor then assigns homework.

For their homework, the counselor asks Brian and Lori to take one day during the next week in which they were to act as if the problem had been resolved. They are not to tell the other spouse which day they choose. The spouse will have to guess which day it is. But each one's job is to act as if the problems had been resolved. If the partner is upset on the "as if" day, the other spouse is to respond as if they were getting along at the 10 level on the scale. Each spouse is instructed to notice how things go on the "as if" day. If some things go better, then they are to ask themselves, "Why did it go better?" When they come back to counseling the next time, they will reveal which day they had chosen. Until then, they have to be content with guessing.

Session 2

When Brian and Lori returned one week later, they agreed that things had gone somewhat better the past week. They had had two major disagreements. However, this was an improvement over their previous pattern. In reviewing the homework, Lori acknowledged having tried to go through a day as if the problems had been resolved. However, Brian said that he had been so busy with work that he had not been able to follow through. However, he did acknowledge that Lori had made an effort to help things go better.

In a problem-centered approach, the counselor would look at their two disagreements. However, coming from a solution-based perspective, the counselor focused on the days that things had gone right. This involved some unexpected cheerleading and encouragement because Brian and Lori were anticipating discussing their failures.

> *Counselor:* From the way you two described it, it sounds as if you got along better than you have in a long time. That's great! How were you able to pull it off?
>
> *Brian:* For one thing, Lori was much nicer. Your idea of pretending that things were okay really worked for her.
>
> *Counselor:* Tell me, Brian, what did you do that helped you two do so well?
>
> *Brian:* Not much. Lori was the one who was different.
>
> *Counselor:* I know that Lori did a lot. But it takes two people to get along. What was your part in it? How did you help?
>
> *Brian:* When I noticed that Lori was trying, I decided to give her a break. So even though things weren't perfect, I decided to be quiet and enjoy what she was doing.

By continuing to ask Brian what he had done, the counselor is educating him in how change with a couple works. The counselor is also reinforcing the possibility that Brian will repeat these actions at a future date.

Sometimes in marital counseling, you will have to do some education and explanation. Conflict management can be one of these areas. It is not unusual for couples to be ignorant about basic techniques of conflict resolution. Frequently it can be more time effective and save strain on the relationship if you explain some of these techniques to a couple rather than just letting them guess for themselves.

In their book *The Marriage Mender,* Thomas Whiteman and Thomas Bartlett suggest seven conflict-resolution principles that couples can use at home.[1] These principles can be effectively practiced in a counseling session, then assigned as homework. Let me list them here and make some observations.

1. *Make it a win-win situation*—In disagreements each spouse should try to find a way both can win rather than attempt to win his or her position at all costs.

2. *Find a way to de-escalate*—Negative interactions are extremely damaging to any relationship. When a disagreement occurs, a couple should take a short break from the discussion if it gets too heated.

3. *Accentuate the positive*—As an alternative to a negative-focused relationship, each partner should focus on the positive things that the other does. This creates a safe base from which to deal with problems.

4. *Use what works*—Couples are encouraged to consider times when they have been successful at resolving conflict. The task then becomes using these skills in overcoming current disagreements.

5. *Stop doing what doesn't work*—As we've seen in previous chapters, people have a tendency to repeat behavior that is not helpful and does not accomplish what they want. In resolving conflict, couples need to identify how they are doing this, then attempt a different tactic.

6. *Keep the big picture in sight*—When improvement occurs, couples tend to keep looking at where they want to go and miss seeing the progress that they have made. They need to step back periodically and recognize where they have come from and the positive steps that they have made toward their goals.

7. *It takes time*—Conflict resolution is a skill that has to be practiced. This can be done by having the couple schedule times when they will discuss minor issues with the steps of conflict resolution in mind. As they grow more proficient, they can then progress to working on more difficult issues.

For Brian and Lori the second session was the time to address the area of conflict management. This involved both some education and some practice. In Brian and Lori's case, the counselor explained only what it meant to work for a win-win, how to de-escalate, and how to accentuate the positive. The counselor used the remaining four principles as homework. Their homework assignment was to review all of the principles together. They were then to sit down at least one time during the week and practice the principles while discussing a small issue on which they disagreed.

In addition to practicing the structured conflict-resolution skills for homework, Brian and Lori were asked to repeat their "as if" days since it had appeared to help. This time Brian agreed to make sure to participate.

Session 3

With couples, you may find that problem behavior can frequently follow some identifiable patterns. Problem patterns are merely similar things that occur or precipitate specific problems. These patterns can include the time that the problem occurs, the location in which it occurs, a tone of voice, nonverbal behavior, or even specific subject matter. When couples begin to note their patterns, they can begin to develop a strategy for doing things differently. This can be an effective way of reducing some problems.

For Brian and Lori their problem pattern emerged in this session. It came up when Brian described what he considered to be problems with Lori's housekeeping. From his perspective the house was a mess most of the time. And even though he repeatedly asked Lori to make some changes, he felt that she purposely ignored him. As soon as Brian brought up this issue, Lori jumped in.

> **Lori:** Brian makes such a mess all the time. It's impossible to keep up with. On top of which he never helps to clean up. I'm not going to be his slave.

> **Counselor:** It seems to me that this is a road you two have traveled many times before. I hate to tell you, but it's still a dead end. What do you need to do to get on a more productive path? (This question caused Brian and Lori to pause a moment, which gave the counselor enough time to redirect them into a more productive focus.) When is this disagreement most likely to happen? What are the times? What are the situations when you find yourselves talking to each other this way, about this subject?

> **Brian:** Usually we get into it like this in the evenings. Especially after dinner.

> **Counselor:** What's similar about those times?

>*Lori:* Brian, they usually happen after you've had a long day at work, and you come home exhausted.
>
>*Brian:* Well, you complain enough about being tired yourself.
>
>*Counselor:* (interrupting before they begin arguing again) When this pattern has changed, even when you both are tired, what do you want the other one to be doing and saying?

This conversation led into their homework assignment. Brian and Lori each were to come up with a list of ten things that the other one could do at those times to communicate caring and understanding. These actions had to be positive (things to do, not things not to do) observable, attainable, specific, and measurable. After developing these lists, they were to exchange them and practice doing one thing from the list each night.

Session 4

Using scaling questions can be useful at various points in a session. You can use them to get an idea of how the couple is progressing in the change process. When you use scaling questions later on in the counseling, they can also help identify and reinforce what is working. In Brian and Lori's case, scaling was helpful to identify a positive pattern that they had not yet noticed.

At the beginning of this session Brian and Lori were asked to again rate their marriage on the 1–10 scale. This time Brian rated it at a 5, and Lori placed it at a 6.

>*Counselor:* That's great. What did you do to get it to that point?
>
>*Brian:* Lori is being a lot nicer to me. I'm beginning to feel that she likes me again.
>
>*Lori:* I've noticed that Brian is trying to make things better. It's as if he wants things to work between us. When he is like that, I feel much better and try harder to be considerate of him.
>
>*Counselor:* That's really encouraging. How were you two able to do this? What is each of you doing to help this change happen?

Brian: I've tried that idea about acting as if things were going better. When I do that, things actually do go better.

Lori: I was thinking about one of our sessions, and I realized that I am not as nice to Brian as I could be. When I work harder at being nicer, then he gets nicer to me.

From this dialogue the counselor began to focus on the positive cycle that the couple was beginning to develop. When one was nicer, the other responded positively, which caused the first one to reciprocate. Pointing out this type of positive pattern, where one change promotes a positive reaction in the other, can be an effective way of educating a couple about the mutuality of change.

Another perspective that is helpful with couples is to focus on how problems end rather than how they begin. This is a perspective that couples may not notice, but it can be extremely helpful. The counselor began to consider this when Brian mentioned that they had gotten into one of their typical arguments the past week, even though it was "nothing compared to what the arguments used to be like."

When the counselor asked Brian and Lori how they ended the argument, Lori said that she had gotten tired of the fight and went for a walk. When she returned, both she and Brian were calm and resumed the rest of the evening's activities without any further disagreement. In addition, Brian was fine with her having done this and thought that it was a good thing to use again. This then became a positive tactic that they could use in the future.

For their homework, Brian and Lori were instructed to read 1 Corinthians 13 and then write a paraphrase of it. The emphasis in their paraphrase had to be on ways that they could apply this Scripture passage. This homework would then be reviewed at the next session.

At this point, the decision was made to start meeting every other week. Everyone agreed that the marriage was definitely going better. Stretching out the time between sessions was a way of reinforcing Brian and Lori's efforts and rewarding them for what they had accomplished. In addition, when positive change is starting to happen on a regular basis, giving more time between sessions can actually facilitate the change rather than detract from it. More time between sessions gives the clients additional time to practice the skills they are learning.

Session 5

Three days before this session Brian called the counselor to express his frustration. He acknowledged that some things were better, but he still was upset with "Lori's constant criticism." Even though he knew it was not "what God wanted," Brian felt that he couldn't forgive her for it. If her criticism continued, he was sure that he would have to leave.

The subject of Brian's frustration was the focus of this session. He was clear that he felt Lori still criticized him too much. It was obvious that Lori did not understand what the problem was, but she was willing to change things if she could.

Initially the counselor attempted to identify the exceptions to this situation. However, when Brian was asked about the times that Lori did not criticize him, he adamantly replied, "There aren't any! And besides, the few times I do anything right are just a fluke, or she gets distracted and doesn't realize what I did."

No matter how hard the counselor pressed, Brian would not acknowledge that there were times when things were different. All the while Lori kept insisting that she would be glad to change if she only knew what he was talking about.

Feeling somewhat stuck, the counselor decided that it was time to change the main thrust of the counseling. Brian was given the task of letting Lori know when he felt that she was criticizing him. He was to do this in the spirit of the conflict-resolution guidelines that they had been working on. However, he was to make sure that he let her know at least three times a day when she was criticizing him. That way she could identify the things that she would have to work on.

This is an example of a problem-solving intervention that involves doing something 180 degrees different. If Brian follows through with it, Lori may very well have the information that she needs to change her patterns. However, with his personality and tendency to be oppositional, Brian may not follow through. Oftentimes when this type of assignment is given, clients actually begin backing away from the problem, and it becomes less significant.

Session 6

When Brian and Lori returned for this session, the counselor first inquired about Brian's homework. Brian replied that he had attempted to do it but was not very successful. He explained, "I didn't want to hurt Lori's feelings. I could tell that she was trying. Even though she frequently would get picky and critical, I didn't want to make her feel bad."

This led immediately to a discussion of the problems that his approached caused. In the course of this discussion, Brian began to acknowledge that it was unfair to Lori for him to be upset with what he perceived to be criticism but not let her know so that she could change it. However, Brian continued to express some reluctance about telling Lori when he felt that she was being critical because he did not want to hurt her feelings. For her part, Lori continued to be adamant that she wanted to know when she was doing this so that she could change. The counselor also reinforced that Brian should continue letting Lori know when he perceived that the problem behavior was occurring.

This method of handling Brian's lack of cooperation is a typical problem-solving strategy. When people tend to be oppositional, often they will not acknowledge progress that others are making. Instead, they will find something to complain about. When working with people like this, a paradoxical approach can break the deadlock. In Brian and Lori's situation, it is a win-win situation. Whether Brian does or doesn't cooperate with the homework, the results will be positive. If Brian can identify legitimate complaints, both win because this cycle can be changed. If Brian continues to be considerate of Lori's feelings, they win because they move closer together.

When you begin a paradoxical intervention, like the one used with Brian, carry it through consistently. It would be a mistake to compliment Brian on his attempts to be considerate of Lori's feelings. To do so could easily tap into his oppositional streak and cause him to increase his criticism.

Session 7

Change can be measured in a variety of ways: frequency, duration, and intensity. When these concepts are used in a solution-based approach, they describe how often the positive change is occurring (frequency), how long the change is lasting (duration), and how satisfying the positive times are (intensity). These concepts give clients another perspective by which to measure change. When you have clients conceptualize change in these terms, frequently they can see progress that they may have overlooked before.

It was helpful for Brian and Lori to see change in these terms. They both acknowledged that they were able to get along significantly more often than they had before entering counseling. The times that they were upset with each other were shorter than times that they perceived as positive and enjoyable. In addition, they both stated that they were enjoying each other more than they had for a long time.

In this session the counselor decided to review Brian and Lori's goals. This included assessing their progress and what they still wanted to change. Both spouses acknowledged that they wanted to feel closer to each other. When they were able to make this more concrete, it became evident that they wanted to have more time in which they could enjoy mutual activities. They acknowledged that in the past they both had enjoyed going out to eat and periodically going to a movie or a concert.

At the counselor's suggestion, Brian and Lori decided to try to do this on a regular basis. They agreed to make a weekly date, alternating who planned it. The activity had to be something that was mutually enjoyable. Certain topics were off-limits to discuss, namely their children, money, and anything else that they classified as controversial. The purpose of this was for them to have an enjoyable time together.

In addition to having Brian and Lori go out on a date before the next session, the counselor gave them another homework assignment. As a way of getting closer and strengthening their marriage, the counselor asked them to begin having a devotional time together. This could be two or three times a week and was to include reading a short devotional or Bible passage and praying together. The emphasis in the prayer was to be praise and thanksgiving for what God was doing in their relationship.

Session 8

It is a sign that the counseling process is effective when clients spontaneously apply what they are learning. Lori was the one who was able to do this. As this session began, she shared that while she had been praying about their marriage, God showed her something.

Lori: God showed me in my prayer time yesterday that I had a critical spirit. I became convicted that I focus too much on Brian's faults.

Counselor: Really! What do you think the Lord wants you to do about that?

Lori: I became convicted that I should look for the changes that Brian is making. My job is just to pay attention to what he is doing right. The rest is up to the Lord to take care of.

Counselor: Lori, that is a significant step to have taken. It sounds as if many things are going well for the two of you. What specific things do you two want to continue in order to keep this positive change moving?

Lori: We are getting along better.

Counselor: How are you getting along better? What are the two of you *doing* that you want to keep up?

Brian: Well, when I ask her a question, she answers me.

Counselor: What else? What are the other changes that you want to continue?

Lori: Brian acts as if he wants to be around me. We went on a short trip this past weekend without the kids, and we had fun together.

Focusing on the positive changes in the relationship is a method of maintaining progress. When you do this, it is helpful to emphasize what the couple needs to do to continue their gains. At the end of this session the counselor suggested scheduling the next session in three weeks. Brian and Lori had made significant progress up to this point. Meeting in three weeks would allow them time to consolidate this progress by practicing the skills that they had learned. In addition, if they were to have significant problems, they could look to the next appointment to help them resolve the issues. In that way Brian and Lori would not have to build any resentment by burying things.

Spreading out the counseling sessions as termination approaches is extremely beneficial. When you do this, you give your clients a vote of confidence. The implied message is that they are doing well enough that they do not need to come to counseling as much as before because they are better able to solve the problems on their own. In addition, when you gradually increase the time between sessions, you wean the clients from the need for counseling. This is one way to counteract the artificial dependency that counseling can create.

Session 9

Toward the end of counseling, the task becomes helping the couple maintain the progress that they have made and expediting any additional change that needs to occur. Maintaining counseling gains can be done by asking the clients some pertinent questions.

- What changes do you two want to continue?
- What do you need to do to maintain the progress that you have made?
- What are you currently doing that you want to make sure you are still doing in a year?

With these types of questions, the couple focuses on what they have accomplished and what they want to continue. If a couple has responded well in the counseling to a straightforward focus on solutions, identifying the progress that they want to continue may be enough to maintain positive change.

However, with some couples another approach can be helpful in addition to highlighting progress. When a couple has a history of sabotaging progress, simply focusing on maintaining gains may not be enough. Also, if one of the spouses can be oppositional or has a need to talk about problems, you may need to focus on problem situations in order to maintain positive change.

In addition, if you have had to use some of the problem-solving interventions, then you may want to use an additional strategy to consolidate progress. Discussing potential setbacks can be an effective strategy with some couples.

When it is necessary to focus on problems for the sake of maintaining progress, help the couple define what it would look like if they had a setback. Questions like these may help:

- What will be the warning signs that you two are starting to slip back to where you were before?
- Which of you would be the most likely to notice that problems are starting to occur again?
- Who else might be able to notice that you are slipping?

The counselor decided to use both approaches because of Brian's tendency to be oppositional and sometimes to sabotage things. With this couple the intervention included an effective twist. First, the counselor had them identify the positive changes that they saw in their relationship. This was fairly easy, as they both mentioned general enjoyment of each other, decreased arguments, a feeling that they understood each other and appreciated each other.

Next the counselor asked Lori and Brian to identify the first small indicator that they might be having a setback. Immediately, Lori identified that she would probably find herself sleeping less and getting short-tempered. This gave the idea that she had caught on to what the principle was. Brian, however, had some difficulty acknowledging that there was a chance of a setback.

The twist to the homework came in two parts. First, the counselor, on the basis of experience, predicted that Brian and Lori would have a setback. "After all, many couples do. You two have made good progress, but you also had times when significant problems came up for you."

The second part of the homework twist involved asking Brian and Lori to plan a small setback. The reasoning was that they would likely have one anyway. If they were to plan one out, it would be in their control. By planning a setback, they could choose the setting so that it would not be detrimental to their relationship. Along with planning the setback, they were to plan how they would get back on track again.

Given the level of progress that Brian and Lori had made up to this point, the next session was scheduled for a month later. This was to assess their ability to maintain the gains they had made by letting them manage the relationship without a counselor's help. The counselor introduced the idea of termination by indicating that if things went well for the two of them during the month, then they might want to consider ending the counseling.

Session 10

When Brian and Lori came back, the first thing the counselor did was to ask about their homework. As expected, Lori and Brian had not been able to carry through with their setback, though they had talked about it. If they had completed the homework, Brian and Lori would have gained useful information about managing potential pitfalls. However, by not completing the assignment, they further reinforced the positive gains they had made. Things continued to be better, and they were excited about the state of their marriage. Both Brian and Lori rated their marriage as an 8 on the 1–10 scale. Even though they were not at the level that they wanted to be, they felt that they had made enough progress to terminate counseling. They both agreed that they had the skills that they needed to continue the change process on their own. They knew what their goals were and what they needed to do to achieve them.

In light of Brian and Lori's decision to terminate counseling, the counselor brought up several issues for them to discuss as a follow-up plan for them.

> *Counselor:* Even though we are ending the counseling at this point, I want you to realize that you can come back at any point in the future. You may find some new problems that you would like some outside help with. Or you may find yourselves sliding back into the old problems. In either case the door is still open for you to come back. It may not be necessary to spend as much time together as we did this time. In fact, if you want to come back for a single session to fine-tune something, that would be great.

> *Brian:* That's encouraging to know. I especially like the idea of coming only a time or two if there's something specific that we want to accomplish.

> *Counselor:* I want you to see this office like your medical doctor's office. You can come when something specific is wrong, and when that is taken care of, you can go on your way.

From that point, the counselor worked with Brian and Lori to identify specific things that they could do not only to maintain their progress but also to reach the 10 level on the scale. In addition, the counselor reviewed the helpful things they had already done and encouraged them to continue doing these. Finally, the counselor suggested two marriage books and encouraged Brian and Lori to read them as part of their maintenance plan.

At the end of this session, the counselor asked Brian and Lori for their evaluation of the counseling—what things were helpful for them and what could have been more helpful. After discussing some of these, Lori stated that one of the most valuable things for her was that the counselor had encouraged them to set goals and then kept them on track by frequently reviewing their progress toward them.

As discussed at the beginning of this chapter, marriage counseling can be difficult. Yet it can also be fulfilling. A solution-based approach coupled with a judicious focus on problems can be an effective method for helping couples change. The techniques that are used in marriage counseling are not much different from the ones that are used in individual counseling. The application of these techniques is what is different in marriage counseling.

12 / WHAT *to* DO WHEN YOU DON'T KNOW WHAT *to* DO

If you need wisdom—if you want to know what God wants you to do—ask him, and he will gladly tell you. He will not resent your asking. But when you ask him, be sure that you really expect him to answer, for a doubtful mind is as unsettled as a wave of the sea that is driven and tossed by the wind.   JAMES 1:5-6

Ever been in this situation? You feel that you have the trust of the client. You understand what the problem is and what the client wants to see happen. You've even clearly defined with the client what the solution will look like. Yet, in spite of all the things you have done right, you are stuck! Counseling is not going where you know it should. In fact, at the moment, it is not progressing at all.

What do you do when you reach this impasse? Even though it is tempting to bluff or give up, these are not good options. However, the situation is not hopeless. You can do a number of things to get the process moving again. What is essential at this point is for you to do something different. Staying with the same approach is merely repeating what does not work and will keep you stuck.

As strange as it seems, getting out of this position actually begins before you find yourself at the standstill. Certain types of clients are more likely than others to get stuck. In addition, certain things that you do or do not do will make it more likely that an impasse will occur later in the therapeutic process. If you begin the therapeutic process with these ideas in mind and take a proactive position, it is possible to lessen the chances of getting into a stalemate. However, even when you are proactive, you can become stuck. When this happens, there are techniques that may help you to get things going again.

CLIENTS THAT WILL GET YOU STUCK

Some clients who come to your office present more difficult situations to work with. This can be due to their specific problems, their life circumstances, or even their own personality styles. Recognize from the beginning that these cases have a greater likelihood of becoming stuck. Let's look at several client types and situations in which the change process could stall.

The Visitor and Complainant Mix

Seventeen-year-old Megan was moderately active in her local church. She had some questions about her faith, but none of these questions were unusual for someone her age. She was actively involved in her youth group and known at her school as a somewhat outspoken Christian. In spite of her overall positive situation, Megan and her parents were at odds with each other, and the tension in her home greatly increased. When her parents brought her to the counseling office, they complained that she was withdrawing from the family. Whenever she was at home, she would spend most of her time in her room, often in the dark. If her parents attempted to encourage her to interact with the rest of the family, she would either not talk to them or respond with a short, rude answer. Recently her grades began to slip, and she had started saying that she was no longer interested in going to college. When Megan's parents brought her to counseling, she was adamant that everything would be fine if her parents would give her "some space." She also complained that they tried to make her decisions for her and would not allow her to do a simple thing like "stay out until 12:30 on a Friday night." When Megan's parents talked with the counselor, they made it clear that they thought that the problem was Megan's and that they would be involved in the counseling only to the extent that was needed to "fix" her.

This situation is set up to reach an impasse very quickly unless you are careful about how it is approached. Obviously, the parents need some education about their part in the problem, but to launch into that immediately will likely alienate them and lead them to withdraw Megan from counseling. To focus immediately on Megan's need to change will quickly result in resistance and passive aggression. If you do not recognize some of the pitfalls in this situation within the first session, this case could easily become deadlocked very fast.

The problem here is that you need to deal with a visitor who is brought to counseling by complainants. None of the clients is a customer; none is willing to change. To manage this problem, you must develop goals and a direction on which the clients can agree. If this is not possible, you may be able to establish different but complimentary goals for each of the clients. Megan may be willing to work toward getting her parents to leave her alone. Her parents may be willing to learn new ways of encouraging and parenting their daughter.

You can run into problems similar to this one whenever you have a mixed situation. A customer-visitor or a customer-complainant combination both have the potential to get stuck.

Difficult Personalities

Megan and her parents are just one example of how the type of client can precipitate a deadlock. People who are typically classified as personality disorders are another type that can end up in a stalemate. This is likely to occur when you do not focus on what these clients want out of treatment. Instead, the counselor begins to focus on the obvious personality and relational problems and subsequently begins to treat the client for things for which the client is not a customer. Three general principles for dealing with this type of client can help avoid a deadlock.

1. *Understand the personality style and dynamics of the client as soon as possible.* Then structure your interventions so that you can work *with* the client's personality rather than against it.

2. *Clearly define the treatment goals immediately.* Establishing goals with these clients is more difficult than with other types of clients. However, if you fail to do so in the first or second session, you are setting yourself up to get stuck. Also, make sure that the goals are what the client wants, not what you think the client needs.

3. *Focus the counseling on the goals, not the personality characteristics.* If it is

necessary to look at the client's personality, make sure the client is also engaged in doing this. Sometimes clients can be motivated to do this when they see that it is necessary to change their relational style in order to reach their goals.

Resistant Clients

Another type of client that can be difficult to help is the one who has a tendency to disagree with the majority of suggestions you make. This is the person who gets labeled passive-aggressive or resistant. In some counseling approaches, you would attempt to explain why the client is behaving in this manner. You might even try to identify how the resistance may help the client. However, in a solution-based approach, what could be termed resistance is seen as a signal that the counseling needs to shift focus slightly. The client is indicating that what is being suggested is not helpful. One way of managing this situation is to go in the same direction as the resistance.

A fifty-six-year-old man came to counseling because he had been depressed for an extended period of time and had barely worked for the past three years. He was a self-employed accountant and had kept his business going, but only at a marginal level. When he came to counseling, he was accompanied by his wife, who had recently returned to the workforce. In the past she had frequently nagged and complained in an effort to get her husband to do more. Despite all of her well-intentioned efforts, he continued to have difficulty simply doing anything that related to work.

After a couple of sessions the man began to express some desire to catch up on the work that he had neglected for so long. In spite of his expressed desire, this client still exhibited what could be classified as some resistance. In counseling he was negative and disagreed with many efforts to reach his goals. He never completed any homework. Yet he continued to insist that he wanted to change. In this vignette, notice how the counselor directs the intervention in the direction of the client's resistance.

> **Husband:** I really think that I should begin to catch up on my work. I have piles of tax papers that I have not filed for a couple of years. I also need to provide an audit for an estate trust; I should have filed

that audit three months ago. I think that I need to begin working on these.

Wife: You're right! You do need to start doing these. I've been telling you that for the last three months.

Counselor: If you think that you should begin catching up on these items, then that could be a good place to start. How would you want to begin doing that?

Husband: Well, I don't know. There is so much to do that I'm afraid I'm going to become overwhelmed. When I begin to think of all that I have to do, it boggles my mind. When I begin to feel like that, I freeze up and can't do anything.

Counselor: That's very astute of you to recognize these potential pitfalls. You really shouldn't do anything that would get you overwhelmed. What is the smallest amount that you could do without getting that feeling?

Husband: Well, I could work for an hour a day maybe.

Wife: What good would that do? You've got months of work to do. You need to get in there and work fifty hours a week until you're caught up.

Counselor: I don't agree. Taking on too much at once can actually make the task feel impossible. What you need to do is start out with a very small amount. Then, when you feel comfortable with that, you can increase the time you put in. You suggested an hour a day. Do you think that would work? Or could that be too much? If that would feel overwhelming, then you might want to start out with only forty-five minutes.

When the client recognizes the need to change, the counselor needs to support that progress. And when the client says that he cannot take on too much, he is probably accurate. If the client were to attempt to do more work than he says he can handle, he is likely to fail. If he is encouraged to push himself, one of two things is likely to occur. He could get overwhelmed easily, or his resistant style could sabotage any attempts at progress. Either way, the client loses. When the counselor agrees with the client's position, it is much less likely that the client will undercut the plan. In fact, sometimes the opposite occurs. When the counselor agrees with the "resistant" position of the client, the client begins to move out of that position and becomes move actively involved in the change process.

THINGS THAT COUNSELORS DO TO GET STUCK

When you approach counseling from a solution-based perspective, you use techniques that differ from the ones you would use in a long-term method. However, you still need to use some basic counseling skills. Empathy is one of these. Working briefly does not mean that counselors neglect to empathize with the clients and communicate a genuine concern and understanding for their situation. If you ignore this basic skill, you could easily cause the counseling process to stall.

Another basic skill that you must continue to employ in brief therapy is the ability to adapt the treatment to the client's basic viewpoint. Clients will not benefit if they think that counselors are pushing their own agenda. This is called establishing rapport. Clients need to feel comfortable in counseling. They need to feel that it is safe to share very personal information. They need to know that they have come to the right place to get the help that they need. If counselors do not establish a good level of rapport, the counseling process will bog down from the start.

Another mistake that counselors make is to use a cookbook approach to counseling, rigidly following a specific technique rather than adapting the technique to the specific situation. Each client and each counseling situation is unique. Failure to recognize that will invite a stalemate.

GETTING UNSTUCK

You can get stuck for a variety of reasons. Sometimes it's because of what clients do. Sometimes it's because of what you do. However it happens, getting stuck is a significant problem. When that happens, you need to figure out how to get things back on track again.

What follows is a menu of "something different" to try. This menu consists of a variety of techniques for getting unstuck and putting the counseling back in a change-focused direction. Not all of these techniques will work in every situation. But they can help.

Discuss the Situation with the Client

This may seem to be a rather obvious tactic, hardly one that you would pay good money to be told. However, it is such an obvious move that it can be easily overlooked. In addition, graduate school training teaches counselors to be the experts. Yet when you are stuck, it may be time to shift perspectives and rely on the expertise of the client. Sometimes clients may have a very good idea about why they are stuck and good suggestions about what to do about it. This is a benign maneuver and should be the first line of attack before attempting to use any more drastic steps.

Shift to an Emotional Focus

Some clients find it difficult to focus on solutions and exceptions. When you ask exception-finding questions, these clients tend to respond, "I don't know," or, "There aren't any."

When this occurs, you end up feeling frustrated and trapped. After all, how can you help someone who will not cooperate in the process? What do you do now? In some situations it can be helpful to continue to probe for exceptions. When clients are not used to thinking in this manner, it may take them some time to shift their thinking process before they can begin to identify exceptions to their problems. However, sometimes it becomes obvious that pursuing this line of interaction will be fruitless.

You may want to shift to a more emotionally centered solution focus. Brief therapists David Kiser, Fred Piercy, and Eve Lipchik suggest that one reason clients may not be able to focus on solutions is the difficulty involved with overcoming strong negative emotions. "The movement in solution-focused therapy from problems to solutions is not automatic. It involves considerable therapeutic skill to help a client move from 'affective congruence' (feeling bad and talking about negative experiences) to 'affective incongruence' (feeling bad and shifting focus to more positive emotions)." [1]

This problem can be overcome by one of the following tactics:

1. *Join with the negative emotion.* This can be done by reflecting to the clients the frustration and negative feelings that they have about their situation.

2. Actively elicit positive feelings. To do this, simply ask the clients about times when they feel positive, happy, content, etc.

3. Use emotions as exceptions. When you use emotions as exceptions, you specifically ask the clients to tell you about a time when they felt different from the way they feel now.

Make the Most of Exceptions

At times a client can have difficulty identifying exceptions to his or her situation. When this occurs, you must not be too quick to accept the client's statements. Going back into the client's past to find times when the situation was different can be helpful. Saying to the client, "Tell me about a time last year when you were able to get along with your wife," can expand the client's perspective and increase the likelihood of being able to identify exceptions.

Another method for helping the client identify unnoticed exceptions is for the counselor to point them out. A man who has been moderately depressed for a number of years cannot identify times when he feels a little better. In this situation the counselor can use the man's coming to counseling as an exception. "Frequently people who are depressed have difficulty accomplishing anything. Yet you were able to come in for counseling and even were able to dress nicely. How were you able to do that? I would not have expected someone who is as depressed as you are to be able to do these things."

Exceptions can also be identified by using the 1–10 scale. After the client rates his or her current situation, work to identify what has helped the client attain a particular level. "What is it that has helped the situation be at a three rather than a two?" The reasons that the client gives for being at that particular level then become exceptions that you can elaborate on.

Review the Goals

As mentioned in chapter 8, one of the most common reasons for counselors getting stuck is unclear treatment goals. For goals to be an adequate road map for treatment, they need to be clear and stated in observable, specific, measurable, attainable, and positive terms. However, it is still possible to have acceptable goals yet find that they are not directing treatment adequately. In this case make sure that you are actually following the goals. When the goal is that the client will reduce the number of anxiety attacks from three to one a day, it slows down the counseling to be talking about getting along with a spouse, unless the relationship with the spouse is contributing to the anxiety.

Take Smaller Steps

It is possible to have well-developed goals and even to be working toward these goals and yet be doing so too fast. Most of the time, progress in counseling comes from taking one small step at a time. Remember that change is generative. One small change leads to another small change. Eventually, the small changes will add up to the result that the client wants.

Sometimes it is possible to attempt to accomplish too much at once. When the steps are too big, the client may not be able to negotiate the process. The desire is for the client first to move from a 2 to a 3 on a 1–10 scale, not to move from a 2 to a 6. When it appears that progress is bogged down, check to make sure that the client is not trying to take too big a step. A frequent reason for getting stuck is that clients are not used to thinking in terms of the small changes. They need to be educated to see things in this manner.

Assess Client Status

It is possible to get stuck simply by attempting to treat visitors or complainants as if they were customers. When this happens, it is time to reassess what category best describes the client that you are working with and shift your approach accordingly.

When working with visitors, find something to compliment them on. Sometimes this is as basic as thanking them for expending the effort to show up. In addition, any homework you give to visitors should be limited to observational tasks since the visitor is not invested in changing. By aligning with visitors, it is possible to find out what they are customers for. Then counseling can progress toward those goals.

In working with complainants, point out that focusing on someone else's problem does not get them to their goal since they cannot change another person. It is necessary to establish what is in the complainant's power to change. When you help them do this, then new treatment goals can be established.

You can also become stuck when you misidentify the stage of change that clients are in. Chapter 2 discussed James Prochaska's model of change.

That model identifies six separate stages for the change process. If clients are in the contemplation stage and if you are working with them as if they are in the action stage, then you and they will get nowhere. It is always appropriate to do a quick reassessment of a client's stage of change when you find yourself at an impasse. Once you are sure of what stage they are in and respond accordingly, you may be able to resume progress.

Assess the Attempted Solution

At times it is possible for clients to be doing things that actually reinforce the problem. It is essential to be sure that attempted solutions are working instead of being just more of the same thing, which will only result in maintaining the problem.

A father comes in for help with his parenting skills. His twelve-year-old daughter will not follow his directions. He tells her, in every way that he can think of, what he wants done. Yet she still continues to ignore him. When he talks to her about it, she shrugs her shoulders and says, "I guess I forgot."

In counseling, the father decides to write out his instructions for his daughter and then hand them to her. This intervention is just more of the same thing that he has already done. He is merely telling her what to do in a different form. He needs to find another approach, such as implementing a system of appropriate consequences to address his daughter's behavior.

Agree with the Client's Perspective

Sometimes, what looks like resistance may actually be an indication that clients do not feel completely understood. As a result, they may overemphasize one point in an attempt to communicate more clearly with the counselor. When this occurs, it can be helpful to agree with their point. To continue with your perspective is only going to get them further entrenched in their position.

Jill frequently stated that she felt that things would go better and she would feel more confident if she could have a regular time of Bible study. Her counselor worked with her to identify times when she was able to do this and what helped her to do the study. Then her counselor gave Jill appropriate homework assignments. However, three sessions later Jill had made no progress. She had only partially completed her homework, and despite discussing her goal from a variety of perspectives in counseling, she was stuck. When her counselor brought up the issue with her, this is what occurred.

> *Counselor:* I know that you sincerely feel that the next step for you would be to make some changes in your spiritual life. You've even mentioned that having a regular Bible study would be the way you would want to move ahead. Yet whatever we come up with to help you do this doesn't seem to work. Do you have any idea how we can get past this problem?
>
> *Jill:* I think the problem is that I just don't have enough confidence. If I were more sure of myself, I would probably do it.
>
> *Counselor:* Help me understand. You said earlier that if you were to have a regular Bible study, it would help your confidence to grow. Yet you can't have a regular study because you don't have enough confidence. Is that right?
>
> *Jill:* Well, that's what I said. But it doesn't make a lot of sense, does it?
>
> *Counselor:* I can understand what you mean, though. If you don't feel comfortable with yourself, it's difficult to start something new, even if it is the thing that you need to do.
>
> *Jill:* Yeah, that's it.
>
> *Counselor:* I think you may be onto something there. Let me ask you this. Suppose you were to develop more confidence. What is the first thing your husband would notice is different? What would be the first small clue to him that you had the confidence?
>
> *Jill:* Actually, I think that has begun to happen. Recently I have begun to talk to him in a more confident manner, and he has paid attention to the things I had to say.

From this point Jill was able to identify several small exceptions, times when she felt that she was displaying more confidence. This session ended with her agreeing to look for the times when she showed the type of confidence that would enable her to do the desired Bible study. This session was a turning point that allowed Jill to move out of the rut and get back on the road of change.

Change the Main Thrust

Two tactics for promoting change have been presented in this book. One tactic focuses on developing solutions. This approach works on identifying exceptions and helping the client do more of the same. The second tactic focuses on problems, which are seen as ineffective attempts at resolving the situation. This approach works to identify the attempted solution and to do something entirely different.

At times in the counseling process, you will find that clients are not responding to a solution focus. Clients can't or won't identify any exceptions. They find it impossible to identify what a miracle would look like or to envision a future without the problem. When this happens, you may find it effective to shift from developing solutions to focusing on problems. This can be accomplished initially by beginning to agree with the client that the situation does look bleak and by suggesting that you explore the problem. From here you begin to look at attempted solutions with a perspective toward having the client do something different.

At times, after focusing on assessing problem-solving techniques and working with the 180-degree change, you realize that the method is not getting the results you want. This is when it can be helpful to begin probing for exceptions. This is a drastic shift because the client has been reinforced for thinking in problem-solving terms. So when you begin to look for exceptions, you will need to give the client ample time to begin thinking in these terms.

Make Sure You're Not Working Too Hard

As a counselor, you can easily become invested in your clients' progress. Sometimes, though, it is possible to become too invested. When this happens, you can begin to put more effort than you should into the counseling. You can spot this happening when you are doing more talking than the clients are. Or you may begin to realize that when clients frequently say, "I don't know," you proceed to answer your own questions. Another indication that you are working too hard is when you have more reaction to the situations in clients' lives than they do.

The result of your working too hard is that clients lose the motivation to figure out their own solutions. It is necessary for clients to struggle sometimes. This struggle is part of the change process. Without it, change may not be lasting.

When you begin to think that you are working harder than clients are working, you need to slow down. Let clients grapple with the issues. If there are long silences in response to your questions, that's fine. Sometimes clients need to think or even feel uncomfortable. The worst that can happen when you quit trying so hard and place the responsibility for change on the clients is that you find out that the clients really do not want to change. In that case you terminate the counseling and move on.

Reframe the Problem

Reframing is a technique that can help clients see the situation from a different perspective and at times encourage new avenues for developing solutions. Reframing simply involves your restating the problem in terms that are gentler and less condemning. When you are able to restate the problem in terms that are more positive, it gives clients a fresh way of looking at the situation. A perspective that is less pathological may help them become more motivated to change. Reframing can also reduce the reluctance to doing something that is new and different.

Reframing provides a logical but totally new way of describing the issue. One example is to call a client's anger intense love. Another would be to label a spouse who is overcontrolling as concerned. Teenage rebellion can become an attempt at normal independence.

One reason that reframing can help clients move from a stuck position is that it allows them to see the problem in a different manner. Thus they can use different approaches to relate to it. They way they will respond when they see themselves as very concerned can be significantly different from the way they will respond when they see themselves as overcontrolling. Reframing opens up new options for acting differently and thus increases the chances that clients will respond in a new way to the problem.

Bring in Other People

In helping people, you can become stuck when you overlook important information about the problem. You can also get stuck when you miss important solutions that are available to clients. These situations can occur when clients become subjective and do not recognize viable options. Also, clients can neglect to give you important information because they do not realize its value. In these situations progress can begin again by bringing in other people who can provide additional information. At times spouses or parents can be valuable consultants.

Consider the case of a fifty-two-year-old man who was in counseling for severe depression after he had seriously considered committing suicide. Part of the factors precipitating the depression was his feeling that his marriage of twenty years was falling apart. He sincerely wanted to repair his marriage, but he was unsure of how to reengage his wife. When his wife was brought in for one session, she revealed that her husband frequently became involved in helping young, single mothers. There was nothing immoral about what the man was doing. He simply felt that it was his ministry to assist these needy women in the church. His help was limited to giving advice and periodic financial assistance, which he was able to provide. However, whenever he got involved in one of these projects, his wife felt left out of his life. She began to feel resentful toward him, and she withdrew.

In this situation, it was essential to have the perspective of the client's wife. He did not see that what he was doing in helping the younger women was a problem. In fact, he saw it as something quite spiritual. He was blind to the injury his ministry involvement caused his wife. He told her that her resistance indicated that she was not allowing the Lord to lead her and that she was hindering his expression of the spiritual gift of helps.

Bringing in the client's wife allowed the man to see the problem in his marriage from a different perspective. It also helped the counselor to help him develop a strategy to solve the problem, which in turn helped his mood to change.

Imagine the Future If Change Doesn't Occur

Another effective strategy for getting the change process moving after it has stalled can be to explore the benefits of not changing. This intervention can either help the client realize the absurdity of remaining in a stagnant position or at times bring to light significant reasons why the client actually does not want to change. If the latter occurs, then the counselor can redirect the process or terminate the counseling; either solution is preferable to remaining stuck.

Brad is a thirty-four-year-old man who came to marital counseling with his wife, Angie. Both were tired of the boisterous arguments that were a regular part of their life. When they finally came for counseling, they had tried every marriage seminar and workshop that they could find. At the advice of their pastor, they sought professional help.

Initially, they began to show progress in counseling. The intensity and frequency of the arguments decreased drastically, with both Brad and Angie working hard to identify and change their part in the marital uproar. However, after about six sessions, progress began to stall as Brad started to complain that his feelings about issues had not changed. Furthermore, Brad claimed that he was merely stuffing his views and if Angie did not start listening to him, the arguments would soon begin again. At this point the counselor began to talk with Brad about what it would look like if he did not change.

> *Counselor:* Brad, let's suppose for a minute that you decide to stop stuffing your views. In fact you decide never to stuff your views again. Your opinions are important, and you want to make sure that Angie knows them and understands them. What do you think would happen if you never stuffed your views again?
>
> *Brad:* There's a good chance that Angie might think about leaving.
>
> *Counselor:* Suppose Angie did that. You let her know your opinion, and she decided she couldn't take it anymore and actually left. What would life be like then?
>
> *Brad:* Things would be pretty lonely if that happened.
>
> *Counselor:* What would you do then, with this lonely life?
>
> *Brad:* I don't know. Things sure would be miserable.

In this instance, exploring the results of not changing was fruitful. It helped Brad realize where his actions were leading. This realization then provided additional motivation for him to become more flexible instead of rigidly holding to his position. This motivation is what was needed to get the counseling moving again.

Getting stuck is a common occurrence in counseling. Sometimes you can be proactive and prevent it by understanding your clients and their personalities or by handling difficult situations in a way that minimizes the likelihood of getting bogged down. However, no matter what you do right, sometimes you just get stuck. When you find yourself in this situation, there are things that you can do. Consciously implementing some of the techniques suggested here may be able to get the counseling moving again. It's worth a try. It is something different.

PART FOUR

Final Considerations

13 / RESEARCH: CAN ANYTHING SO SIMPLE BE SO EFFECTIVE?

Science can only ascertain what is, but not what should be, and outside of its domain, value judgments of all kinds remain necessary.
ALBERT EINSTEIN, *Out of My Later Years*

Sound research based on scientific reasoning can lead us to a better understanding of the techniques that we use in our offices. Perhaps more important, well-conducted research studies deepen our knowledge of our Creator and his general revelation. Not only can this discipline help guide us into truth, but it also helps us discern fact from fiction. Of course, scientific methodology is not intended to be the sole basis of decisions and reasoning. We as Christians must weigh the claims of science against the teachings of the Bible. When this is done appropriately, high quality research endeavors become another important tool to use when examining the techniques we use in our offices. Perhaps more important, sound research allows us to understand the effectiveness of our work.

Most of the research we will present is well conducted, rigorous, and insightful. Where noted, several of the studies cited need follow-up work and provide only tentative conclusions. Read on to learn more about the scientific evidence about brief therapy. Even if research doesn't interest you, take some time to walk through this important information with us. We hope that it will give you a better understanding of the workings of brief therapy as well the scientific rationale for the model we have chosen to explain.

Research on Brief Therapy

In their comprehensive review of the literature on brief therapy, Mary Koss and Julia Shiang make four valid points in relation to brief therapy and the comprehensive body of research collected on it.

1. It is now generally recognized that when patients enter psychological treatment, they do not anticipate that their therapy will be prolonged but believe that their problems will require a few sessions at most.
2. Brief therapy models, once thought to be appropriate only for less severe problems, have actually been shown to be effective in treating a wide range of psychological and health-related problems, including severe and chronic problems, if treatment goals are kept reasonable.
3. Brief treatment methods have generally reported the same success rates as longer treatment programs.
4. Brief therapy is seen as a means to treat emotional difficulties effectively at a relatively reasonable cost.[1]

Wow! These are powerful statements that have far-reaching effects on the effectiveness of brief therapy! If they have any merit, then perhaps this brief therapy is deserving of further attention.

For over fifty years, researchers have examined the effects of psychotherapy. Fortunately for all of us in the people-helping professions, we get to keep our jobs. At least for now. After thousands of studies and millions of dollars, the large body of data collected on psychotherapy suggests that it is effective. In general, therapy has an effect on individuals so that those who seek treatment are significantly better off than those who do not seek treatment for a variety of conditions.[2] This is good news! After all, it would be disappointing to find that counseling really has no meaningful effect in people's lives.

We know that therapeutic interventions are generally helpful; however, what about this brief stuff? We know that in general brief therapy is helpful and as effective as long-term modalities.[3] Research conducted on brief therapy suggests that it is useful for a number of diagnostic conditions. Empirical evidence also suggests that brief therapy may be useful in the treatment of a number of disorders, including depression, anxiety disorders, maladaptive interpersonal functioning, and panic disorders.[4] Research even suggests some utility of brief models for the treatment of personality disorders.[5] The data suggest that brief therapy may be effective for a number of the problems for which our clients come to us for help. But what kind of brief therapy is helpful? Are specific types of treatment better for certain people? Are certain ways of thinking more helpful for specific problems? Let's look further at the research on brief therapy.

Models of Brief Therapy Contrasted

In general, research on brief therapy has focused on cognitive-behavioral and psychodynamic therapies. With hundreds of studies conducted to test the effectiveness of these types of treatment, we have a large body of research to examine. Fortunately, new techniques allow researchers to compare a large number of studies, thus examining a more significant body of data. For example, in a well-controlled study, Paul Crits-Christoph of the University of Pennsylvania School of Medicine compared eleven studies to examine the efficacy of brief psychodynamic treatment.[6] This researcher included only studies of cases that involved fewer than twelve sessions, used experienced therapists, used real subjects, and employed a control group or comparison group. In other words, only rigorously conducted studies were included. His findings suggest that brief psychodynamic therapies showed large effects in comparison to control groups. These brief psychodynamically treated clients truly benefited from counseling as the average client receiving brief psychodynamic therapies was better off than 62 percent of the clients in the comparison group.[7]

Similarly, data examining brief cognitive-behavioral therapy have found it to be effective for a number of presenting problems.[8] Like brief psychodynamic therapies, brief cognitive-behavioral therapy is efficacious. While brief cognitive-behavioral treatments have been found to be slightly better for the treatment of a handful of conditions, the research generally finds minimal or no differences when comparing brief psychodynamic to brief cognitive-behavioral therapies. For example, brief cognitive, cognitive-behavioral, and psychodynamic therapies have all been found to be helpful for the treatment of depression.[9]

The most comprehensive and thorough research endeavor, the NIMH Collaborative Study of Depression, provides further insight into the effectiveness of different types of brief therapy.[10] Four modalities of treatment were compared, including brief interpersonal therapy, cognitive-behavioral therapy, imipramine plus clinical management, and a placebo control plus clinical management. With 250 subjects, this research suggests that imipramine plus clinical management was the most effective means of treatment, with the placebo plus clinical management being the least effective means. The two brief therapies fell in between and appeared to be effective, even though there were no significant differences between the two types of therapy.

Their studies and others suggest that brief therapy is effective for a variety of diagnostic categories and that it is equally as effective as long-term treatment in many cases.[11] The above findings also provide varied reviews on the comparative effectiveness of different types of brief treatments. Even so, it seems that there are few significant differences among the various modalities of treatments.[12] At the same time, "specific approaches may outperform others when applied to a particular client problem."[13]

Counterpoint

In 1995, *Consumer Reports* conducted a unique research study in which 180,000 of their readers were asked twenty-six questions about the mental health services they had received.[14] Just as these readers rated the fit and finish of their new cars or the speed of a food processor, they rated the quality of counseling services. The methodology used in this study varies drastically from traditional psychotherapy research. In place of extensive outcome testing and controlled conditions emerges the importance of personal rating and testimony. While some have criticized this methodology, it provides important information that challenges a large body of the data that we have just mentioned.[15]

In addition to numerous other findings, the *Consumer Reports* study found that long-term therapy produced greater improvements than short-term therapy. This finding was reported to be statistically robust. In addition, respondents whose choice of duration of care was limited by their insurance company tended to do worse than those who had a choice.

These are important findings that cannot be ignored. While they provide an interesting contrast to most other research on the effectiveness of brief counseling, there are several limitations to these findings because of the way the research was conducted. We recognize that the case for or against brief therapy is not closed. We include this new data to spur additional discussions and research.

WHY BE BRIEF?

When Does Change Really Happen?

Perhaps the most striking studies about brief therapy are those that examine the time in which change occurs in therapy. Using a sample of twenty-four hundred subjects with data from thirty years of experimentation, psychologist and researcher Kenneth Howard and colleagues provide a comprehensive study to summarize the literature comparing the length of treatment to therapy outcome.[16] They note in their body of research that 15 percent of patients showed measurable improvement before attending the first session; 50 percent of patients were significantly improved after six to eight sessions; and 75 percent of the patients showed measurable improvement by the twenty-sixth session. Further research indicates that 75 percent of those clients who benefit from therapy do so within the first six months of treatment.[17] Whether you are a brief therapist or a long-term therapist, this is important information. Not only do many people begin to change before they attend their first session, but half of all therapy clients have demonstrated significant improvement by the sixth session.

Client Expectations

Perhaps even more striking are the expectations our clients have of the length of therapy. Psychologist and researcher Gene Pekarik surveyed therapy clients, and they had some interesting things to say. Over two-thirds of the people in his sample expected therapy to last ten or fewer sessions. They even expected that they would feel better by the fifth session. In addition, it was noted that 75 percent of all community mental health patients and more than half of all private patients terminate by the tenth session.[18]

This research sounds a wake-up call for us to listen to our clients and their expectations. Perhaps even more alarming is research by Gene

Pekarik and Karen Finney-Owen, in which it was reported that of 173 therapists, the majority overestimated actual treatment lengths while underestimating dropout rates.[19] In short, our expectations about the length of treatment seem to differ from those of our clients.

Single-Session Therapy

Let's look at the research on really brief therapy. While it may be surprising and even alarming, research tells us that the most frequent (modal) number of sessions is one. That's right—one session of counseling! While many of us consider one session to be a treatment failure, Bernard Bloom of the University of Colorado researched those who attended only one session of therapy, and he found that single-session treatment can be effective.[20] Psychologist Moshe Talmon also researched people who attended only one session of treatment, and he found that the majority of these clients received help for that problem in just one session.[21]

Does Brief Therapy Really Lead to Change?

Some have called brief therapy a Band-Aid approach, claiming that no lasting change can occur from eight or ten sessions of treatment. While brief therapy focuses on specific goals and leads to specific and measurable behavioral changes, research indicates that brief treatment may also lead to lasting changes in psychological structures. John Exner and Anne Andronikof-Sanglade, noted researchers on the Rorschach test, treated two groups of thirty-five people with brief therapy and long-term therapy.[22] The group receiving brief therapy received an average of 14.2 sessions of treatment, in contrast to the long-term group, which received an average of 47 therapy sessions. The Rorschach inkblot test was given to both groups before treatment, at termination, and again at eight to twelve months after termination. Not only did both groups report significantly fewer symptoms at termination and at eight to twelve months after termination, but in both groups the Rorschach data suggested that there was considerable improvement in psychological organization. Brief therapy caused changes that were more than skin deep.

Another study by the University of Sheffield's Gillian Hardy and his colleagues examined the effects of brief cognitive-behavioral and interpersonal therapy on clients diagnosed with cluster C personality disorders along with depression.[23] These included clients with avoidant, obsessive-compulsive, or dependent personality disorder. When compared to depressed patients who were not diagnosed with a personality disorder, it was found that rates of improvement were similar for both groups. Those with cluster C personality disorders responded to brief therapy, and they responded no more slowly than those without diagnosed personality disorders.

THE EFFICACY OF SOLUTION-BASED THERAPY

At this point, we have reason to believe that therapy helps our clients. We also have reason to believe that brief therapy is effective for a number of people with a number of problems. What about solution-based brief therapy? Is there anything to support the use of the techniques about which you have just spent hours reading? Let's look at the research on solution-based models and see if these ideas really hold water.

At the Brief Therapy Training Center in Milwaukee, Steve de Shazer and his colleagues have collected data. Because this research was conducted by de Shazer, a strong proponent of solution-focused brief therapy, it may be subject to bias. Even so, I think it is worth examining. De Shazer and colleagues note that between 1978 and 1983, 1,600 cases were seen in their clinic, each averaging six sessions. Follow-up phone calls by an outside source were made to a representative sample of 400. From this, 72 percent of those contacted either noted that they met their goals in therapy or felt as if they had made enough progress so that further treatment was not needed. De Shazer and colleagues also note that of those presenting with vague or ill-defined goals, 23 of 28 patients contacted after termination reported that their complaints were better after therapy than before. Of this same group, 23 of 28 also noted that changes accomplished in therapy had endured.[24]

In a similar study, David Kiser followed the outcome of 164 clients treated in the Brief Family Therapy Center for six, twelve, and eighteen months after therapy.[25] He used a questionnaire similar to the one used by the MRI group in 1974, where they reported that about 75 percent of their cases had at least some relief from their presenting complaint.[26] Kiser found even better results.

Of 69 cases receiving 4 to 10 sessions, 64 clients, or nearly 93 percent, felt they had met or made progress on their treatment goal (about 77 percent of the 64 met the goal, and more than 14 percent made progress). At the 18 month follow-up, of all 164 clients (94 percent of whom had 10 or fewer sessions), about 51 percent reported the presenting problem was still resolved, while about 35 percent said it was not as bad as when they had initiated therapy. In other words about 85 percent of the clients reported full or partial success.[27]

The research conducted at the Brief Family Therapy Center gives us a broad idea that solution-based therapy was at least helpful for many of the people seen in the Milwaukee clinic. While this cannot be considered rigorous or unbiased work, the numbers are still impressive. In addition to the research conducted in Milwaukee, other studies speak to solution-focused therapy. School psychologist James Morrison and colleagues employed a solution-focused, family-systems model to treat those presenting with behavior problems in school.[28] For 30 families who participated in the study, 67 percent of the students completely met their goals. Behavioral changes were maintained over a one- to two-year period. Another 10 percent of the students reported making partial progress toward stated goals. Relapse rate was also reported: 22 percent of those studied were later referred for behavioral problems.

Even with the research that touts the effectiveness of solution-based therapies, you may be wondering about the interventions used by this model. Do they work? For example, why do exception-finding questions make a difference? Greer Melidonis and Brenna Bry examined four families who were referred to treatment because of adolescent behavior problems.[29] Specifically, they wanted to know if exception-finding questions would reduce the number of blaming statements made by family members since distressed families have been found to engage in more blaming statements and are unable to transition from blame to supportive communication.

To test this hypothesis, each family was seen for two sessions of therapy. In the first session, exception-finding questions were pursued, and the therapist responded only to reports of positive adolescent behavior. During the second session, the therapist returned to baseline behavior and ceased asking exception-finding questions. Perhaps not surprisingly, when the therapist asked exception-finding questions, blaming statements made by the family decreased significantly. Even more important, when the therapist stopped asking exception-finding questions in the second session, blame increased and positive statements decreased.

In a similar study, family-therapy researchers Cleveland Shields, Douglas Sprenkle, and John Constantine examined initial interviewing skills and tested solution-focused questions to determine their effect on outcome in family therapy.[30] Again, when examining solution-focused interviewing skills, it was found that the probability of family members discussing solutions or goals in the first session was significantly related to their outcome in therapy. Early introduction of solution-focused principles may, in fact, lay the groundwork for future changes.

Pre-Session Changes

Solution-based therapy recognizes that people begin to change before they even enter our offices. In fact, some people may change between the time they schedule their appointment and later appear for their first session. To further examine this, Michele Weiner-Davis, Steve de Shazer, and Wallace Gingerich developed three questions to be used to assess pre-session change with all clients who presented for treatment in their agency. They include:

1. Many times people notice in between the time they make the appointment for therapy and the first session that things already seem different. What have you noticed about your situation?
2. (If yes to #1): Do these changes relate to the reason you came for therapy?
3. (If yes to #1): Are these the kinds of changes you would like to continue to have happen?[31]

Thirty cases in which at least one parent and an adolescent were seen were assessed for pre-session change. The authors found that 20 of 30 people interviewed reported pre-session changes. All 20 also answered yes to questions 2 and 3, suggesting that the kinds of changes they were looking for had already begun. In addition, of the 10 who reported no changes, the authors report that many of them were later able to identify pre-session changes. These authors further note that the frame of reference of the therapist determines whether or not these changes will be seen as significant and amplified. For example, some therapists may see them as a flight into health, while others may view them as changes that can make a difference. Michele Weiner-Davis and her colleagues note, "The approach we have found useful is to view 'flights into health' as real change (although admittedly new and somewhat 'out of character'). We then try to 'keep 'em flying' by transforming these 'flights' into real lasting change." [32]

Formula First-Session Task

Researchers and psychologists Jerome Adams, Fred Piercy, and Joan Jurich examined solution-focused family therapy as the formula first-session task (FFST) was contrasted to strategic-structural interventions.[33] Specifically, the FFST asks family members in the first session to observe for the next week what things they would like to continue to see happen. It was noted that, after one week, the groups in which the FFST was prescribed showed higher levels of family compliance, clarity of treatment goals, and improvement in the presenting problem. While there was no difference in outcome between the groups following ten weeks of treatment, it seems that the formula first-session task may have made the initial stages of therapy more effective.

RESEARCH ON THE PROBLEM-SOLVING MODELS OF BRIEF THERAPY

With an understanding of some of the research on the solution-based models, let's take a look at the outcome studies that examine the MRI school. Similar to the research conducted by Steve de Shazer at his clinic, John Weakland and his colleagues made follow-up contacts to ninety-seven clients who received counseling at the MRI clinic in Palo Alto, California. The researchers were interested in two broad areas of outcome as measured by the following questions: "Has behavior changed as planned?" "Has the complaint been resolved?"[34]

Answers to these questions were broken down into three categories, which included

1. complete resolution of the problem
2. clear and considerable change but not complete resolution
3. little or no change

Consistent with our knowledge of the effectiveness of brief therapy, Weakland and his colleagues found that 40 percent of the clients reported complete resolution of their problems. Another 32 percent reported significant improvement, and only 28 percent reported no change.[35] While this cannot be considered rigorous research, it does demonstrate the general effectiveness of the MRI model, at least according to clients' reports of outcome.

Efficiency of the MRI Model

In California in the mid 1980s, Kaiser Permanente, a large managed-care organization, experimented with the MRI model. According to Hendron Chubb and Eldon Evans, the MRI model was exclusively implemented at its clinic in Pleasanton, California. In contrast, traditional models, including those of a psychodynamic nature, were maintained at other area clinics that were treating similar populations. Several variables including utilization, length of stay, and hospitalizations were measured. The Pleasanton clinic was compared to other facilities in the area.[36]

In examining the data, it was found that the clinic using the MRI model was able to see significantly more clients and allocate fewer staff resources. Remarkably, 82 percent more patients were seen in the Pleasanton clinic than were seen in the other area facilities. While comparable facilities in the area had up to twenty-two-week waiting lists, the Pleasanton clinic never had to have a client wait for services. In addition, only 11.1 percent of the clients receiving the MRI model were seen more than five times. This is in sharp contrast to the average of the other clinics in which 27.9 percent were seen more than five times. Perhaps even more notable, only 0.1 percent of clients treated using the MRI model were seen more than twenty times. Therapists' time was used more efficiently.

Of course, these statistics are of little value if clients were not helped. While no formal outcome measures were reported, the clinic using the MRI model had the lowest hospitalization rate of any of the clinics in the area. In addition, patient satisfaction with treatment was measured. The

Pleasanton facility, which used the MRI model exclusively, consistently reported a 90 percent satisfaction rate with services rendered.

While this does not meet the requirements for rigorous outcome research, these are several findings that speak directly to the efficiency and utility of the MRI model. Not only were clients helped in a timely manner and kept out of the hospital, but the limited resources of staff were better used to help a greater number of people.

Strategic/Problem-Solving Treatment of Phobic Disorders

Based on the MRI principle that the attempted solutions become the problem, Giorgio Nardone describes a model of brief, strategic therapy based on the MRI writings. Forty-one cases of people with serious phobic disorders including agoraphobia, panic attacks, and serious anxiety attacks were treated with this model. Because of the high rate of relapse in severe phobic disorders, cases were followed at three, six, and twelve months after termination.[37] In this unique model, the social support system of the client is seen as part of the problem. Consistent with Weakland's presuppositions, the social support system is seen as part of the attempted solution that becomes part of the problem.[38] By reframing the client's need for the support in combination with other strategic methods, change in the phobic condition is begun. (For a comprehensive examination of this treatment model, see Nardone.)

For example, 41 patients in Italy, ranging in age from eighteen to seventy-one years, were treated under these conditions. At a one-year follow-up, 32 of the patients were successfully treated with no relapse; 7 patients showed moderate improvement; and 2 patients showed some improvement, although they had not fully recovered from their condition. In addition, Nardone reports that 80.7 percent of the cases were treated in fewer than twenty sessions.

PRINCIPLES UNDERLYING THE SOLUTION-BASED AND PROBLEM-SOLVING MODELS

Behavior, Then Insight

Many contemporary theories of change rest on the assumption that behavior changes after some learning or insight occurs. These theories hold that lasting change occurs only after the "aha" experience. While many therapists implicitly believe this, a large body of data suggests otherwise. In contrast to many contemporary theories, the MRI model and, to a large extent, the solution-based models, take a different approach. For the problem-solving or solution-based practitioner, no insight is needed or relevant. By doing something different, the counselor and client evoke prescriptions to change behaviors, actions, relationships, and sometimes attitudes. These theorists realize that insight may eventually follow "doing something different."

In his comprehensive work in the field of social psychology, Philip Zimbardo notes the power of having people role-play behaviors or enact behaviors that are contrary to their current beliefs. In doing so, attitudes often follow. Hard to imagine? Let's look at some research.

In 1965, social scientists Irving Janis and Leon Mann designed a study that demonstrates the value of changing behavior, realizing that attitudes will soon follow.[39] In this research, college women who smoked at least fifteen cigarettes a day were recruited as subjects. Half of these women were assigned to a role-playing condition where they played the role of a woman who had a bad cough and went to the doctor to find that she had lung cancer and needed immediate surgery. Over the course of their visits to the doctor, women in this treatment group role-played a scene in which the only chance for successful treatment was for them to quit smoking. Each woman in the experimental group played the role of a woman talking to her doctor about the fact that she may die because of her heavy smoking. The other half of the women were assigned to a control group. Rather than acting out the role of the dying woman, they merely listened to tapes of the role-plays.

The results of this study clearly suggest the value of changing behavior, even if it is just for the purposes of a role-play. The women in the experimental group expressed much stronger beliefs about the negative effects of smoking following the experiment, and they noted a significantly stronger desire to quit smoking. Talk is cheap. Did this really lead to any changes in smoking behavior? At two weeks following the experiment, both groups of women were again contacted. The experimental group reported smoking 10.5 fewer cigarettes per day, on average. Women in the control group were also affected; however, not to the same degree. They reported smoking 4.8 fewer cigarettes per day.

How does this work, and what difference does it make? The field of social psychology provides important insights into our work with brief therapy. When behavior is changed, self-attributions may also change. That is, we frequently infer our attitudes and beliefs from our experiences. For the women in the smoking studies, their self-attributions changed as they attributed new meanings to their new behaviors and recognized the need to decrease their smoking behaviors. This research recognizes the value of encouraging people to try something new, realizing that they may attribute new meanings to it at a later time.

Paradoxical Interventions

The problem-solving models, like other strategic therapies, suggest the use of paradox and/or paradoxical intervention. This remains a debated therapeutic technique. Research on process and outcome in therapy is concerned with measuring the therapeutic interventions used and their relationship to client outcome. Believe it or not, the research conducted on process and outcome in therapy indicates that paradox may be one of the most consistent ways to bring about change. That's right! When used appropriately, paradox has been found to be highly related to the effectiveness of counseling and psychotherapy.

In their comprehensive 1994 review of the research on process and outcome in psychotherapy, noted researchers David Orlinsky, Klaus Grawe, and Barbara Parks summarize the current studies conducted on the use of paradoxical intention in counseling. "The most impressive record of effectiveness has been established for the technique of paradoxical intention in a number of simulated therapy experiments. [There are] 11 studies in which all 13 findings showed positive associations with outcome, and 2 meta-analyses showing substantial effect sizes." [40]

When compared to other commonly used techniques including interpretation, reflection, clarification, experiential confrontation, and self-disclosure, paradoxical intention headed the list of interventions that appear to be most highly related to patient outcome. While these authors note the importance of exercising caution with this intervention, they conclude their chapter by saying, "The experimental evidence on paradoxical intention is remarkably consistent, demonstrating a very robust association with outcome in situations where it can be used effectively. Other therapist interventions and response modes show a less consistent association with outcome."[41]

~ Goal Setting

Similar to the value of paradoxical intention, both the solution-based and problem-solving models of brief therapy rely heavily on well-executed goal setting as well as the consensus of goals between client and therapist. Orlinsky, Grawe, and Parks also looked at the relationship between goal consensus of clients and therapists and its relationship to outcome in therapy. In their examination of thirty-five research studies, they found that goal consensus, as measured from the client's perspective, tended to be an important variable when measuring outcome.[42] Surprisingly, goal consensus as measured by the therapist was not related to outcome. Our perspective doesn't mean much here. Somehow we must work to make sure that our clients perceive a consensus of goals. Most important, these findings suggest that when our clients believe that they are in agreement with their therapist on the goals of treatment, they are more likely to have a favorable outcome.

RESEARCH DIFFERENCES BETWEEN SOLUTION-BASED AND PROBLEM-SOLVING MODELS

You may be wondering whether solution-based models have ever been compared to the MRI problem-solving model. Perhaps there are advantages to one of these models. Karen Jordan and William Quinn provide an interesting comparison of the solution-based model and the problem-solving models, at least on a micro level.[43] Specifically, they believe that it is necessary to look at single-session outcomes on a micro level to determine the effectiveness of specific interventions. Here's what they did. Jordan and Quinn note that both the MRI and solution-based models rely on the formula first-session task. However, each model does something different with it in the second session. While both models ask clients to observe what it is they would like to continue to see happening in their lives, solution-based models follow this with exception-finding questions in the second session. In contrast, the MRI therapist uses this question to understand the problem better, while helping the client develop new problem-solving behaviors.

To examine these differences, Jordan and Quinn compared second-session outcomes in a controlled study of therapists who used either MRI or solution-based methods following the introduction of the formula first-session task. The authors suggest a careful interpretation of their results because no significant findings were made when all variables are considered. However, when individual variables are examined, there are several important differences. Specifically, those receiving solution-based interventions following the FFST showed significant perceived problem improvement. In addition, outcome expectancy and session positivity were also greater for the solution-based clients. When these are examined as a group, it seems that the focus on strengths and positive attributes may actually provide hope and encouragement, even in the second session of treatment. One additional difference between the two models emerged: Those receiving solution-based interventions reported their sessions to be more smooth and of greater depth.

These findings again point to the value of a positive, strength-based approach to counseling. While there appear to be benefits of a solution-based model, there were not clear differences of a great enough magnitude to discourage the use of the MRI model.

MAKING SENSE OF ALL OF THIS

These are but a few of the research studies that describe the effectiveness and utility of brief therapy, as well as of the solution-based and MRI models. Some of this research is especially rigorous and impressive. Other studies are helpful but lack scientific rigor. Follow-up research is needed. Even so, we know that brief therapy is generally helpful and as effective as long-term modalities.[44] Brief therapy is effective with a number of diagnostic categories.[45]

We are also beginning to see the value of the solution-based approaches as the research on exception questions, the formula first-session task, and a general solution-based orientation suggests that these interventions appear to impact clients positively and in a time-effective manner. In addition, the problem-solving techniques of paradoxical intention and the importance of goal setting have a large body of support that further validates their effectiveness.

In an age that is built on the principles of empiricism, it is important that we adequately understand and defend the integrity of the work we do. Sound scientific reasoning can guide us further into truth. Accordingly, a strong case can be made for the use of brief therapy, as well as many of the interventions explained in this book. Even so, we recognize that no scientific data are ever meant to supplant biblical truth. Let this chapter be a guide to help you understand the value of brief therapy, especially as sound research might expand our understanding of general revelation. In so doing, it is our hope that biblical truth will take precedence when there are areas of discrepancy or dispute.

14/ PUTTING IT ALL TOGETHER

When I look up into the night skies and see the work of your fingers—the moon and the stars you have made—I cannot understand how you can bother with mere puny man, to pay any attention to him!

And yet you have made him only a little lower than the angels, and placed a crown of glory and honor upon his head.

You have put him in charge of everything you made; everything is put under his authority.   PSALM 8:3-6, TLB

Brief therapy, as demanded by managed care and preferred by an increasing number of clients, has become the treatment of necessity for a significant segment of the population. Regardless of counselors' primary orientation, many of them have found it essential to have a brief-therapy tool in their therapeutic toolbox.

That is one of several reasons why AACC and Tyndale asked us to write a clinical book that would provide professional, pastoral, and lay Christian counselors with a brief-therapy tool for their counseling ministry. We've tried to do just that. Our intention has been to present an integrative model we've called solution-based brief therapy as one of several time-effective ways to help people change. Our intention has not been to coerce, convince, or convert but to encourage, inform, describe, and demonstrate.

We've seen our approach effectively used by and with a variety of people from a variety of theological persuasions. It doesn't matter whether you are charismatic or fundamental, use only the King James Version or prefer the New Living Translation, like the old hymns or contemporary praise music, sprinkle or dunk, are dispensational or Reformed, solution-based brief therapy can be a powerful tool.

A SOUND PSYCHOLOGY

It is our hope that after reading this book you will understand that, regardless of the demands of a managed-care environment, brief therapy that emphasizes solutions more than problems can be used of God to help many people experience meaningful change.

This book is a call for counselors to prepare ahead of time for each session, to maximize the critical first session, to remain active and highly focused throughout each session, to give specific homework assignments, to be able to do effective work within a limited number of sessions, and to know when a different and perhaps longer-term approach might be necessary.

We've tried to give you more than a textbook, step-by-step approach. We want to help you see what it's like to "think brief" and encourage you to begin to integrate these insights into what you already do. We don't believe that all problems can be solved in a short period of time. We agree that good questions and an optimistic, solution-based approach are not magic. Some people have complex problems that take a longer period of time and greater work to solve, even with good questions. We do believe and have experienced that most problems can be solved in twenty or fewer sessions and that many people can receive meaningful help in fewer than ten sessions.

We have tried to challenge you to consider the brief approach in order to increase your efficiency and positive treatment outcomes. We encourage you to incorporate aspects of this model into approaches and techniques you are already using.

A SOUND THEOLOGY

In our own practice we try to make sure that what we do is consistent with sound psychological principles. However, that's not the foundation of what we do. We believe that you cannot have a sound psychology that is not based or at least consistent with a sound theology. The key for being an effective tool in God's hand to speak the truths of historic Christianity into the hearts and lives of people today starts with an intimate heart knowledge of who God is, what he has revealed to us, and who he has designed us to become. Understanding who we are in Christ must precede what we attempt to do for Christ.

Colossians 2:8 warns us not to allow philosophy and deception to take our thoughts captive. It's easy for Christian counselors to become so fascinated or enamored by the theories and techniques of different psychological schools of thought that we forget what is most important. While some aspects of psychology can provide helpful insights and tools for the counselor, what it means to be a whole person can be understood only within the context of a personal life-changing relationship with Jesus Christ. Our vertical relationship with him defines, informs, and instructs our horizontal relationship with others.

We value science and respect the results of sound, solid psychological research; we use the aspects of both that we find consistent with the Bible. But we believe that divine revelation in Scripture is more reliable, more dependable, and more authoritative than the discoveries and theories of science. We believe that the Bible is the sufficient and final authority for faith and clinical practice.

The approach to brief therapy we have shared with you is an integrative model that builds on a solid biblical anthropology and uses insights from three change models: the cognitive-behavioral, the MRI model (find out what doesn't work, and do something different), and the solution-focused model (find out what does work, and do more of it).

Our approach to brief therapy involves a fresh combination of techniques and tools that are consistent with what we understand to be an orthodox biblical and theological foundation. Its pragmatic focus is on *how* people change rather than on a philosophical, metaphysical, or theological view of *who* people are. However, our view of *who* people are determines the kinds of change that are ultimately helpful.

A SOUND BIBLICAL FOUNDATION

A sound theology is dependent on a sound biblical foundation. We join with Henry Blackaby and Claude King, who, in their best-selling book *Experiencing God,* lament the fact that Christians are relying less and less on the Bible as a guide for faith and practice. "Because Christians have become disoriented to the Bible, they turn to worldly solutions, programs, and methods that appear to be the answer to spiritual problems. I use the Word of God as a guide to what we should be doing. Some people say, 'Henry, that is not practical.' They want to move me away from the Bible and rely on the world's ways or on personal experience. As a Christian disciple, I cannot abandon the guidance I find in the Bible. The Bible is my guide for faith and practice."[1]

As Christian counselors we cannot abandon the guidance we find in the Bible. It is our guide for faith, practice, and clinical work. What does it have to say about who God is and who people are? The Bible tells us that God the Son became flesh and lived among us. Jesus died a humiliating and painful death on the cross to save us from the consequences of our sins and to give us eternal life. We call that justification. Christ sent the Holy Spirit to indwell us and help us "to be conformed to the likeness of his Son" (Rom. 8:29, NIV). We call that sanctification.

Christ shed his blood to make a radical and eternal difference in our lives. It's sad to say that for some Christians, the difference they experience is primarily external or at best intellectual. They continue to be influenced by old thought patterns and controlled by their emotions. Their lives are still dominated by fear, hurt, frustration, anger, or depression. They have become stuck in relational and emotional ruts and rarely experience the joy of their salvation.

We've talked with many people who get discouraged and feel guilty because they still have those struggles. This creates a problem for them. Do they share their questions and struggles with others and risk appearing immature and unspiritual? Or do they deny their problems and pretend that everything is going great? Rather than risk the humiliation and possible rejection that might come from sharing their feelings, many Christians ignore their problems and stuff their emotions. Eventually this creates an even greater problem. We can pretend for only so long.

Part of this problem has been caused by a misunderstanding of 2 Corinthians 5:17. In the King James translation we read: "Therefore if any man be in Christ, he is a new creature: old things are passed away; behold, all things are become new." As a young Christian I (Gary) remember hearing some radio preachers say that if you still struggle with old habits and patterns, then it is clear that *all* things haven't become new and maybe you aren't really saved.

While it's true that many miraculous and wonderful things take place when we ask Christ into our heart, not *all* things become new. Our body and soul (personality) aren't immediately and totally transformed. When I was born again, God became my Father, my spirit was transformed, and I was transferred from the kingdom of darkness to the kingdom of light.

Unfortunately, I didn't receive a new body (I would have liked one), and I didn't get a new soul or personality. My mind didn't become more intelligent, and painful memories did not magically disappear overnight. I found that I continued to struggle with emotions of anger, lust, and depression. My will and its deeply ingrained habit patterns didn't immediately vanish. Becoming "conformed to the likeness of his Son" takes time (Rom. 8:29, NIV). Maturity is indeed a process.

The Bible tells us that when we ask Christ into our hearts, a radical transformation takes place (John 3:16; Rom. 6:23). At the same time, the consequences of sin on our mind, will, and emotions do not immediately disappear. I believe that an important part of the process of sanctification involves the healing of our damaged emotions. Helping people move toward wholeness is a significant part of what God calls us to do as Christian counselors.

At the core of our personhood is our creation in God's image. We bear the image of and, in specific ways, resemble our Creator. Even though the image of God in men and women is damaged and distorted by sin, we are still image-bearers.

When God created us in his image, he gave us a mind, a will, and emotions. As image bearers we have the capacity to feel, to think, and to make choices. Francis Schaeffer said, "As God is a person, He feels, thinks, and acts: so I am a person, who feels, thinks and acts."

It is unfortunate that over the years, many Christians have emphasized the mind and the will to the exclusion of the emotions. They are more comfortable with facts than with feelings, with ideas than with people. Many of us have been led to believe that spiritual maturity consists primarily of the acquisition of facts or head knowledge. The more propositional truth we can cram into our cranium, the more spiritual we will become.

John Stott often told his students in London that God didn't call preachers and teachers (and we might add Christian counselors) to the business of "breeding tadpoles." Stott said, "A tadpole is a little creature with a huge head and nothing much else besides. Certainly there are some Christian tadpoles around. Their heads are bulging with sound theology, but that is all there is to them. No, we are concerned to help people to develop not only a Christian mind, but also a Christian heart, a Christian spirit, a Christian conscience and a Christian will, in fact to become whole Christian persons, thoroughly integrated under the lordship of Christ."[2]

It's easy for Christian counselors to become tadpole breeders and emphasize the acquisition of truth and ignore the critical role of practical application. Information without application leads to desperation, but information with application can lead to transformation. The Bible is a practical book that has a lot to say about application.

For example, the psalmist emphasizes the importance of self-awareness when he writes, "Search me, O God, and know my heart; test me and know my thoughts. . . . And lead me along the path of everlasting life" (Ps. 139:23-24).

Scripture also is clear that our thoughts have a powerful influence on our growth. Romans 8:5 tells us that "those who are dominated by the sinful nature think about sinful things, but those who are controlled by the Holy Spirit think about things that please the Spirit." In Romans 12:2 Paul writes, "Don't copy the behavior and customs of this world, but let God transform you into a new person by changing the way you think. Then you will know what God wants you to do, and you will know how good and pleasing and perfect his will really is."

In Philippians 4:8-9 Paul writes, "Fix your thoughts on what is true and honorable and right. Think about things that are pure and lovely and admirable. Think about things that are excellent and worthy of praise." But Paul doesn't just stop there. He doesn't say that change is merely a matter of walking around having nice thoughts. He moves the reader to activate the will, to make some different choices. He writes, "Keep putting into practice all you learned from me and heard from me and saw me doing, and the God of peace will be with you."

God has built into every person the ability to change. But positive change doesn't just happen. Change involves identifying what hasn't worked and choosing to do something different. Ephesians 4:22-24 tells us, "Throw off your old evil nature and your former way of life, which is rotten through and through, full of lust and deception. Instead, there must be a spiritual renewal of your thoughts and attitudes. You must display a new nature because you are a new person, created in God's likeness—righteous, holy, and true."

It is important that as Christians we don't spend so much time looking back at the past that we fail to grow in the present. While the past is important, we need to look ahead. Christians are new creatures, born again in Jesus Christ. Therefore, we need not live in the past. Isaiah 43:18-19 says, "Forget the former things; do not dwell on the past. See, I am doing a new thing! Now it springs up; do you not perceive it?" (NIV).

In the Gospels we find that on different occasions Jesus invited people to imagine a new life story. He said to several men, "Come, be my disciples, and I will show you how to fish for people" (Mark 1:17). One of the joys of counseling Christians for intentional change is to see the emergence of increased hope, the awareness of new possibilities for growth, and a new appreciation for the relevance of God's Word, God's Spirit, and the body of Christ in the change process. Using a solution-based perspective has inspired us to ask questions that cultivate the client's ability to search for and discover new ways to apply God's Word in the present, to move beyond the *acquisition* of truth to the *application* of truth.

The Bible encourages us to live as if the miracle has happened. That's because the ultimate miracle has. In Romans 6:11 Paul commands us to consider ourselves as dead to sin and alive to God in Christ Jesus. Paul exhorts us to set our sights on the realities of heaven, where Christ sits at God's right hand in the place of honor and power (Col. 3:1-2). He goes on to encourage us to engage in doing more of what works through active behavior change and the "putting on" of the new self.

A SOUND PERSONAL RELATIONSHIP

While sound psychology, sound theology, and sound biblical foundations are important, there is still one piece missing. Effective Christian counseling involves the integration of four components: sound psychology, sound theology, sound biblical foundation, and sound spirituality. But the starting place and the sustaining place is the one that so often gets left out of discussions of integration and Christian counseling. If you forget everything you've read up till now, please don't forget this.

It is our firm conviction that the most vital component of being a successful Christian counselor is your own passionate love relationship with Jesus Christ.

We believe that an effective Christian counselor is someone who has been born again, takes the Bible seriously and actively uses it in the counseling process, takes the power of the Holy Spirit seriously, takes sin seriously, takes prayer seriously, takes spiritual warfare seriously, takes involvement in the local church seriously, takes personal holiness seriously, and actively cultivates a growing love relationship with Jesus Christ and seeks his guidance in every aspect of the counseling process.

We agree with Mark McMinn when he writes in his book *Psychology, Theology, and Spirituality in Christian Counseling,* "The professionalization of counseling has led to the myth that all that is relevant are those things that clients observe, such as a counselor's demeanor, affective response, and display of empathy. I disagree: The kind of therapeutic relationships that foster healing are not formed merely from well-chosen techniques but grow out of the person's inner life. In this sense, counseling is both professional and personal."[3]

It's easy for us to spend so much time on professional growth and development that we ignore the more important dimension of spiritual formation, the practice of the spiritual disciplines, and the pursuit of holiness. Because of this tendency, a number of personal friends, who at one time were capable and committed Christian counselors, are no longer serving the King.

Effective counseling is more than just a truth dump. It's about our relationship with God. God in all his wholeness, fullness, and power has invaded our lives. Because we are empowered by the Holy Spirit, because our redemption is sealed and guaranteed, because the power that raised Jesus from the dead is in us, we can help people move toward wholeness.

After his resurrection, Christ meets Peter at the Sea of Galilee. Remember, this is after Peter had played Zorro on the Mount of Olives, after he had denied Christ three times, and after he had run away and hidden during the Crucifixion. Not exactly a stellar example of courage and spiritual maturity. Three times Jesus looks Peter straight in the eyes and asks him the same question: "Do you love me?" Wow! Can you imagine what Peter must have felt when he heard Christ say those words?

If Christ were to appear to you right now, look you straight in the eyes, and ask you the same question, what would be your answer? What recent activities and choices could you point to in support of your answer? Have you allowed your desire to pursue a sound psychology and perhaps even a sound theology to crowd out the time needed to cultivate an intimate and growing love relationship with your Savior? How is your spiritual pulse? What is your prayer life like? Do you look forward to spending time in the Word? Do you have a hunger and thirst for righteousness?

The bottom line is that each one of us is inadequate apart from the Lord. In John 15:1-5 Christ made it clear that we can do nothing without him. When we abide in him, when we rely on him, when we are filled with his Spirit, when we allow his love to flow through us, then the fruit will come. Oswald Chambers said, "The resounding evidence of the Holy Spirit in a person's life is the unmistakable family likeness to Jesus Christ and the freedom from everything which is not like Him."[4]

When we start each day by turning to Jesus and praising his name, we will see in our counseling a power and a purpose that transcend our training, our degrees, and our years of experience. Consider the words of the Lord given through the apostle Paul, who clearly stated the task and ultimate goal of every Christian counselor—knowing him and making him known.

The *real* believers are the ones the Spirit of God leads to work away at this ministry, filling the air with Christ's praise as we do it. We couldn't carry this off by our own efforts, and we know it—even though we can list what many might think are impressive credentials. . . .

The very credentials these people are waving around as something special, I'm tearing up and throwing out with the trash—along with everything else I used to take credit for. And why? Because of Christ. Yes, all the things I once thought were so important are gone from my life. Compared to the high privilege of knowing Christ Jesus as my master, firsthand, everything I once thought I had going for me is insignificant. . . . I've dumped it all in the trash so that I could embrace Christ and be embraced by him. I didn't want some petty, inferior brand of righteousness that comes from keeping a list of rules when I could get the robust kind that comes from trusting Christ—*God's* righteousness.

I gave up all that inferior stuff so I could know Christ personally, experience his resurrection power, be a partner in his suffering, and go all the way with him to death itself. . . . Friends, don't get me wrong: By no means do I count myself an expert in all of this, but I've got my eye on the goal, where God is beckoning us onward—to Jesus. I'm off and running, and I'm not turning back.

So let's keep focused on that goal. (Phil. 3:3-13, THE MESSAGE)

APPENDIX

Solution-based counseling is more than a theory or a group of techniques. Instead, it is a mind-set that sees possibilities rather than impossibilities, exceptions rather than uninterrupted problems, and strength instead of weakness. A solution-based mind-set necessitates setting small and attainable goals while watching expectantly for change to occur. As God's grace fills our lives, it becomes easier to look for the positive, find exceptions, and build on existing strengths.

Solution-based principles are not relegated solely to the counseling room or to professionally trained counselors. In fact, many of the principles outlined in this book have direct application to ministry in the local church. Pastors, teachers, ministry leaders, and lay people can all benefit from solution-based counseling techniques. Following are several examples of the application of solution-based principles to a church setting. From prayer and evangelism to the way you conduct board meetings or deal with people in crisis, these techniques can be applied in many ways. Read on and allow yourself to think of other ways to implement these tools in your church. With a little creativity you may come up with other practical ways to use the principles outlined in this book in your ministry.

CRISIS COUNSELING

Since the time of the Old Testament, God's house has been a place of refuge for people in crisis. Jesus commands his church to reach out to the poor, the sick, and the oppressed. As we in the church take these teachings seriously, we frequently encounter people who experience significant emotional and psychological distress. Unfortunately, as people's problems become increasingly complex, the helpers in the church can feel less equipped, less able to help. We have found some of the techniques of solution-based and problem-solving brief therapies especially helpful in crisis counseling. Whether you are in full-time ministry or involved in a lay position, these principles may give you some additional tools when you work with people in crisis.

A situation in my own church demonstrates the value of solution-based counseling in a crisis situation. John, a thirty-year-old man, expressed deep feelings of despair in Sunday school after he disclosed that he was infected with HIV and was becoming increasingly ill. The leaders and members of the class felt great compassion; however, they were also unsure how to handle this deeply discouraged man. Solution-based principles helped this man feel stabilized while allowing him to draw upon experiences and resources he had used in previous times of crisis.

When John answered a series of exception-finding questions, he was able to identify that when he had felt depressed at an earlier point in his life, he had found it effective to pray, read his Bible, and talk to his friends. While a quick recollection of these resources gave him a glimmer of hope, he quickly noted that he was unable to pray or read his Bible the way he used to because of poor concentration, anger, and significant worry. Scaling questions then helped John to set simple and realistic goals he could achieve. For example, he rated himself a 1 on a scale that measured hopelessness. He noted he might move to a 2 if he could read his Bible for five minutes each day this week. Because he was unsure he could actually read his Bible, he agreed simply to look at it, attempting to concentrate on the words. He also wanted to know that others were praying for him. Members of the group agreed to pray for him, and they suggested specific passages that would provide comfort and hope.

A member of the class who was trained in solution-based brief therapy followed up with John over the course of several weeks. He continued to build on exceptions, used scaling questions to promote additional growth, and helped guide John toward Christ and the support of other members of the church. While John continued to struggle with his illness, he moved from isolation and depression to increased hope and connectedness by continuing to do more of what had worked for him in the past.

You can be an effective helper by helping people in crisis to recall thoughts, feelings, and behaviors that have helped them through previous difficulties. Other techniques like the miracle question, the formula first-session task, and setting reasonable goals can be valuable tools.

Crisis counseling requires discernment and wisdom, and this certainly applies to the principles explained in this book. For example, using the miracle question with a terminally ill person may actually reinforce feelings of hopelessness. Even so, the miracle question can be very helpful in other situations. For example, a woman who has recently lost a job may find the miracle question a meaningful way to imagine God working in her life to provide a new position. In addition, it may help her set goals and make a plan to obtain a new job.

Crisis counseling requires sensitivity and discernment, especially with people who become suicidal or homicidal. Solution-based and problem-solving brief therapy provides practical, hands-on tools that people in the church can use. Even so, it is important to seek outside consultation with difficult and potentially dangerous people.

SOLUTION-BASED PRAYER

Solution-based principles can also be applied to prayer. One of the primary solution-based principles is that change comes in small increments. Have you ever thought of praying for small changes? You can pray that your neighbor, who is antagonistic toward anything spiritual, will receive Christ. For that neighbor to turn from a totally antagonistic position to surrender to Christ is a big step. It is not likely that this will occur in the space of a short time. When you pray for the large change, you can be discouraged when you see no movement.

However, you can pray differently. Instead of praying for the neighbor's salvation, which is the ultimate goal, you can pray for the small steps that would eventually lead to that. First, you can pray that the neighbor would begin to acknowledge that spiritual things are valuable for some people. This change in attitude is certainly not enough to secure salvation; however, it is a small step in that direction. And this small step moves your neighbor a little closer to listening seriously to the gospel.

I'm not suggesting that praying this way will change how the Holy Spirit moves in people's lives. But it may open your eyes to what God is doing and specific ways that he might be answering your prayers. If God is working in a situation or a person's life through one small change at a time, you are more likely to recognize it and be encouraged when you pray. While God is certainly capable of working miraculously and in big ways, my experience is that frequently he chooses to work through small changes.

This idea of God working in small increments is not a new concept. As God revealed himself to the human race, he did so a little bit at a time. He did not reveal all that he wanted us to know to Moses, for example. Rather, what he revealed to Moses was a foundation for the prophets, who came later. When the New Testament was written, the Holy Spirit built on the foundation that was laid in the Old Testament.

The solution-based principle of a positive focus is another perspective that you can incorporate into your prayer life. When you ask God to help you overcome a fault, do you pray in a negatively focused manner and asked God to help you stop doing something? Or have you tried praying in a positively focused manner and asked God to help you do something different instead? Remember, when you want to stop a behavior, it is easier if you focus on what to do than on what not to do.

Applying the counseling principles that we have suggested in this book to your prayer life can influence your spiritual life. These ideas may not drastically change your relationship with God or revolutionize your ministry, but they have the potential to strengthen what you do. Praying in positive small steps with an eye toward seeing God move in a new and different manner can be exciting. At the very least, attempting to implement these suggestions can help you to be more aware of God's activity in your life.

OTHER APPLICATIONS

Crisis counseling and prayer are only two ways in which the principles we have suggested in this book can be applied to your spiritual life and ministry. There are a variety of other ways that these ideas could enhance the effectiveness of individual or church ministry.

Church committee meetings are an excellent place to think of creatively applying some of the counseling perspectives we have presented. The next time you sit on a committee, you may want to look for the ways that you can either work on doing something different or focus on what you are already doing successfully and do more of it.

Some of these basic principles could be applied to preaching or teaching. The ideas in this book could help you think differently as you try to find new and effective ways to communicate the gospel to non-Christians. The counseling principles that we have presented are not some totally new perspective that can provide all of the answers for the ministry problems with which you struggle. However, these principles can give you a different perspective from which you can approach them. Sometimes that is all you need to get back on track.

In these few pages we have presented some ways that you can apply the principles presented in this book to your church ministry. These suggestions are meant to stimulate your thinking. See them as new ways to view and experience how God can work. May they be a small stepping stone in your own process of serving our Lord.

ENDNOTES

Chapter 1: The Long Road to Brief Therapy

1. H. W. Robinson, "Call Us Irresponsible," *Christianity Today* (4 April 1994): 15.
2. S. L. Garfield, "Research on Client Variables in Psychotherapy," in *Handbook of Psychotherapy and Behavior Change: An Empirical Analysis,* in 3rd ed., ed. S. L. Garfield and A. E. Bergin (New York: John Wiley & Sons, 1986), 213–56, 662.
3. S. H. Budman and A. S. Gurman, *Theory and Practice of Brief Therapy* (New York: Guilford, 1988), 4.
4. J. Preston, N. Varzos, and D. Liebert, *Every Session Counts: Making the Most of Your Brief Therapy* (San Luis Obispo, Calif.: Impact Publishers, 1995), 26.

Chapter 2: Change Happens, but Growth Takes Work

1. M. J. Mahoney, *Human Change Processes: The Scientific Foundation of Psychotherapy* (New York: Basic Books, 1991), 5.
2. Taken from a message given on *Back to the Bible* Broadcast.
3. T. Hansel, *Holy Sweat* (Dallas: Word, 1987), 54–5.
4. Some of this material was adapted from H. N. Wright and G. J. Oliver, *How to Bring Out the Best in Your Spouse* (Ann Arbor, Mich.: Servant, 1996).
5. C. R. Swindoll, *Come Before Winter . . . And Share My Hope* (Portland, Oreg.: Multnomah, 1985), 331–2.
6. J. O. Prochaska, C. C. DiClemente, and J. Norcross, *Changing for Good* (New York: William Morrow, 1994), 57.
7. Ibid., 32.
8. Ibid., 34.
9. Ibid., 43.
10. Ibid., 45.
11. Ibid., 39.
12. Ibid., 15.
13. Ibid., 16.
14. B. McFarland, *Brief Therapy and Eating Disorders* (San Francisco: Jossey-Bass, 1995), 78.
15. D. Dillon, *Short-Term Counseling* (Dallas: Word, 1992), 31.

Chapter 3: What Is Brief Therapy?

1. S. L. Garfield, *The Practice of Brief Psychotherapy* (New York: Pergamon Press, 1989), 19.

2. S. L. Garfield, "Research on Client Variables in Psychotherapy," in *Handbook of Psychotherapy and Behavior Change: An Empirical Analysis*, in 3d ed., ed. S. L. Garfield and A. E. Bergin (New York: John Wiley & Sons, 1986), 213–56.

3. Garfield, *The Practice of Brief Psychotherapy*, 1–10; S. H. Budman and A. S. Gurman, *Theory and Practice of Brief Therapy* (New York: Guilford, 1988), 1–4.

4. N. A. Cummings and M. Sayama, *Focused Psychotherapy: A Casebook of Brief Intermittent Psychotherapy throughout the Life Cycle* (New York: Brunner/Mazel, 1995), 25.

5. E. L. Phillips and D. N. Wiener, *Short-Term Psychotherapy and Structured Behavior Change* (New York: McGraw, 1966), vii.

6. B. Duncan et al., "Brief Therapy Addiction: The Secret Compulsion," *Family Therapy News* (November/December, 1990): n.p.

7. J. F. Cooper, *A Primer of Brief Psychotherapy* (New York: W. W. Norton, 1995), 28.

8. Phillips and Wiener, *Short-Term Psychotherapy and Structured Behavior Change*, 2.

9. Cooper, *A Primer of Brief Psychotherapy*, 15.

10. S. H. Budman and A. S. Gurman, *Theory and Practice of Brief Therapy* (New York: Guilford, 1988), 278.

11. Garfield, *The Practice of Brief Psychotherapy*, 11.

12. M. P. Koss, and J. N. Butcher, "Research on Brief Psychotherapy," in *Handbook of Psychotherapy and Behavior Change: An Empirical Analysis*, in 3rd ed., ed. S. L. Garfield and A. E. Bergin (New York: John Wiley & Sons, 1986), 642.

13. Cummings and Sayama, *Focused Psychotherapy*, 6.

14. H. Levenson, *Time-Limited Dynamic Psychotherapy: A Guide to Clinical Practice* (New York: Basic Books, 1995), 6.

15. Garfield, *The Practice of Brief Psychotherapy*, 6.

16. S. H. Budman and A. S. Gurman, "The Practice of Brief Therapy," *Professional Psychology: Research and Practice* 14, no. 3 (1983): 277–92.

17. M. D. Selekman, *Pathways to Change: Brief Therapy Solutions with Difficult Adolescents* (New York: Guilford, 1993), 41.

18. J. Mann and R. Goldman, *A Casebook in Time-Limited Psychotherapy* (Cambridge: Harvard University Press, 1973), x.

19. S. de Shazer, Foreword in Y. M. Dolan, *Resolving Sexual Abuse* (New York: W. W. Norton, 1991), x.

20. M. F. Basch, *Doing Brief Psychotherapy* (New York: Basic Books, 1995), xii.

21. A. Maslow, *The Psychology of Science: A Reconnaissance* (New York: HarperCollins, 1966), 15–6.

22. N. A. Cummings and G. Vanden Bosk, "The General Practice of Psychology," *Professional Psychology* 10 (1979): 430–40.

23. D. Saleeby, ed., *The Strengths Perspective in Social Work Practice* (New York: Longman, 1992), 171.

24. R. Fisch, J. H. Weakland, and L. Segal, *The Tactics of Change: Doing Therapy Briefly* (San Francisco: Jossey-Bass, 1982), ix.

25. P. Watzlawick, J. Weakland, and R. Fisch, *Change: Principles of Problem Formation and Problem Resolution* (New York: W. W. Norton, 1974), 9–11.

26. L. R. Wolberg, ed., *Short-Term Psychotherapy* (New York: Grune & Stratton, 1965), 140.

Chapter 4: Problem-Solving Brief-Therapy Models

1. For more information about the history of the MRI model, see M. Nichols and R. Swartz, *Family Therapy: Concepts and Methods,* 3d ed. (Needham, Mass.: Allyn & Bacon, 1995), 408–43.

2. J. H. Weakland et al., "Brief Therapy: Focused Problem Resolution," *Family Process* 13 (1974): 141–68.

3. P. Watzlawick, J. Weakland, and R. Fisch, *Change: Principles of Problem Formation and Problem Resolution* (New York: W. W. Norton, 1974), 31–9.

4. P. Watzlawick, K. Anger, and B. Anger-Diaz, *MRI Intensive Brief Therapy Training* (Palo Alto, Calif.: Personal Communication, 1995), n.p.

5. In the MRI model, the *customer* for treatment is the person who seeks assistance. This differs from the definition the solution-based model has for *customer.* Please refer to chapter 8 for a thorough definition of *customer, visitor,* and *complainant.* The MRI *customer* may be the same as the solution-based *customer* or *complainant.*

6. R. Fisch, J. H. Weakland, and L. Segal, *The Tactics of Change: Doing Therapy Briefly* (San Francisco: Jossey-Bass, 1982), 18–19, 69–88.

7. Ibid, 13–14.

8. Watzlawick, Anger, and Anger-Diaz, *MRI Intensive Brief Therapy Training.*

9. C. A. Kiesler, *The Psychology of Commitment: Experiments Linking Behavior to Belief* (New York: Academic, 1971).

10. C. D. Batson and W. L. Ventis, *The Religious Experience* (New York: Oxford University Press, 1982), 199–200.

11. W. B. Swann Jr., B. W. Pelham, and T. R. Chidester, "Change through Paradox: Using Self-Verification to Alter Beliefs," *Journal of Personality and Social Psychology* (1988): 54, 268–73.

12. Fisch, Weakland, and Segal, *The Tactics of Change.*

13. Watzlawick, Anger, and Anger-Diaz, *MRI Intensive Brief Therapy Training.*

14. Watzlawick, Weakland, and Fisch, *Change: Principles of Problem Formation and Problem Resolution.*

Chapter 5: From Problem-Focused to Solution-Focused

1. B. O'Hanlon, "The Third Wave: Can a Brief Therapy Open Doors to Transformation?" *Family Therapy Networker* (November/December 1994): 23.

2. S. de Shazer et al., "Brief Therapy: Focused Solution Development," *Family Process* (1986): 208.
3. W. O'Hanlon, "The Third Wave," 23.
4. Ibid.
5. W. O'Hanlon and M. Weiner-Davis, *In Search of Solutions: A New Direction in Psychotherapy* (New York: W. W. Norton, 1989); J. Walter and J. Peller, *Becoming Solution-Focused in Brief Therapy* (New York: Brunner/Mazel, 1992); M. D. Selekman, *Pathways to Change: Brief Therapy Solutions with Difficult Adolescents* (New York: Guilford, 1993).
6. S. de Shazer and I. K. Berg, "The Brief Therapy Tradition," in *Propagations: Thirty Years of Influence from the Mental Research Institute,* ed. J. H. Weakland and W. A. Ray (New York: Haworth Press, 1995), 249, 252.
7. I. K. Berg, *Family-Based Services: A Solution-Focused Approach* (New York: W. W. Norton, 1994), x.
8. Ibid., 14.
9. I. K. Berg and S. de Shazer, "Making Numbers Talk: Language in Therapy," in *The New Language of Change: Constructive Collaboration in Psychotherapy,* ed. S. Friedman (New York: Guilford, 1993), 22.
10. Berg, *Family Based Services,* 12–3.
11. M. Weiner-Davis, S. de Shazer, and W. J. Gingerich, "Building on Pretreatment Change to Construct the Therapeutic Solution: An Exploratory Study," *Journal of Marital and Family Therapy* 13 (1987): 359.
12. From a lecture given by Insoo Kim Berg at the Brief Family Therapy Center in Milwaukee, Wisconsin, in 1994.
13. S. de Shazer, *Keys to Solution in Brief Therapy* (New York: W. W. Norton, 1985).
14. Ibid.; S. de Shazer, *Clues: Investigating Solutions in Brief Therapy* (New York: W. W. Norton, 1988).
15. de Shazer, *Keys to Solution in Brief Therapy,* 137.
16. de Shazer, *Clues: Investigating Solutions in Brief Therapy,* 52.
17. J. O. Prochaska, C. C. DiClemente, and J. Norcross, *Changing for Good* (New York: William Morrow, 1994), 43.
18. H. N. Wright and G. J. Oliver, *How to Change Your Spouse without Ruining Your Marriage* (Ann Arbor, Mich.: Servant, 1994).
19. M. S. Wylie, "Brief Therapy on the Couch," *Family Therapy Networker* 14, no. 2 (1990): 26–35, 66.
20. J. S. Efran, and M. D. Schenker, "A Potpourri of Solutions: How New and Different Is Solution-Focused Therapy?" *Family Therapy Networker,* 17, no. 3 (May/June 1993): 73.
21. C. Storm, "The Remaining Thread: Matching Change and Stability Signals," *Journal of Strategic and Systemic Therapies* 10 (1991): 114–7.
22. D. Efron and K. Veenendall, "Suppose a Miracle Doesn't Happen?" *Journal of Systemic Therapies* 13, no. 1 (1994): 17.

23. J. S. Fraser, "Process, Problems, and Solutions in Brief Therapy," *Journal of Marital and Family Therapy* 21, no. 3 (1995): 265–79.
24. E. Lipchik, " 'Both/And' Solutions," in *The New Language of Change: Constructive Collaboration in Psychotherapy*, ed. S. Friedman (New York: Guilford, 1993), 27.
25. M. Weiner-Davis, "Pro-constructed Realities," in *Therapeutic Conversations*, ed. S. Gilligan and R. Price (New York: W. W. Norton, 1993), 157.
26. D. Mostert, "Letters to the Editor," *Journal of Systemic Therapies* 14, no. 1 (1995): 80.

Chapter 6: Assumptions of Solution-Based Therapy

1. J. Walter and J. Peller, *Becoming Solution-Focused in Brief Therapy* (New York: Brunner/Mazel, 1992), 10–36.
2. S. de Shazer et al., "Brief Therapy: Focused Solution Development," *Family Process* 25 (1986): 207–22; S. de Shazer, *Clues: Investigating Solutions in Brief Therapy* (New York: W. W. Norton, 1988); W. O'Hanlon and M. Weiner-Davis, *In Search of Solutions: A New Direction in Psychotherapy* (New York: W.W. Norton, 1989); J. Peller and J. Walter, "When Doesn't the Problem Happen?" in *Brief Therapy Approach to Treating Anxiety and Depression*, ed. M. Yapko (New York: Brunner/Mazel, 1989); J. Peller and J. Walter, *Becoming Solution-Focused in Brief Therapy* (New York: Brunner/Mazel, 1992).
3. Walter and Peller, *Becoming Solution-Focused in Brief Therapy*, 13.
4. Ibid., 14.
5. Ibid., 21.
6. Ibid., 23.

Chapter 7: The First Session

1. For further discusssion on single-session therapy, see S. H. Budman, M. F. Hoyt, and S. Friedman, eds., *The First Session in Brief Therapy* (New York: Guilford, 1992), 59–86.
2. M. Weiner-Davis, S. de Shazer, and W. J. Gingerich, "Building on Pretreatment Change to Construct the Therapeutic Solution: An Exploratory Study," *Journal of Marital and Family Therapy* 13 (1987): 359–63.

Chapter 8: Developing and Maintaining a Clear Focus in Treatment

1. I. K. Berg, *Family Based Services: A Solution-Focused Approach* (New York: W. W. Norton, 1994), 63.
2. I. K. Berg, "Of Visitors, Complainants, and Customers: Is There Really Such a Thing As 'Resistance'?," *Family Therapy Networker* (January/February, 1989): 21.
3. J. Walter and J. Peller, *Becoming Solution-Focused in Brief Therapy* (New York: Brunner/Mazel, 1992), 188–99.
4. Berg, "Of Visitors, Complainants, and Customers," 21.

5. Walter and Peller, *Becoming Solution-Focused in Brief Therapy*, 188–99.
6. J. Gale, ed., *Conversation Analysis of Therapeutic Discourse: The Pursuit of a Therapeutic Agenda*, vol. 41 (Norwood, N.J.: Ablex Publishing Corporation, 1991), 42–5.

Chapter 9: After the First Session: Keeping Change Going
1. I. K. Berg and S. Miller, *Working with the Problem Drinker* (New York: W.W. Norton, 1992), 131.
2. M. D. Selekman, *Pathways to Change: Brief Therapy Solutions with Difficult Adolescents* (New York: Guilford, 1993), 79–80.
3. Berg and Miller, *Working with the Problem Drinker*, 137.
4. B. McFarland, *Brief Therapy and Eating Disorders* (San Francisco: Jossey-Bass, 1995), 129.
5. See chapter 2.
6. I. K. Berg, *Family Based Services: A Solution-Focused Approach* (New York: W. W. Norton, 1994), 137.
7. M. McMinn, *Psychology, Theology, and Spirituality in Christian Counseling* (Wheaton, Ill: Tyndale, 1996), 65.
8. N. A. Cummings and M. Sayama, *Focused Psychotherapy: A Casebook of Brief, Intermittent Psychotherapy throughout the Life Cycle* (New York: Brunner/Mazel, 1995), 2–5.

Chapter 10: Adolescents: Sometimes It's Got to Be Brief
1. M. D. Selekman, *Pathways to Change: Brief Therapy Solutions with Difficult Adolescents* (New York: Guilford, 1993), 19–24, 46–48.
2. Ibid, 52.
3. Ibid.
4. S. de Shazer, "Muddles, Bewilderment, and Practice Theory," *Family Process* 3 (1991): 3, 453–8; S. de Shazer, *Clues: Investigating Solutions in Brief Therapy* (New York: Guilford, 1993).
5. Selekman, *Pathways to Change*, 63.
6. de Shazer, "Muddles, Bewilderment, and Practice Theory," 3, 453–8.
7. Selekman, *Pathways to Change*, 58.
8. Ibid., 72.

Chapter 11: Promoting Change in Marriages
1. T. A. Whiteman and T. G. Bartlett, *The Marriage Mender* (Colorado Springs, Colo.: NavPress, 1996), 167–71.

Chapter 12: What to Do When You Don't Know What to Do
1. D. J. Kiser, F. P. Piercy, and E. Lipchik, "The Integration of Emotion in Solution Focused Therapy," *Journal of Marital and Family Therapy* 19 (1993): 233–42.

Chapter 13: Research: Can Anything So Simple Be So Effective?

1. M. P. Koss and J. Shiang, "Research on Brief Psychotherapy" in *Handbook of Psychotherapy and Behavior Change,* ed. A. E. Bergin and S. L. Garfield, 4th ed. (New York: John Wiley & Sons, 1994), 664.

2. M. J. Lambert and A. E. Bergin, "The Effectiveness of Psychotherapy," in *Handbook of Psychotherapy and Behavior Change,* ed. A. E. Bergin and S. L. Garfield, 4th ed. (New York: John Wiley & Sons, 1994): 143–89.

3. Koss and Shiang, "Research on Brief Psychotherapy," 662; B. N. Steenbarger, "Toward a Science-Practice Integration in Brief Counseling and Therapy," *The Counseling Psychologist* 20 (1992): 403–50.

4. For information about depression, see I. Elkin et al., "National Institute of Mental Health Treatment of Depression Collaborative Research Study," *Archives of General Psychiatry* 46 (1989): 971–82. For information about anxiety disorders, see J. S. Klosko et al., "A Comparison of Alprazolam and Behavior Therapy in Treatment of Panic Disorder," *Journal of Consulting and Clinical Psychology* 58 (1990): 77–84. For information about maladaptive interpersonal functioning, see H. H. Strupp and J. L. Binder, *Psychotherapy in a New Key: A Guide to Time-Limited Dynamic Psychotherapy* (New York: Basic Books, 1984). For more information about panic disorders, see A. T. Beck et al., "A Crossover Study of Focused Cognitive Therapy for Panic Disorder," *American Journal of Psychiatry* 149 (1992): 778–83; L. Michelson et al., "Panic Disorder: Cognitive-Behavioral Treatment," *Behavior Research and Therapy* 28 (1990): 141–51.

5. L. Alden, "Short-Term Structured Treatment for Avoidant Personality Disorder," *Journal of Consulting and Clinical Psychology* 57 (1989): 756–64.

6. P. Crits-Christoph, "The Efficacy of Brief Dynamic Psychotherapy: A Meta-Analysis," *American Journal of Psychiatry* 149 (1992): 151–8.

7. M. P. Koss and J. Shiang, "Research on Brief Psychotherapy," 664.

8. Ibid.; S. D. Hollon and A. T. Beck, "Cognitive and Cognitive-Behavioral Therapies," in *Handbook of Psychotherapy and Behavior Change,* ed. A. E. Bergin and S. L. Garfield, 4th ed. (New York: John Wiley & Sons, 1994), 664–700.

9. L. Thompson, D. Gallagher, and J. Breckenridge, "Comparative Effectiveness of Psychotherapies for Depressed Elders," *Journal of Consulting and Clinical Psychology* 55 (1987): 385–90.

10. Elkin et al., "National Institute of Mental Health Treatment of Depression Collaborative Research Study," 971–82.

11. B. N. Steenbarger, "Toward a Science-Practice Integration in Brief Counseling and Therapy," *The Counseling Psychologist* 20 (1992):403–50.

12. M. P. Koss and J. Butcher, "Research on Brief Psychotherapy," in *Handbook of Psychotherapy and Behavior Change: An Empirical Analysis,* ed. A. E. Bergin and S. L. Garfield, 3d ed. (New York: John Wiley & Sons, 1986), 627–70;

Steenbarger, "Toward a Science-Practice Integration in Brief Counseling and Therapy," 403–50.

13. Steenbarger, "Toward a Science-Practice Integration in Brief Counseling and Therapy," 416.

14. "Mental Health: Does Therapy Help?" *Consumer Reports* (November 1995): 734–9.

15. M. E. P. Seligman, "The Effectiveness of Psychotherapy: The *Consumer Reports* Study," *American Psychologist* 50, no. 12 (1995): 965–83.

16. K. I. Howard et al., "The Dose-Effect Relationship in Psychotherapy," *American Psychologist* 41 (1986): 159–64.

17. M. J. Lambert, D. A. Shapiro, and A. E. Bergin, "The Effectiveness of Psychotherapy," in *Handbook of Psychotherapy and Behavior Change: An Empirical Analysis,* ed. A. E. Bergin and S. L. Garfield, 3d ed. (New York: John Wiley & Sons, 1986), 157–212; Koss and Shiang, "Research on Brief Psychotherapy," 664.

18. G. Pekarik, "The Effects of Employing Different Termination Classifications Criteria in Dropout Research," *Psychotherapy* 22 (1985): 86–91; G. Pekarik and M. Wierzbicki, "The Relationship between Clients' Expected and Actual Treatment Duration," *Psychotherapy* 23 (1986): 532–4.

19. G. Pekarik and K. Finney-Owen, "Outpatient Clinic Therapist Attitudes and Beliefs Relevant to Client Drop-Out," *Community Mental Health Journal* 23 (1987): 120–30.

20. B. L. Bloom, *Planned Short-Term Psychotherapy* (Boston: Allyn & Bacon, 1992), 97–121.

21. M. Talmon, *Single-Session Therapy: Maximizing the Effect of the First (and Often Only) Therapeutic Encounter* (San Francisco: Jossey-Bass, 1990), 1–17.

22. J. E. Exner and A. Andronikof-Sanglade, "Rorschach Changes Following Brief and Short-Term Therapy," *Journal of Personality Assessment* 59 (1992): 59–71.

23. G. E. Hardy et al., "Impact of Cluster C Personality Disorders on Outcome of Contrasting Brief Psychotherapies for Depression," *Journal of Consulting and Clinical Psychology* (1995): 997–1004.

24. S. de Shazer et al., "Brief Therapy: Focused Solution Development," *Family Process* 25 (1986): 207–21.

25. M. S. Wylie, "Brief Therapy on the Couch," *Family Therapy Networker* 14, no. 2 (1990): 26–35, 66.

26. J. H. Weakland et al., "Brief Therapy: Focused Problem Resolution," *Family Process* 13 (1974): 163.

27. Wylie, "Brief Therapy on the Couch," 34–5.

28. J. A. Morrison et al., "The Application of Family Systems Approaches to School Behavior Problems on a School-Level Discipline Board: An Outcome Study," *Elementary School Guidance and Counseling* 27 (1993): 258–72.

29. G. Melidonis and B. H. Bry, "Effects of Therapist Exceptions Questions on Blaming and Positive Statements in Families with Adolescent Behavior Problems," *Journal of Family Psychology* 9 (1995): 451–7.
30. C. G. Shields, D. H. Sprenkle, and J. A. Constantine, "Anatomy of an Initial Interview: The Importance of Joining and Structuring Skills," *The American Journal of Family Therapy* 19 (1991): 3–14.
31. M. Weiner-Davis, S. de Shazer, and W. J. Gingerich, "Building on Pretreatment Change to Construct the Therapeutic Solution: An Exploratory Study," *Journal of Marital and Family Therapy* 13 (1987): 359–63.
32. Ibid., 362.
33. J. F. Adams, F. P. Piercy, and J. A. Jurich, "Effects of Solution Focused Therapy's 'Formula First Session Task' on Compliance and Outcome in Family Therapy," *Journal of Marital and Family Therapy* 17 (1991): 277–90.
34. J. H. Weakland et al., "Brief Therapy: Focused Problem Resolution," 163.
35. Ibid., 141–68.
36. H. Chubb and E. L. Evans, "Therapist Efficiency and Clinic Accessibility with the Mental Research Institute Brief Therapy Model," *Community Mental Health Journal* (1990): 139–49.
37. G. Nardone, "Brief Strategic Therapy of Phobic Disorders: A Model of Therapy and Evaluation Research," in *Propogations: Thirty Years of Influence of the Mental Research Institute,* ed. J. Weakland and W. A. Ray (New York: Haworth Press, 1995), 91–106.
38. Weakland et al., "Brief Therapy: Focused Problem Resolution," 141–68.
39. I. L. Janis and L. Mann, "Effectiveness of Emotional Role-Playing in Modifying Smoking Habits and Attitudes," *Journal of Experimental Research in Personality* 1 (1965): 84–90.
40. D. E. Orlinsky, K. Grawe, and B. K. Parks, "Process and Outcome in Psychotherapy—Noch Einmal," in *Handbook of Psychotherapy and Behavior Change,* ed. A. E. Bergin and S. L. Garfield, 4th ed. (New York: John Wiley & Sons, 1994), 306. (See chapter 8 of Bergin and Garfield for further clarification.)
41. Ibid., 339.
42. Ibid., 270–376.
43. K. Jordan and W. H. Quinn, "Session Two Outcome of the Formula First Session Task in Problem- and Solution-Focused Approaches," *The American Journal of Family Therapy* 22 (1994): 3–15.
44. Koss and Shiang, "Research on Brief Psychotherapy," 664; Steenbarger, "Toward a Science-Practice Integration in Brief Counseling and Therapy," 403–50.
45. Ibid., 664.

Chapter 14: Putting It All Together

1. H. Blackaby and C. King, *Experiencing God* (Nashville: Broadman and Holman, 1994), 14.
2. J. Stott, *The Contemporary Christian* (Downers Grove, Ill.: InterVarsity, 1992), 119.
3. M. McMinn, *Psychology, Theology, and Spirituality in Christian Counseling* (Wheaton, Ill.: Tyndale, 1996), 13.
4. O. Chambers, *My Utmost for His Highest: An Updated Edition in Today's Language,* ed. J. Reimann (Grand Rapids: Discovery House, 1992), entry for Feb. 8.

BIBLIOGRAPHY

Adams, J. F., F. P. Piercy, and J. A. Jurich. "Effects of Solution Focused Therapy's 'Formula First Session Task' on Compliance and Outcome in Family Therapy." *Journal of Marital and Family Therapy* 17 (1991): 277–90.

Alden, L. "Short-Term Structured Treatment for Avoidant Personality Disorder." *Journal of Consulting and Clinical Psychology* 57 (1989): 756–64.

Basch, M. F. *Doing Brief Psychotherapy.* New York: Basic Books, 1995.

Batson, C. D., and W. L. Ventis. *The Religious Experience.* New York: Oxford University Press, 1982.

Beck, A. T., L. Sokol, D. A. Clark, R. Berchick, and F. Wright. "A Crossover Study of Focused Cognitive Therapy for Panic Disorder." *American Journal of Psychiatry* 149 (1992): 778–83.

Berg, I. K. "Of Visitors, Complainants, and Customers: Is There Really Such a Thing As 'Resistance'?" *Family Therapy Networker* (January/February 1989): 21.

———. *Family Based Services: A Solution-Focused Approach.* New York: W. W. Norton, 1994.

———. "A Wolf in Disguise Is Not a Grandmother." *Journal of Systemic Therapies* 13, no. 1 (1994): 14.

Berg, I. K., and S. de Shazer. "Making Numbers Talk: Language in Therapy." In *The New Language of Change: Constructive Collaboration in Psychotherapy.* Edited by S. Friedman. New York: Guilford, 1993.

Berg, I. K., and S. Miller. *Working with the Problem Drinker.* New York: W. W. Norton, 1992.

Bierenbaum, H., M. P. Nichols, and A. J. Schwartz. "Effects of Varying Length and Frequency in Brief Emotive Psychotherapy." *Journal of Consulting and Clinical Psychology* 44 (1976): 790–8.

Bloom, B. L. *Planned Short-Term Psychotherapy.* Boston: Allyn & Bacon, 1992.

Budman, S. H., and A. S. Gurman. "The Practice of Brief Therapy." *Professional Psychology: Research and Practice* 14, no. 3 (1983): 277–92.

———. *Theory and Practice of Brief Therapy.* New York: Guilford, 1988.

Budman, S. H. "Training Experienced Clinicians to Do Brief Treatment—Silk Purses into Sow's Ears." Paper presented at the 97th annual convention of the American Psychological Association, New Orleans, Louisiana, 1992.

Budman, S. H., M. F. Hoyt, and S. Friedman, eds. *The First Session in Brief Therapy.* New York: Guilford, 1992.

Chubb, H., and E. L. Evans. "Therapist Efficiency and Clinic Accessibility with the Mental Research Institute Brief Therapy Model." *Community Mental Health Journal* (1990): 139–49.

Cooper, J. F. *A Primer of Brief Psychotherapy.* New York: W. W. Norton, 1995.

Crits-Christoph, P. "The Efficacy of Brief Dynamic Psychotherapy: A Meta-Analysis." *American Journal of Psychiatry* 149 (1992): 151–8.

Cummings, N. A. "Prolonged (Ideal) Versus Short-Term (Realistic) Psychotherapy." *Professional Psychology* 8: 491–501.

Cummings, N. A., and M. Sayama. *Focused Psychotherapy: A Casebook of Brief Intermittent Psychotherapy throughout the Life Cycle.* New York: Brunner/Mazel, 1995.

Cummings, N. A., and G. Vanden Bosk. "The General Practice of Psychology." *Professional Psychology* 10 (1979): 430–40.

de Shazer, S. *Patterns of Brief Family Therapy.* New York: Guilford, 1982.

———. *Keys to Solution in Brief Therapy.* New York: W. W. Norton, 1985.

———. *Clues: Investigating Solutions in Brief Therapy.* New York: W. W. Norton, 1988.

———. *Putting Difference to Work.* New York: W. W. Norton, 1991.

———. Foreword to *Resolving Sexual Abuse* by Y. M. Dolan. New York: Norton, 1991.

———. "Muddles, Bewilderment, and Practice Theory." *Family Process* 3 (1991): 453–8.

de Shazer, S., and I. K. Berg. "Doing Therapy: A Post-Structural Revision." *Journal of Marital and Family Therapy* 18 (1992): 71–81.

———. "The Brief Therapy Tradition." In *Propagations: Thirty Years of Influence from the Mental Research Institute.* Edited by J. H. Weakland and W. A. Ray. New York: Haworth Press, 1995: 249–52.

de Shazer, S., I. K. Berg, E. Lipchik, E. Nunnally, A. Molnar, W. Gingerich, and M. Weiner-Davis. "Brief Therapy: Focused Solution Development." *Family Process* 25 (1986): 207–22.

de Shazer, S., and R. Kral, eds. *Indirect Approaches in Brief Therapy.* Rockville, Md.: Aspen Publishers, 1986.

Diagnostic and Statistical Manual of Mental Disorders. 4th ed. Washington, D.C.: American Psychiatric Association, 1994.

Dillon, D. *Short-Term Counseling.* Dallas: Word, 1992.

Duncan, B., S. Drewry, M. Hubble, G. Rusk, and P. Breuning. "Brief Therapy Addiction: The Secret Compulsion." *Family Therapy News* (November/December 1990).

Efran, J. S., and M. D. Schenker. "A Potpourri of Solutions: How New and Different Is Solution-Focused Therapy?" *The Family Therapy Networker* (May/June 1993): 73.

Efron, D., and K. Veenendall. "Suppose a Miracle Doesn't Happen?" *Journal of Systemic Therapies* (1993).

Elkin, I., M. T. Shea, J. T. Watkins, S. D. Imber, S. M. Sotsky, J. F. Collins, D. R. Glass, P. A. Pilkonis, W. R. Leber, J. P. Docherty, S. J. Fiester, and M. B. Parloff. "National Institute of Mental Health Treatment of Depression Collaborative Research Study." *Archives of General Psychiatry* 46 (1989): 971–82.

Erickson, M. H. "Special Techniques of Brief Hypnotherapy." *Journal of Clinical and Experimental Hypnosis* 2 (1954): 109–29.

Exner, J. E., and A. Andronikof-Sanglade. "Rorschach Changes Following Brief and Short-Term Therapy." *Journal of Personality Assessment* 59 (1992): 59–71.

Fisch, R., J. H. Weakland, and L. Segal. *The Tactics of Change: Doing Therapy Briefly.* San Francisco: Jossey-Bass, 1982.

Frank, J. D. *Persuasion and Healing.* 2d ed. Baltimore: Johns Hopkins University Press, 1973.

Fraser, J. S. "Process, Problems, and Solutions in Brief Therapy." *Journal of Marital and Family Therapy* 21, no.3 (1995): 265–79.

Furman, B., and T. Ahola. *Solution Talk: Hosting Therapeutic Conversations.* New York: W. W. Norton, 1992.

Gale, J., ed. *Conversation Analysis of Therapeutic Discourse: The Pursuit of a Therapeutic Agenda.* Norwood, N. J.: Ablex Publishing Corporation, 1991.

Gale, J., and N. Newfield. "A Conversational Analysis of a Solution-Focused Marital Therapy Session." *Journal of Marital and Family Therapy* 18 (1992): 153–65.

Garfield, S. L. "Research on Client Variables in Psychotherapy." In *Handbook of Psychotherapy and Behavior Change.* 2d ed. Edited by S. L. Garfield and A. E. Bergin. New York: John Wiley & Sons, 1978.

———. "Research on Client Variables in Psychotherapy." In *Handbook of Psychotherapy and Behavior Change: An Empirical Analysis.* 3d ed. Edited by S. L. Garfield and A. E. Bergin. New York: John Wiley & Sons, 1986.

———. *The Practice of Brief Psychotherapy.* New York: Pergamon Press, 1989.

———. "Research on Client Variables in Psychotherapy." In *Handbook of Psychotherapy and Behavior Change.* 4th ed. Edited by S. L. Garfield and A. E. Bergin. New York: John Wiley & Sons, 1994.

Haley, J. *Problem-Solving Therapy.* New York: Harper Colophon Books, 1976.

———. *Uncommon Therapy.* New York: W. W. Norton, 1986.

Hansel, T. *Holy Sweat.* Dallas: Word, 1987.

Hardy, G. E., M. Barkham, D. A. Shapiro, W. B. Stiles, A. Rees, and S. Reynolds. "Impact of Cluster C Personality Disorders on Outcome of Contrasting Brief Psychotherapies for Depression." *Journal of Consulting and Clinical Psychology* (1995): 997–1004.

Hollon, S. D., and A. T. Beck. "Cognitive and Cognitive-Behavioral Therapies." In *Handbook of Psychotherapy and Behavior Change.* 4th ed. Edited by A. E. Bergin and S. L. Garfield. New York: John Wiley & Sons, 1994.

Howard, K. I., S. M. Kopta, M. S. Kraus, and D. E. Orlinsky. "The Dose-Effect Relationship in Psychotherapy." *American Psychologist* 41 (1986): 159–64.

Huber, C. H., and B. A. Backlund. *The Twenty-Minute Counselor.* New York: Crossroad, 1995.

Janis, I. L., and L. Mann. "Effectiveness of Emotional Role-Playing in Modifying Smoking Habits and Attitudes." *Journal of Experimental Research in Personality* 1 (1965):84–90.

Jordan, K., and W. H. Quinn. "Session Two Outcome of the Formula First Session Task in Problem- and Solution-Focused Approaches." *The American Journal of Family Therapy* 22 (1994): 3–15.

Kiesler, C. A. *The Psychology of Commitment: Experiments Linking Behavior to Belief.* New York: Academic, 1971.

Kiser, D. J., F. P. Piercy, and E. Lipchik. "The Integration of Emotion in Solution Focused Therapy." *Journal of Marital and Family Therapy* 19 (1993): 233–42.

Klosko, J. S., D. H. Barlow, R. Tassinari, and J. A. Cerny. "A Comparison of Alprazolam and Behavior Therapy in Treatment of Panic Disorder." *Journal of Consulting and Clinical Psychology* 58 (1990): 77–84.

Koss, M. P., and J. N. Butcher. "Research on Brief Psychotherapy." In *Handbook of Psychotherapy and Behavior Change: An Empirical Analysis.* 3d ed. Edited by S. L. Garfield and A. E. Bergin. New York: John Wiley & Sons, 1986.

Koss, M. P., and J. Shiang. "Research on Brief Psychotherapy." In *Handbook of Psychotherapy and Behavior Change.* 4th ed. Edited by A. E. Bergin and S. L. Garfield. New York: John Wiley & Sons, 1994.

Lambert, M. J., D. A. Shapiro, and A. E. Bergin. "The Effectiveness of Psychotherapy." In *Handbook of Psychotherapy and Behavior Change: An Empirical Analysis.* 3d ed. Edited by A. E. Bergin and S. L. Garfield. New York: John Wiley & Sons, 1986.

Lambert, M. J., and A. E. Bergin. "The Effectiveness of Psychotherapy." In *Handbook of Psychotherapy and Behavior Change.* 4th ed. Edited by A. E. Bergin and S. L. Garfield. New York: John Wiley & Sons, 1994.

Lankton, S. R., and K. K. Erickson, eds. *The Essence of a Single-Session Success.* New York: Brunner/Mazel, 1994.

Levenson, H. *Time-Limited Dynamic Psychotherapy: A Guide to Clinical Practice.* New York: Basic Books, 1995.

Lipchik, E. "'Both/And' Solutions." In *The New Language of Change: Constructive Collaboration in Psychotherapy.* Edited by S. Friedman. New York: Guilford, 1993.

Luborsky, L., B. Singer, and L. Luborsky. "Comparative Studies of Psychotherapies." *Archives of General Psychiatry* 32 (1975): 995–1008.

MacKenzie, K. R. "Recent Developments in Brief Psychotherapy." *Hospital and Community Psychiatry* 39, no. 7 (July 1988): 742–52.

Mahoney, M. J. *Human Change Processes: The Scientific Foundation of Psychotherapy.* New York: Basic Books, 1991.

Mann, J., and R. Goldman. *A Casebook in Time-Limited Psychotherapy.* Reprint, Washington, D.C.: American Psychiatric Press, 1987.

Maslow, A. *The Psychology of Science: A Reconnaissance.* New York: HarperCollins, 1966.

McFarland, B. *Brief Therapy and Eating Disorders.* San Francisco: Jossey-Bass, 1995.

McMinn, M. *Psychology, Theology, and Spirituality in Christian Counseling.* Wheaton, Ill.: Tyndale, 1996.

Melidonis, G., and B. H. Bry. "Effects of Therapist Exceptions Questions on Blaming and Positive Statements in Families with Adolescent Behavior Problems." *Journal of Family Psychology* 9 (1995): 451–7.

"Mental Health: Does Therapy Help?" *Consumer Reports* (November 1995): 734–9.

Michelson, L., K. Marchione, M. Greenwald, and L. Glanz. "Panic Disorder: Cognitive-Behavioral Treatment." *Behavior Research and Therapy* 28 (1990): 141–51.

Morrison, J. A., K. Olivos, G. Dominguez, D. Gomer, et al. "The Application of Family Systems Approaches to School Behavior Problems on a School-Level Discipline Board: An Outcome Study." *Elementary School Guidance and Counseling* 27 (1993): 258–72.

Mostert, D. "Letters to the Editor." *Journal of Systemic Therapies* 14, no. 1 (1995): 80.

Nardone, G. "Brief Strategic Therapy of Phobic Disorders: A Model of Therapy and Evaluation Research." In *Propagations: Thirty Years of Influence of the Mental Research Institute.* Edited by J. Weakland and W. A. Ray. New York: Hayworth Press, 1995.

Nichols, M., and R. Schwartz. *Family Therapy: Concepts and Methods.* 3d ed. Needham, Mass.: Allyn & Bacon, 1995.

O'Hanlon, B. "The Third Wave: Can a Brief Therapy Open Doors to Transformation?" *Family Therapy Networker* (November/December 1994): 19–29.

O'Hanlon, W., and M. Weiner-Davis. *In Search of Solutions: A New Direction in Psychotherapy.* New York: W. W. Norton, 1989.

Oliver, G. J., and H. N. Wright. *Good Women Get Angry.* Ann Arbor, Mich.: Servant, 1996.

Orlinsky, D. E., K. Grawe, and B. K. Parks. "Process and Outcome in Psychotherapy—Noch Einmal." In *Handbook of Psychotherapy and Behavior Change.* 4th ed. Edited by A. E. Bergin and S. L. Garfield. New York: John Wiley & Sons, 1994.

Orlinsky, D., and K. Howard. "Process and Outcome in Psychotherapy." In *Handbook of Psychotherapy and Behavior Change: An Empirical Analysis.* 3d ed. Edited by S. Garfield and A. Bergin. New York: John Wiley & Sons, 1986.

Pekarik, G. "The Effects of Employing Different Termination Classifications Criteria in Dropout Research." *Psychotherapy* 22 (1985): 86–91.

Pekarik, G., and G. K. Finney-Owen. "Outpatient Clinic Therapists' Attitudes and Beliefs Relevant to Client Drop-Out." *Community Mental Health Journal* 23, no. 2 (1987): 120–30.

Pekarik, G., and M. Wierzbicki. "The Relationship between Clients' Expected and Actual Treatment Duration." *Psychotherapy* 23 (1986): 532–4.

Peller, J., and J. Walter. "When Doesn't the Problem Happen?" In *Brief Therapy Approaches to Treating Anxiety and Depression.* Edited by M. Yapko. New York: Brunner/Mazel, 1989.

Phillips, E. L., and D. N. Wiener. *Short-Term Psychotherapy and Structured Behavior Change.* New York: McGraw, 1966.

Preston, J., N. Varzos, and D. Liebert. *Every Session Counts: Making the Most of Your Brief Therapy.* San Luis Obispo, Calif.: Impact Publishers, 1995.

Prochaska, J. O., C. C. DiClemente, and J. Norcross. *Changing for Good.* New York: William Morrow, 1994.

Quick, E. K. *Doing What Works in Brief Therapy: A Strategic Solution Focused Approach.* San Diego: Academic Press, 1996.

Robinson, H. W. "Call Us Irresponsible." *Christianity Today* (4 April 1994): 15.

Saleeby, D., ed. *The Strengths Perspective in Social Work Practice.* New York: Longman, 1992.

Selekman, M. D. *Pathways to Change: Brief Therapy Solutions with Difficult Adolescents.* New York: Guilford, 1993.

Seligman, M. E. P. "The Effectiveness of Psychotherapy: The *Consumer Reports* Study." *American Psychologist* 50, no. 12 (1995): 965–83.

Shields, C. G., D. H. Sprenkle, and J. A. Constantine. "Anatomy of an Initial Interview: The Importance of Joining and Structuring Skills." *The American Journal of Family Therapy* 19 (1991): 3–14.

Sifneos, P. E. *Short-Term Psychotherapy and Emotional Crisis.* Cambridge, Mass.: Harvard University Press, 1972.

Smith, M. L., and G. V. Glass. "Meta-Analysis of Psychotherapy Outcome Studies." *American Psychologist* 32 (1977): 752–60.

Smith, M. L., G. V. Glass, and T. I. Miller. *The Benefits of Psychotherapy.* Baltimore: Johns Hopkins University Press, 1980.

Steenbarger, B. N. "Toward a Science-Practice Integration in Brief Counseling and Therapy." In *The Counseling Psychologist* 20 (1992): 403–50.

Storm, C. "The Remaining Thread: Matching Change and Stability Signals." *Journal of Strategic and Systemic Therapies* 10 (1991): 114–7.

Strupp, H. H., and J. L. Binder. *Psychotherapy in a New Key: A Guide to Time-Limited Dynamic Psychotherapy.* New York: Basic Books, 1984.

Svartberg, M., and T. C. Stiles. "Comparative Effects of Short-Term Psychodynamic Psychotherapy: A Meta-Analysis." *Journal of Consulting and Clinical Psychology* 59 (1991): 704–14.

Swann, W. B. Jr., B. W. Pelham, and T. R. Chidester. "Change through Paradox: Using Self-Verification to Alter Beliefs." *Journal of Personality and Social Psychology* (1988).

Swindoll, C. R. *Come Before Winter . . . And Share My Hope.* Portland, Ore.: Multnomah, 1986.

Talmon, M. *Single-Session Solutions: A Guide to Practical, Effective, and Affordable Therapy.* Reading, Mass.: Addison-Wesley, 1993.

———. *Single-Session Therapy: Maximizing the Effect of the First (and Often Only) Therapeutic Encounter.* San Francisco: Jossey-Bass, 1990.

Thompson, L., D. Gallagher, and J. Breckenridge. "Comparative Effectiveness of Psychotherapies for Depressed Elders." *Journal of Consulting and Clinical Psychology* 55 (1987): 385–90.

Walter, J., and J. Peller. *Becoming Solution-Focused in Brief Therapy.* New York: Brunner/Mazel, 1992.

Watzlawick, P., J. Weakland, and R. Fisch. *Change: Principles of Problem Formation and Problem Resolution.* New York: W. W. Norton, 1974.

Watzlawick, P., K. Anger, and B. Anger-Diaz. *MRI Intensive Brief Therapy Training.* Palo Alto, Calif.: Personal Communication, 1995.

Weakland, J. H., R. Fisch, P. Watzlawick, and A. M. Bodin. "Brief Therapy: Focused Problem Resolution." *Family Process* 13 (1974): 141–68.

Weiner-Davis, M. "In Praise of Solutions." *Family Therapy Networker* 14, no. 2 (1990): 42–8.

———. "Pro-constructed Realities." *Therapeutic Conversations.* Edited by S. Gilligan and R. Price. New York: W. W. Norton, 1993.

Weiner-Davis, M., S. de Shazer, and W. J. Gingerich. "Building on Pretreatment Change to Construct the Therapeutic Solution: An Exploratory Study." *Journal of Marital and Family Therapy* 13 (1987): 359–63.

Wells, R. A. "Clinical Strategies in Brief Psychotherapy." In *Casebook of the Brief Psychotherapies.* Edited by R. A. Wells and V. J. Gianetti. New York: Plenum, 1993.

Whiteman, T. A., and T. G. Bartlett. *The Marriage Mender.* Colorado Springs, Colo.: NavPress, 1996.

Wolberg, L. R., ed. *Short-Term Psychotherapy.* New York: Grune & Stratton, 1965.

Worschel, J. "Short-Term Dynamic Psychotherapy." In *Handbook of Brief Psychotherapies.* Edited by R. A. Wells and V. J. Giannetti. New York: Plenum, 1990.

Wright, H. N., and G. J. Oliver. *How to Bring Out the Best in Your Spouse.* Ann Arbor, Mich.: Servant, 1996.

Wright, H. N., and G. J. Oliver. *How to Change Your Spouse without Ruining Your Marriage.* Ann Arbor, Mich.: Servant, 1994.

Wylie, M. S. "Brief Therapy on the Couch." *Family Therapy Networker* 14, no. 2 (1990): 26–35, 66.

Zimbardo, P. G., and M. R. Leippe. *The Psychology of Attitude Change and Social Influence.* Philadelphia: Temple University Press, 1991.

ABOUT THE AUTHORS

Gary J. Oliver, Ph.D., has over thirty years of experience in counseling. Dr. Oliver serves as the clinical director of Southwest Counseling Associates in Littleton, Colorado, as well as an associate professor and the program director of the D.Min. in Marriage and Family Counseling program at Denver Seminary. Dr. Oliver has earned degrees from Biola University, Talbot Theological Seminary, Fuller Theological Seminary, and University of Nebraska. He has written *How to Get It Right after You've Gotten It Wrong, Real Men Have Feelings Too,* and *Masculinity at the Crossroads,* as well as nine books cowritten with Norm Wright, including *How to Change Your Spouse without Ruining Your Marriage, Good Women Get Angry,* and *When Anger Hits Home.* Dr. Oliver is a contributing editor for *Christian Parenting Today, New Man Magazine,* and *Marriage and Family: A Christian Journal.* Gary, his wife, Carrie, and their three sons live in Littleton, Colorado.

Monte Hasz, Psy.D., a licensed clinical psychologist at Southwest Clinical Associates holds degrees from Biola University, Denver Seminary, and Rose-mead School of Psychology. Dr. Hasz is an adjunct faculty member at Denver Seminary. He has also done extensive work in crisis evaluation in hospital settings and has worked for ten years in church ministry. Monte, his wife, Susan, and their three children live in Highlands Ranch, Colorado.

Matthew Richburg, M.A., is a licensed professional counselor at Southwest Clinical Associates and an adjunct faculty member and clinical supervisor at Denver Seminary. Richburg, who has earned degrees from Bethel College in St. Paul, Minnesota, and the University of Denver, is presently a Ph.D. candidate in the Counseling Psychology program at the University of Denver. Matt and his wife, Sara, live in Denver, Colorado.